The "Girl Problem"

The
"Girl Problem"

Female Sexual Delinquency
in New York, 1900–1930

Ruth M. Alexander

Cornell University Press   *Ithaca and London*

First published 1995 by Cornell University Press.

Printed in the United States of America

∞ The paper in this book meets the minimum requirements
of the American National Standard for Information Sciences—
Permanence of Paper for Printed Library Materials. ANSI Z39.48-1984.

Library of Congress Cataloging-in-Publication Data

Alexander, Ruth M., 1954–
The "girl problem" : female sexual delinquency in New York,
1900–1930 / Ruth M. Alexander.
    p.   cm.
Includes bibliographical references and index.
ISBN 0-8014-2821-1 (alk. paper)
1. Delinquent girls—New York (State)—Case studies.
2. Delinquent girls—New York (State)—Rehabilitation. 3. Juvenile
delinquency—New York (State)—Case studies. 4. Juvenile
delinquency—New York (State)—History. 5. Juvenile corrections—
New York (State)—Case studies. I. Title.
HV9105.N7A67   1995
364.3'6'082—dc20
                                                    94-47525

For my mother and
in memory of my father

Contents

Acknowledgments

I am pleased to acknowledge the many individuals and institutions who supported my work on this book. Mary Beth Norton's encouragement and guidance sustained me during several years of research and writing; her careful reading of drafts and many thoughtful suggestions added immeasurably to the quality of my work. Isabel V. Hull and Joan Jacobs Brumberg also gave generously of their time and insight.

Funding for research and writing came from several sources. At Cornell University I was the recipient of awards from the Graduate Research Fellowship program, the Gertrude A. Gilmore endowment, and the Sage Continuing Graduate Fellowship program. A New York State Archives Research Award supported several months of uninterrupted archival research. At Colorado State University, grants from the Professional Development program in the College of Liberal Arts and the Career Enhancement program in the Office of Equal Opportunity allowed me to hire research assistants and travel to research collections during critical stages of my work. Research for this project was also facilitated by librarians and archivists at several repositories, especially Richard Andress, Duncan O. McCollum, and Christine W. Ward at the New York State Archives, Elizabeth Norris at the YWCA National Board Library, Sue Weiland at the Jewish Board of Family and Children's Services, and the librarians in the Inter-Library Loan offices at Cornell and Colorado State universities.

I am fortunate to work among congenial and supportive historians at Colorado State University. Special thanks go to Mark Gilderhus, chair of the History Department during my first five years at CSU, for helping me achieve a productive balance between writing and teaching and for taking an interest in research that was far afield from his own area of specialization. Andrea Russo and Mary Bauer, graduate students in history, tracked down important sources with alacrity and great resourcefulness. Linda Carlson, curator of the Historic Costume and Textile Collection at CSU, helped me date historic photographs. Linda McNamara provided expert computer assistance.

Peter Agree, my editor at Cornell University Press, deserves thanks for shepherding me into the world of book publishing; he answered my numerous (and often naive) questions with unfailing grace and precision. I also acknowledge the University of Kansas Press for permission to use material from my previously published article, "'The Only Thing I Wanted Was Freedom': Wayward Girls in New York, 1900–1930," which appeared in *Small Worlds: Children and Adolescents in America, 1850–1950*, ed. Elliott West and Paula Petrik (1992), © 1992 by the University Press of Kansas.

Many individuals took time from their own busy schedules to read or comment on my work. I am especially indebted to Estelle B. Freedman for critiquing the manuscript at two stages and for offering observations on organization, conceptualization, and language that greatly enhanced the finished book. Susan Porter Benson and Kathleen Kennedy also made helpful and timely comments on the revised manuscript. Elizabeth Lunbeck and Peggy Pascoe commented on a conference paper written during my work on this project, and Joanne Meyerowitz carefully critiqued two dissertation chapters as well as an early conference paper. Cynthia Eckert, Nan Enstad, Regina Kunzel, and Mary Odem generously shared insights from their own research.

Family members and friends have supplied moral support and social diversion in equal measure. I especially thank my mother for her interest and encouragement and Tine Buchman for many years of friendship. Robbin Bell, John Mark Garrison, Leslee Becker, Pattie Cowell, Sherry Pomering, and Michael Wilson deserve special credit for keeping my spirits high. Finally, Maggie Boys has been an unstinting champion of my work on the "girl problem." Her companionship, endless hours of conversation, and practical assistance made this book possible.

R. M. A.

The "Girl Problem"

Introduction:
A New Adolescent Female

This book is about young women who "got into trouble" as they tried to reinvent female adolescence and found themselves in two of New York State's reformatories for women. During the early twentieth century young women and girls from across the socioeconomic spectrum self-consciously rejected the behavioral conventions and moral values of the nineteenth century, substituting self-assertion and conspicuous heterosexuality for deference and sexual purity. Working girls flocked to commercial dance halls and other amusements, engaging in social rituals that celebrated heterosexual romance, the autonomy of youth, and the purchase of fun. Middle-class girls in high schools and colleges became unabashed advocates of unchaperoned dating, "necking," and "petting." As patrons of a newly eroticized entertainment industry and participants in urban youth subcultures, young women tried to wrest themselves from parental controls, the strictures of marriage, and the stigma of prostitution.

Young women's rebellion against Victorian moral conventions took place in the context of striking transformations in the lives of parents and youths, women and men. As the United States became an industrial and urban society, the family became a consumer rather than a productive unit and specially trained "experts" in public schools, government agencies, community organizations, medical offices, and mental-health clinics took over many functions previously performed by parents. Parents lost authority as sons and daughters in their teens and early twenties were drawn outside their homes to work in low-paying jobs, attend public high schools, socialize with their peers, and listen to the advice of professional "experts" on the options available to them in a modern society. These changes gave adolescents a taste of independence, but in many instances they were also cause for youthful insecurity. In fact, adolescence emerged as an increasingly distinct stage of life marked by prolonged and complex preparation for adulthood, crises of identity, and occasional displays of antisocial conduct.

Simultaneously, as new institutions and industries affected families, upsetting traditional patterns of interaction between parents and their children, American women began to invent new models of womanhood, forsaking Victorian gender conventions. These so-called new women moved beyond the confines of their homes and assumed an increasingly conspicuous role in public life as consumers, wage earners, students, professionals, social reformers, labor activists, entertainers, and cinematic "sex symbols." They were affluent and impoverished, black and white, immigrant and native-born, old and young; they pursued various (often competing) agendas and offered divergent visions of the future. And yet, despite their differences, all the "new women" challenged masculine dominance, redefining the place of women in society and in their families.

Over time, young women scored a relative triumph as agents of sexual innovation and cultural change. At first, reformers and public officials condemned the young women's claims to social and sexual autonomy: they found rebellious working girls virtually indistinguishable from prostitutes and saw more affluent young women as threats to the moral foundation of middle-class families. Parents of all social backgrounds complained that their "modern" daughters were disrespectful and unlikely to attract decent husbands. Adolescent females, however, were unwilling to cave in to the criticism and anxieties of their elders. Aided by the increasing convergence of working- and middle-class ways of life and by the public's growing familiarity with Freudian theories of psychosexual development, young women won from their adult critics a grudging acceptance of female adolescent autonomy and sexual expression. Through a process of negotiation and compromise, young women and girls redesigned the terms of their passage to womanhood.

Of course, "modern" young women did not gain complete sexual and social freedom; nor did they fully reject received definitions of morality. A persistent double standard, limited access to birth control, a discriminatory job market, homogenizing forces in mass culture, and misogynist interpretations of psycholanalytic theory all worked together to shape and constrain young women's choices and identities. Still, despite these varied cultural checks on their individuality, by the 1910s and 1920s female adolescents explored the meaning of womanhood within the context of an emerging liberal social and sexual order. Demands for purity and for submission to family claims held them more lightly than in the generation past. Indeed, the popular culture of the day admired them for their ambition, spunk, and sexual attractiveness.

The early twentieth century need not be interpreted solely in terms of a white middle-class drive for social control; clearly, young women and girls were historical actors rather than powerless victims of convention and authority. Yet we should not imagine that female adolescents shifted without confusion, conflict, or hazard from one set of values to another. Nor should we assume that the new sexual order meant the same thing for young women of different socioeconomic, cultural, or racial groups. Although not denying the agency of adolescent females or the newness of their ideas and behavior, this book looks beyond the cultural values these young women helped to invent and examines their sometimes pained and thwarted efforts to construct a new sense of self. It investigates the lives and identities of young women who, in embracing the modern, collided with the limits of change, with inequalities of gender, race, ethnicity, and class and with powerful agents of repression and control. Rebellion and innovation entailed risk; even as some forward-looking parents, professionals, and social reformers tried to accommodate the reinvention of female adolescence, others forcefully resisted a phenomenon they called the "girl problem," certain that to do otherwise was to invite moral corruption, family dissolution, and community degradation.

The women studied here were incarcerated in New York State's two reformatories for women between 1900 and 1930: the New York State Reformatory for Women at Bedford Hills, just north of New York City, and the Western House of Refuge for Women at Albion, approximately thirty miles west of Rochester. The reformatory at Albion opened in 1893, serving the western and northern counties of New York, and was renamed the Albion State Training School in 1923. Bedford Hills opened its doors in 1901 and served the counties of the New York metropolitan area and the Hudson River valley. Albion usually had an inmate population of approximately two hundred; Bedford's inmate population was usually closer to four hundred. The two institutions were established to reform "delinquent" young women (usually in their late teens or early twenties) who had transgressed Victorian standards of feminine virtue but were not yet "hardened" criminals or thoroughly "degraded" females. The young women were most often committed for prostitution and solicitation, incorrigibility and "waywardness," disorderly conduct, and petty larceny. Although the reformatories sometimes resorted to harsh discipline, they preferred to use their female staff to teach inmates, by instruction and example, to become hardworking, deferential, and chaste. This book examines in close detail the experiences of one hundred inmates, fifty-one from Bedford Hills and forty-nine from Albion. Of all the inmates in my sample, eighty-five were between the ages of sixteen and twenty-two at the time of commitment; only fifteen were between the ages of twenty-three and thirty, and these women's case histories often revealed experiences during adolescence that were similar to those of the younger inmates.[1]

Significantly, the inmates at the reformatories came from homes and communities of little privilege; with few exceptions they were from working-class, immigrant, and African American homes. Their low social status was not accidental, and it raises critical questions about the ways in which race, class, ethnicity, and gender intersected to define both the "girl problem" and state-mandated "reform" in modern America. How did low status and familial disadvantage shape young women's pursuit of autonomy and their attempts to weigh the merits and hazards of nonconformity? Why, in an era of growing sexual permissiveness and youthful independence, were these particular young women arrested and incarcerated for evincing an interest in erotic expression or resisting parental rule? Many of these young women were apparently prostitutes, but what, precisely, did prostitution mean in post-Victorian America? Finally, what impact did arrest and incarceration have on young women's social and sexual identities and on their relationships with their families and communities; to what extent was state-mandated reform a despised source of repression and shame, to what extent a valued source of aid and direction?

In examining the experiences of these young women, I have relied on a variety of sources. Recent historical works on early-twentieth-century sexuality, the family, adolescence, womanhood, and the Progressive crusade against prostitution provide an essential backdrop to my work; this secondary literature is referenced in the bibliographic essay at the end of the book. Where appropriate, these and other relevant secondary sources are also referenced in the notes. Among primary sources, I have turned to the annual reports of the Bedford Hills and Albion reformatories, newspapers, advice books to parents, the reports of vice commissions and social-service agencies, and the published and unpublished articles, books, and speeches of probation officers, social workers, mental-health professionals, and sex educators. Most important, I have used the unpublished case files of the Bedford Hills and Albion reformatories, now in Albany. My sample of one hundred files, admittedly a small one, is extraordinarily rich. Many of the case files include official records, interview notes, and correspondence (both official and censored). These documents reveal the goals and methods of institutional authorities, the concerns and coping strategies of family members, and the values and self-perceptions of young females who were labeled and treated as delinquents.

At the time of my research, not all of the reformatory records for Bedford Hills and Albion had been accessioned by the New York State Archives at Albany, so I could not attempt a statistically representative study of the inmate populations.[2] Because of the limitations and relative disorder of the reformatory records collection, I selected files that were unusually well documented, trying at the same time to find cases representing a variety of offenses and involving young women who were white and of color, immigrant and native born.[3]

I began by examining Albion cases, one for each year from 1900 to 1914. These early files usually contain little more than the original commitment papers and an occasional piece of correspondence on the case; they are complemented by Albion's admission ledgers, which offer sketchy accounts of the inmates' family background, conduct, work in the institution, and record on parole. I chose files in which some correspondence accompanied the case file, supplementing the stingy recital of facts in the admission ledgers and commitment papers. This close reading of a few early cases provided a starting point from which to analyze and compare the histories of the inmates who stayed at the reformatories in later years.[4]

The remaining eighty-five young women in my sample were committed to the reformatories at Bedford Hills and Albion between 1915 and 1930; fifty to Bedford, thirty-four to Albion. The quality and depth of the Albion records had been much improved by the hiring of Flora P. Daniels as superintendent in 1916; she had been influenced by the new case-method techniques of modern social workers. Daniels instituted the practice of interviewing each inmate who arrived at Albion and recording a brief history of her upbringing and "delinquencies." The files from Bedford Hills for the period after 1915 are richer still. By this time, under an arrangement worked out with Katharine Bement Davis, Bedford's first superintendent, the Rockefeller Foundation had established at Bedford Hills the Laboratory of

Social Hygiene, which provided staff and funding for an elaborate system of investigation of the inmates. A team of social workers, psychologists, and psychiatrists delved into the histories of the young women, trying to assess social, psychological, familial, and industrial factors that contributed to their delinquency.[5] Thanks to these investigations, some files from the mid-1910s include very detailed case histories. Some also include psychological examination reports, conduct reports, and parole applications. When the Rockefeller Foundation withdrew its funding in 1918 and forced Bedford Hills to close the laboratory and narrow the scope of its investigations, the reformatory still continued to record information from intake interviews and to compile data for conduct reports and parole applications.

Just as the two institutions began to keep better formal records after 1915, they also began to save correspondence with greater care, including letters between the families of the inmates and the superintendents of the institutions, letters between the superintendents and young women on parole, letters between the reformatory and social agencies or employers involved in probation or parole programs, and letters sent to or from the inmates that were held back by the reformatory censors. More than any other source, the case-file correspondence disclosed the often competing (yet sometimes overlapping) interests of reformatory officials, inmates, and inmate family members, and the discrepant power of the different groups to define "delinquency" and "reform."

Of course, one must read formal correspondence, interview results, and official case histories with extreme care. In letters to the reformatories, family members and parolees may have occasionally disguised their sentiments or activities as they told the superintendents what they thought the officials wanted to hear or tried to protect their privacy and independence. Similarly, during interviews with reformatory staff, young women, family members, and others may have often tailored their responses to deflect or satisfy the intentions of their interrogators; moreover, interviewers sometimes paraphrased respondents' answers and explanations, perhaps distorting their meaning. Nonetheless this material is illuminating. Inmates' self-conscious efforts to represent and explain their character and values provide important clues about the politics of state-mandated reform. Moreover, the cautious self-disclosure of inmates and family members in formal or ritualized contexts often may be balanced against correspondence, conduct reports, and the like in which young women and their kin reveal great urgency, deliberately questioning reformatory authorities. Especially when read in conjunction with letters that failed to pass reformatory censors precisely because they showed too much of the writers' real feelings and thoughts, the formal case materials are a valuable historical resource.

Part I, "Getting into Trouble," investigates how and why working-class, immigrant, and nonwhite young women were arrested and incarcerated as "delinquents." In analyzing how these women found themselves so labeled, the chapters in this section stress several interactive themes: conflict within families over competing models of female adolescence; disadvantaged young women's investment in rebellion and their limited powers of self-protection; social reformers' "discovery" of the "girl problem" and their attempts to contain it; the cultural construction of a new and relatively permissive model of female adolescence by middle-class "experts" in the emerging field of mental hygiene; and, finally, the state's resistance to modern notions of female adolescence and its use of class and racial assumptions in responding to female adolescent sexuality.

Part II, "Going Straight," analyzes the young women and the process of reform. It explores the values, expectations, and methods of reformatory officials and staff; the inmates' sense of themselves as "delinquents" and their efforts to resist state authority or shape the terms of reform; and finally, the roles played by kin, community, and peers in shaping delinquent girls' understanding of and responses to state authority.

Exploring the experience, perceptions, and agency of "delinquent" adolescent females is a great challenge, for these young women can be understood only if we connect them to the values and authority of the adults and institutions around them. Their lives must be thoroughly contextualized, viewed in relation to cultural narratives and forces that acted to define and contain them as dangerous and immoral. And yet, as one documents and evaluates the ideas and regulatory strategies of parents, professionals, reformers, and state agencies, it is surprisingly easy to lose sight of the young women who became objects of condemnation and social control. They tend to slip into shadow beside their outspoken and authoritative critics. Resisting this tendency, I have tried to restore the young women who became the "girl problem" to the status of historical subjects engaged in reflection, gesture, and action. Although remaining attentive to the figures around them, I have allowed adolescent females, not adults, to claim center stage.

PART ONE

Getting into Trouble

CHAPTER ONE

"Going Around with a Bad Crowd of Girls":
Young Women and the Lure of City Streets

Nellie Roberts was sent to the New York State Reformatory for Women at Bedford Hills in mid-1917, after a Port Jervis magistrate concluded that she was a menace to the community. Sixteen-year-old Nellie, the daughter of an illiterate laborer, first captured the attention of the police in Port Jervis, a city of smoke-filled railroad yards and glass factories, when she and her sister Susan started to stand along local roads "hailing men on motorcycles and asking them for rides." The girls' hitchhiking began in late 1916, and over the next several months police officers also observed Nellie loitering "out on the streets" and heard that she was one of the girls "hanging around" the soldiers at a nearby army training camp. Worried that Nellie might expose the servicemen to forbidden sexual pleasures and venereal disease, the police placed her under close watch. Soon they went a step further, arresting her in a local hotel restaurant, at the request of the proprietor's outraged daughter, for engaging in an "immoral act" with one of the hotel's male guests. Although the arresting officer failed to produce any witnesses to the alleged offense in court, Nellie was convicted of "travelling about the city entering saloons and committing acts of prostitution" and received a standard three-year sentence to Bedford Hills.[1]

Pieced together, the basic facts of Nellie's "criminal history" offer a compelling narrative of moral conflict, social inequality, and state-imposed strategies of behavioral control. Nellie, a young woman of working-class origins, was an active participant in the nation's emerging urban youth culture.

Through lively use of America's streets and consumer commodities, and bold explorations of heterosexuality, she and her peers were reinventing female adolescence, rejecting Victorian standards of girlhood virtue to lay claim to sexual desire, erotic expression, and social autonomy. But rebellion inevitably invited reaction; to the "respectable" element in Port Jervis, Nellie demonstrated a disgraceful willingness to narrow the social distance between herself and the degraded prostitute, her moral indifference serving as vivid evidence of an escalating "girl problem." Moreover, power still belonged to the middle-class champions of Victorian morality, and town officials, making use of both local and federal laws, wasted little time in throwing restraints around the teenage girl.[2] The reinvention of female adolescence was not an exclusively working-class undertaking, but, as Nellie discovered, it was usually girls of low status who suffered public reproach. Unlike the affluent young women—some of them students at elite urban colleges such as Barnard and the University of Chicago—who escaped legal sanction though they patronized cheap dance halls, entertained men in their rooms, and indulged in premarital sex, Nellie became a "female delinquent."[3]

Historians are well acquainted with early-twentieth-century reformers' determined efforts to resist working-class young women's rebellion against "respectable" morality. Mark Connelly, Ruth Rosen, Kathy Peiss, and others have shown how doctors, lawyers, settlement workers, government officials, and juvenile-court advocates leaned on the correctional arm of the state to control prostitutes and other renegade females. As adept propagandists, these middle-class elites also created compelling media images of disorderly and immoral young working girls, arousing public antipathy to social change and regenerating faith in Victorian notions of girlhood purity.

Nellie nicely fits this picture of a rebellious working girl stigmatized by middle-class authorities; in fact, Nellie recognized and condemned their agenda for social control. During interviews with staff members at Bedford Hills, she spoke resentfully of the "cops and things" who "think they [can] reform the girls here." Then, unwilling to let stand the state's representation of her behavior, Nellie recast the meaning of the "girl problem" to draw attention to the "real" predicament of being classed unfairly as a girl in need of correction. Substituting her own values for those of Port Jervis's court magistrate, Nellie insisted that she should never have been judged a prostitute because her interest in soldiers was neither financially opportunistic nor sexually exploitative. Rather, she liked spending time with the uniformed men "because they were going off to war and she felt sorry for them. . . . they were always good to her and never used bad language." Nellie could see in herself little evidence of serious wrongdoing and no grounds for the court's harsh treatment. As she put it so plainly, "[I] didn't deserve to come here. . . . Lots of girls as bad as me."[4]

Nevertheless, even as Nellie acknowledged (and tried to repudiate) the disciplinary tactics of New York's criminal justice system, she also spoke of family dynamics that operated independently of the state's moralism yet made her susceptible to its selective strategies of repression. Complicating the meaning of the "girl problem," the teenager claimed that her father, a common laborer who was frequently unemployed, drunk, and violent, bore more responsibility for her plight than Port Jervis's narrow-minded arbiters of morality.

According to Nellie, the Roberts home was "quite happy" while her mother was alive, and all the children were treated "equally." But after Mrs. Roberts' death in 1915, Nellie's father made her "take the blame for everything." Unable to find or keep a job, he often arrived home intoxicated and in a belligerent mood. To make matters worse, he had also had incestuous relations with his elder daughter, Susan, and on more than one occasion "got fresh" with Nellie as well. On several occasions Nellie had left home to stay with a friendly aunt and uncle. More often, looking for respite from her impoverished and turbulent home, she spent time on the streets and in the arms of young men. Usually her boyfriends were "good to her," but she had also been vulnerable to mistreatment, and at least one encounter with a man ended in sexual assault.[5]

Vulnerable or not, Nellie continued to explore heterosexuality in public venues. She used immodesty as a form of defiance against her father's unjust treatment and took her chances, refusing to alter her conduct even after she became aware of close scrutiny by the police. In the end, the teenager held her father accountable for her arrest and incarceration: claiming that he had asked the police to watch her because she "went out nights," Nellie interpreted her reformatory sentence as punishment for refusing to submit to his unreasonable demands and violent temper.[6] She saw her father as her greatest "problem" and could neither explain nor make sense of her incarceration without assessing the conflict and unhappiness that she had known with him in recent years.

Though the details of Nellie's story are unique, its fundamental elements—unhappiness at home and a troubled search for self in the sexualized subcultures of working-class urban youth—are echoed in the case files of other young women who were sent to New York's state reformatories between 1900 and 1930. Of course, as Chapter 2 will show, formal accusations and convictions for sexual and social delinquency took place within a framework of institutionalized class, cultural, or racial bias; with few exceptions, the criminal justice system looked for illicit or blatant instances of youthful gender transgression in working-class, immigrant, or nonwhite neighborhoods. Still, if we are to understand what it meant to young women to be placed in a reformatory, we must recognize that discord or dissatisfaction with kin played a critical role in their entry into the ranks of the "delinquent." For New York's delinquent females, the "girl problem" began at home, began in family circumstances that often prompted disadvantaged young women to participate in the life of the street in a manifestly unguarded manner.

The young inmates at Bedford Hills and Albion between 1900 and 1930 had grown up in families that struggled to maintain a modicum of stability and social respectability, dodging or fighting adversity of many kinds. The fathers of the one hundred delinquents had a variety of occupations, but few held jobs that conferred security, status, or more than a modest income. Rather, as day laborers, skilled tradesmen, farmers, factory workers, truck drivers, and railroad workers, they suffered seasonal layoffs or periodic unemployment and knew the difficulties of trying to stretch an inelastic dollar.[7] Even the seventeen men who provided reasonably comfortable homes for their families as small shopkeepers, builders, or craftsmen must have been keenly aware of their vulnerability to the vicissitudes of the economy. And in an era when the consumer market served more and more Americans as a critical source of pleasure, social identity, and self-esteem, it is likely that only one father, a prosperous veterinarian, was able to satisfy his dependents' physical needs and indulge their material desires.

Bowing to economic necessity, the mothers of many delinquent young women also worked for wages. Among the one hundred Bedford and Albion inmates in my sample, twenty-seven had working mothers, a rate well above national rates of employment for married women from 1900 to 1930.[8] Moreover, most of the young women had abandoned school at an early age, taking domestic, factory, or waitressing jobs or helping with housework and childcare to relieve the burdens of their hard-pressed families. Nellie Roberts had quit school at the age of fifteen, after completing only six grades, and she had worked in four low-paying domestic and factory jobs before her arrest. Deborah Herman, another Bedford inmate, had left school at the age of sixteen because of "eye trouble" and to care for a sickly younger sister while her mother went out to work; she also had reached only the sixth grade. Within a year or so, Deborah was supplementing the income of the family "by doing domestic work in families nearby her home."⁹ Just nineteen of the one hundred inmates had attended high school, although compulsory education laws and the shift to a skilled white-collar work force prompted the national rates of attendance at public secondary schools to rise from 11 percent to 51 percent of all fourteen- to seventeen-year-olds between 1900 and 1930. Acknowledging the importance of academic and vocational training to social mobility, many working-class, African American, and immigrant parents made short-term economic sacrifices to keep their teen-agers in school. But few of the young women who became reformatory inmates came from families willing or able to affirm the value of education.¹⁰

Economic uncertainty was not all that troubled these households. Many of the Bedford and Albion inmates grew up in immigrant homes whose members daily confronted the trials of cultural dislocation and assimilation. Only twelve of the delinquents were born outside the United States, but at least thirty-nine young women had immigrant mothers and fathers, and six others had one foreign-born parent. Most of these parents struggled to situate themselves in an unfamiliar society, to make sense of new commercial and industrial practices, strange cultural values, and xenophobic attitudes. After nearly twenty years in the United States, Anna Levinson's Russian Jewish parents still felt ill at ease in their adopted country. Anna's father provided well for his family, working as an independent carpenter, but he resented working on the Sabbath and grew increasingly aware of his cultural marginality after the family relocated from their immigrant community in the Bronx to an upwardly mobile gentile neighborhood in Westchester County, north of New York City. The move to the suburbs was visible proof of the family's successful integration into America's economic mainstream, but Mr. Levinson and his wife were still loath to pursue cultural assimilation and would not allow their children to mix with the Christian youths in the neighborhood.¹¹

The immigrant families in this study were not the only ones isolated from America's cultural and economic mainstream. Thirteen of the delinquents were the daughters of African American or West Indian parents and two were Native Americans. They and their kin lived in an era in which whites deliberately crafted scientific theories, legal doctrines, and patterns of terror-ism to bolster racism and block the aspirations of people of color. Subtle and overt forms of racism contributed to the hardship that marked the lives of delinquent nonwhite young women, limiting their independence and depressing their standard of living. Caroline Browning, for example, was raised by a grandmother in New Orleans while her mother worked as a laundress, one of the few occupations open to black women. And Sonya Arnett, the daughter of a Mohican Indian father and French Indian mother, had been placed in a reservation school in Ohio when she was young, while her parents eked out a living as peddlers who "travelled around" selling patent medicines.[12]

Millions of working-class families in the early twentieth century lived with economic worries, ethnic or racial prejudices, and cultural dilemmas like those confronting the families of New York's delinquent females. Parents coped with their difficulties in many ways: they sent children and adolescents into the workforce; they turned to relatives for psychological and economic support; they took paying boarders into their homes; they joined immigrant and African American social clubs, mutual-aid societies, and homeowners' associations; they sought help from sympathetic settlement workers and charities; they went to priests, ministers, or rabbis for aid and guidance; and occasionally they joined labor unions.[13] Incomplete evidence suggests that the mothers and fathers of New York's delinquent girls also followed this pattern, turning, for example, to a Jewish charity for medical assistance or to grandmothers for regular childcare.[14]

But coping strategies were not always equal to the problems at hand, and sooner or later some disadvantaged families experienced profound distress. Struggling as they did with serious economic woes, social marginalization, and cultural alienation, the majority of the families of our one hundred female delinquents eventually succumbed to domestic disorder and calamity: sixty-one women came from homes broken by the death, desertion, separation, or divorce of parents. At least twenty-four young women grew up amid severe and ongoing conflict or abuse, including marital disagreement, wife battering, child abuse, and incest. Alcoholism, drug use, or serious parental illness also destabilized numerous families.[15]

Some families confronted several problems simultaneously, each one reinforcing the others. Clearly, Nellie Roberts's family was devastated by the cumulative effects of multiple crises: the recent death of Nellie's mother, abuse, incest, alcoholism, and acute poverty. Violence, alcoholism, and poverty also afflicted the Pomrenke household. Mildred Pomrenke's father, an illiterate immigrant, had difficulty finding work and was arrested repeatedly for alcoholism and physical abuse of his wife and children; on one occasion he beat his wife so badly that she miscarried and for a while had to forfeit her role as the family's principal breadwinner.[16] And for young Deborah Herman, poverty, racism, and paternal desertion were the defining features of domestic life. Deborah was raised in Bellport, Long Island, by a working mother, her father having deserted the family when she was six years old. An illiterate black woman, Deborah's mother could find no employment except as a poorly paid domestic servant in her semirural community; it is likely that racial prejudice also contributed to the inferior housing conditions in which the Hermans lived, "a one room hut in the depth of the woods in the most primitive surroundings."[17]

At best, a fragile equilibrium prevailed in the homes of New York's delinquent females, and as the girls entered adolescence and young adulthood, many found that home life compared poorly with the buoyant mood and youthful companionship to be found in city streets, dance halls, and amusement parks. Disadvantaged and troubled young women yearned for a place, a way of life, an identity outside the family circle. They longed for a life different from what their families could offer, and many saw in New York's urban youth culture and commercial amusements the means to attain it.

Thus at the age of eighteen Deborah Herman became romantically involved with a young man who urged her to make a new life for herself. She quit her job as a domestic servant, ignoring her family's pressing monetary needs. No longer a shy and dependable daughter, Deborah devoted herself to pleasure, traveling from her small community on Long Island to larger towns nearby, where she went to dance halls and stayed out late at night.[18]

Sophie Polentz, the daughter of Austrian parents, also looked for ways to improve her rather grim existence. The Polentzes lived in a stable residential neighborhood in the Bronx, but both of Sophie's parents were ill, her father with tuberculosis, and the family had very little money. The atmosphere at home was poisoned by frequent quarrels between Sophie's parents and her brothers over the boys' poor work habits and fondness for pool halls. At fifteen, Sophie left school, where she was doing poorly, and went to work, first in a printing company and then in a hat factory. Obliged to turn her wages over to her mother, the teenager nonetheless enjoyed her jobs, making friends with young women who offered to show her New York's dance halls and cabarets. Not surprisingly, Sophie's father disapproved of her new associates. Sophie resented, and perhaps feared, her father's sharp tongue; during a period of unemployment, she ran away from home, pairing up with a girlfriend who was also out of work. Over a period of months the girls lived together in two different apartments in Harlem, where they had "good times" while being supported by newly acquired boyfriends.[19]

Even when young women could find no way to reach a lively town, they found ways to rebel against trying domestic circumstances. Anabel Rider, the orphaned daughter of an Anglo-American mother and a Seneca Indian father, was placed in a succession of foster homes by the New York Charities Aid Society and lived during her mid-teens with a devoutly Christian woman in a small Long Island town. The foster mother claimed that the young woman was "not treated as a maid but as a member of the family" and allowed her to attend church and community socials "with the best girls of the town." But Anabel did not respond gratefully to these charitable gestures, and renouncing her moralistic guardian and subordinate social status, she picked up strange men on the street and telephoned the police and fire departments and various local businesses to flirt with their male employees.[20]

The rebellious acts of these three young women, like those of many others, gained definition and efficacy from a highly specific cultural context. The girls used city streets as well as the technological and commercial inventions of an urban industrial society—telephones, dance halls, automobiles, and nightclubs—to acquire the autonomy they desired. They pursued a romantic and erotic identity, an identity reified by the movies, songs, fashions, and dance steps of urban America. The result of dramatic social and economic developments in the late nineteenth and early twentieth centuries, this urban-industrial-consumer environment enabled masses of young women, including Deborah, Sophie, and Anabel, to challenge a family-centered identity and construct a sense of self dedicated to independence from kin, to peer interaction, and to self-conscious heterosexuality.[21]

In fact, with the growth of cities and the vast expansion of the nation's economy, female adolescence acquired cultural and social meanings that marked it as strikingly different from nineteenth-century girlhood. During the nineteenth century, the great majority of unmarried young women lived under the close supervision of adults—parents, teachers, employers, or slaveholders—and had little opportunity to mingle freely with their peers or to elaborate the values and rituals of an adolescent subculture. Few were able to imagine a future that did not include social and economic dependence on a father or husband, and, in the case of blacks, domination by whites. They could ill afford to strike a fiercely self-reliant pose.[22]

Moreover, whether they were rich or poor, white or black, young women in the nineteenth century were profoundly affected by the moral and sexual values of domestic ideology. Parents, popular writers, physicians, teachers, and social reformers endlessly extolled the principles of feminine domesticity. They adjured young women to place devotion to the family above personal freedom, claiming that women and girls were likely to lose their health and respectability if they tried to invade the "masculine" world of politics, business, and higher education. Social authorities considered sexual purity the most important virtue of all, and they warned young women of the great costs of ignoring the moral precepts of domesticity. Nineteenth-century Americans honored the "pure" woman by setting up the "fallen" or "impure" woman as her foil, and young white women from both humble and prosperous homes learned that they risked losing their reputations, their chances of marriage, and their hopes of economic security if they lost their sexual virtue. By contrast, young African American women, though they might honor moral dignity or "purity" in their hearts, discovered that white men refused to admit blacks' capacity for virtue and thus rationalized their own sexual license and abuse.[23]

Of course, some young women in Victorian America tried to inject a measure of autonomy into their lives. White middle-class girls sought intellectual fulfillment in female seminaries and colleges and questioned the possibilities for marital happiness in a society that required men and women to cultivate disparate mental, emotional, and behavioral traits. Young black women in the South balked at maternal supervision (intended primarily as a shield against the sexual advances of white men) and engaged in youthful romances with black males their own age. The adolescent daughters of New England farmers took jobs in the region's early textile mills and soon began to challenge their employers' narrow definition of virtuous womanhood, forming labor associations and organizing strikes to demand higher wages. And in New York City the adolescent daughters of the laboring poor joined the predominantly male working-class youth culture flourishing along the Bowery, using factory wages and the proceeds of casual prostitution to finance a rough equality with their male peers. But these challenges were not sufficiently powerful to crack the social, economic, and ideological framework of Victorian girlhood.[24]

Still, female adolescence was not immutable, and this life stage was dramatically affected by the nation's rapid industrialization and urbanization. During the late nineteenth and early twentieth centuries, millions of white women and girls from immigrant and native-born homes were drawn into the urban work force as unskilled factory workers, retail clerks, and wait-resses. Though most girls took up wage labor to help their struggling families, employment also exposed them to a new world of experience and values. At work, previously sheltered teenage girls met young people who shared newly acquired ideas about fashion, recreation, and sex. At night, putting these ideas into practice, stylishly dressed working girls flocked to new commercial dance halls, nickelodeon theaters, and amusement parks to explore pos-sibilities for heterosexual romance. Substituting an "up-to-date" lifestyle for Victorian and Old World standards of girlhood decorum, the daughters of the working class produced a distinctly modern rendering of female adolescence.[25]

African American young women also found ways to use city streets and urban amusements to create new social and sexual identities for themselves. Thousands of young unmarried black women abandoned the agricultural South and migrated without their parents to northern cities during the early twentieth century, determined to leave behind both rural poverty and the stifling world of Jim Crow. Denied positions in factories or retail stores, many of them found work as servants and laundresses for middle-class whites in New York, Chicago, Philadelphia, and other cities. Others became ser-vants or performers in the whiskey joints, nightclubs, and brothels that catered to blacks, and learned about the open sex trade operating in the emerging African American ghettos. They found their way to moving-picture houses, theaters, and dance halls, where unrestrained displays of sensuality and romance were commonplace among both performers and patrons. Although some of the young migrants may have been frightened or offended by their new settings, others willingly exchanged the sexual terror-ism of southern whites and the restrictive moralism of rural churchgoing parents for the easy eroticism and cultural sophistication of black city life.[26]

Before long, even the sheltered daughters of the middle class began to participate in the reinvention of female adolescence. As students in the nation's proliferating high schools and colleges, middle-class young women joined their male peers in mocking the stuffy values of parents and teachers. Educators and community leaders tried to distract them from the "vulgar" amusements and habits of poorer youths but, by the 1910s, affluent young women in urban areas also were going to dance halls, movie theaters, and amusement parks, trading in the romance and desire that circulated as youth's common cultural currency. As one well-heeled young woman admit-ted to her scandalized mother after spending successive nights dancing, drinking, and smoking with a married man in Manhattan's fashionable cabarets, "I was dazzled by the glamour of the white lights and the music and dancing on Broadway." And when asked to share her thoughts on America's college women with a New York City audience of social workers and girls' club leaders, Mabel Ulrich, a Minneapolis physician and sex educator, concluded, "The college girl today [1915] is an entirely different girl from the girl of fifteen years ago. I have the reputation in my town of being dangerously radical, but with these girls I feel I belong to an older generation. . . . What they are particularly interested in is the excitement and thrill of the love which is to come to them. They have an entirely new conception of love and they talk about it."[27]

The reinvention of female adolescence continued during World War I, as both working- and middle-class girls succumbed to "khaki fever" and eagerly pursued romantic liaisons with the nation's young uniformed men, a pursuit that caused social workers and government officials to complain that "the lure of the uniform and the romance of the soldier have proved too much for a great many young girls."[28] And in the 1920s young people in high schools and on college campuses engaged in increasingly open sexual behaviors. The decade's middle-class "flappers" or "new girls" rejected their parents' sexual taboos and, along with their male peers, substituted a peer-regulated dating system for parent-regulated courtship. They defended unchaperoned heterosexual interaction as a prerogative of youth and took advantage of the privacy afforded by the newly popular automobile to engage in ritualized expressions of romance and sexual intimacy.[29]

America's twentieth-century female adolescents were sexual rebels and cultural innovators. But for all their boldness, candor, and enthusiasm, they confronted obstacles and resistance to their new-found sensuality and self-assertion at almost every turn. As public schools and college campuses became key sites of cultural innovation, girls (and boys) encountered school administrators and teachers who tried to subvert adolescent autonomy by establishing dress codes and elaborate rules of conduct. Simultaneously, the rising rate of attendance at high school meant that growing numbers of young women and men remained dependent on their parents for support and shelter well into their late teens or early twenties. Prolonged dependence on parents sharpened adolescents' sense of indeterminacy, promoting anxiety about social and sexual identity and a keen desire for adult status.[30]

Significantly, for most girls, prolonged dependence on parents was matched by an altogether new dependence on male peers. Having limited access to money because they attended school or earned low wages in a discriminatory labor market, young women counted on their male peers to pay for recreation and dining. Young men parlayed their relatively greater economic resources into social and sexual prerogatives: they assumed monetary responsibility for their dates' entertainment but expected deference and sexual favors in return. Not surprisingly, adolescent girls had difficulty deciding whether their own desires coincided with the expectations of their partners. Many young women may have engaged in sexual intercourse more or less willingly, but a persistent double standard discouraged others from advancing beyond "petting" for fear of damaging their reputations. They could hardly afford to do otherwise, especially because state and federal laws and customary medical practices restricted young women's access to contraception and abortion, preventing them from gaining full control over their sexual and reproductive lives.[31]

New cultural representations also emerged to define and constrain female adolescent autonomy. As Kathy Peiss notes, working-class young women's fascination with stylish dress served as "a particularly potent way to display and play with notions of respectability, allure, independence, and status and to assert a distinctive identity and presence." But while young women "put on style" to assert their independence and individuality, fashion advertisers and movie makers emphasized the importance of conformity, defining young women's value narrowly in terms of "sex appeal," clothes, cosmetics, and hairstyles. And at high schools and on college campuses, peer-group gossip pressured young women to accept competitive and essentially conformist patterns of behavior in hopes of becoming popular and attracting numerous dates. Woe to the girl who lacked a slim figure, winning personality, pretty face, and stylish wardrobe.[32]

Although young women of every class and ethnic category became familiar with these models and constraints, the impediments to female adolescent self-assertion were not spread evenly across the social spectrum. Those from working-class immigrant households may well have encountered more opposition from parents than did young women from white middle-class homes. Parents of all social ranks were caught off guard by the rapid transformation of female adolescence in the early twentieth century, but immigrant parents were especially unnerved and offended by the novel habits and amusements of young women and girls, seeing them as a threat to family integrity and morality. Immigrants survived the trials of migration by strengthening ties of reciprocal obligation to kin; convinced that survival in America demanded self-sacrifice and the submergence of individual identity in the claims of the family, they were loath to forfeit the right to demand deference and chastity from their daughters. Thus parents from eastern and southern Europe bickered and quarreled with their adolescent daughters over chaperonage, curfews, clothes, cosmetics, entertainment, and money, often insisting that daughters contribute all of their wages to the family economy and spend their hours away from work helping with housework or participating in home-centered amusements. Italian parents were especially strict, fearing that their daughters' virtue and marriageability would be compromised by exposure to commercial amusements and urban youth cultures.[33]

Certainly, our inmates knew firsthand the intransigence of immigrant parents. Julia Kramer spoke bitterly of an Austrian Jewish father who allowed her no leisure and required her to work long hours in his dry-goods store every afternoon, regardless of school assignments to be completed. She often "had to cry to be released." Sophie Polentz's father, also an Austrian Jew, "objected to her going out with boys" and "wanted her first time she met a fellow to bring him up to the house." And Janine Rosen, the daughter of Orthodox Jewish Romanians, was permitted friends and leisure but incurred her father's wrath by staying out until two or three o'clock in the morning. Rosa Covello complained that her Italian Jewish father, a frankfurter and ice-cream peddler, allowed her only the recreation to be found at Italian holiday celebrations; she "used to get hit" when she wanted to go out.[34]

Ambitious and hard-working African American parents also struggled determinedly to control their daughters' access to city life, hoping to protect their families' fragile social status, to shield their girls from sexual exploitation, and to differentiate themselves from the impoverished and uneducated black masses.[35] Thus Althea Davies, the orphaned daughter of West Indian parents, was raised by a married sister who "brought [her] up strict," refusing to let her play in Harlem's streets. Althea occasionally went to movies, public dances, and the YWCA but only in the company of family or friends of the family. And while growing up in a small community in Virginia, Margaret Jackson went to the movies once a week but she was "not allowed to attend any public dances."[36]

In contrast, white middle-class parents' experience and interests may have encouraged somewhat greater tolerance of their daughters' fascination with commercial amusements and heterosexuality. Most were absorbed in an adult version of the culture of consumption that so captivated their daughters. And many were trying to enliven their own marriages with a modern appreciation for sex and romance. Moreover, twentieth-century middle-class parents, acknowledging that their own authority was diminished by the "expertise" of teachers, club leaders, social workers, and physicians, began to embrace a democratic family ideal to replace the hierarchical model of the nineteenth century. Although parents and daughters argued over spending allowances, curfews, clothes, and the like, their shared values and assumptions probably facilitated negotiation and compromise.[37] Moreover, as we will see in the next chapter, middle-class families benefited directly from the intervention of mental-hygiene professionals, who in the 1920s tried to ease the tension and misunderstanding between affluent parents and their "modern" daughters.

Young women of low social status may also have had less power in their relations with young men than did more privileged girls. Middle-class men were inclined to treat working-class young women as sexual objects or "pickups"; one study of female delinquents in New Haven, Connecticut, concluded that the male students of Yale University took deliberate sexual advantage of the town's working-class girls.[38] And even with men of their own background, working-class young women were likely to have limited leverage. As John Modell points out, girls who left school at an early age and frequently changed jobs may have had little access to the "effective, school-based, same-age peer group that oversaw behavior within the dating system." Through gossip and peer pressure, the high school and college dating system held women to a stricter standard of behavior than men, warning those who indulged too freely in petting or intercourse that they might never attract a husband, for marriage was still the prescribed goal of women. By pressuring women to limit their sexual activity, the dating system also demanded restraint from young men and offered "good" young women at least some protection from sexual exploitation, rape, and premarital pregnancy.[39]

Disadvantaged young women did not readily acquiesce either to familial disapprobation or to male privilege; indeed, they often found ways to mitigate or circumvent these obstacles without sacrificing emotional or physical security. Like their more privileged sisters, some worked out compromises with their parents or engaged in occasional subterfuge to gain privacy and freedom; many deflected unwanted sexual advances through delay and prevarication. Yet for all their spunk and determination, disadvantaged girls often found themselves unable to gain mastery over their young lives.[40]

Nowhere do the vulnerabilities of adolescent girls stand out more clearly than in the familial reactions some of them provoked by investing in an imperfect autonomy. Familial condemnation and conflict were prominent features in the lives of New York's delinquent girls, hampering their autonomy and, ultimately, creating the circumstances that led to their arrest and incarceration. The efforts made by these young women to surmount familial criticism were often unsuccessful, marred by their lack of social authority as well as by their recklessness and inexperience. The adolescent girls who most desired autonomy were often those least able to attain it.

The uneven and sometimes incomplete documentation in the one hundred reformatory case files suggests that irreconcilable conflict between girls and their elders clouded the lives of at least fifty-one of the inmates. Parents and guardians were committed to moral values and gender conventions that enhanced family survival; because their social, domestic, and economic difficulties were so acute, loyalty to the family and to inflexible notions of feminine virtue offered them some semblance of security, some faith in their ability to survive in a changeable and daunting world. To these parents, a young woman's assertion of self was far more than the ingenuous proclamation of a "modern" sensibility. It represented an unbearable threat to the survival of a precarious family unit, a display of disloyalty to cultural values already under siege. But paradoxically, in commanding daughters to rededicate themselves to feminine virtue and the family claim, angry and worried guardians often produced the effect they least desired, intensifying young women's dedication to displays of willfulness, ambition, and desire.

Sexual deportment was the most common source of controversy between the young women who became "delinquents" and their close relatives. Parents and guardians displayed anxiety about the reputations of their sexually active daughters and dismay and outrage at the girls' obstinance and disregard for the advice and authority of their elders. Typically, their daughters responded with disdain and further defiance. For example, when Lena Meyerhoff's Russian Jewish parents told their teenage daughter that her romantic interest in a "colored" chauffeur was unacceptable, Lena's attachment to the young man deepened and she began to spend nights with him in Harlem. Put on the defensive, Lena's lover told the parents that "he would rather shed blood than separate from Lena," and so exacerbated their anger and anxiety. Similarly, when Nora Patterson's parents told their seventeen-year-old daughter that she was too young to marry, she and her boyfriend had sexual intercourse anyway, apparently in deliberate rebellion; shortly thereafter Nora ran away from home.[41]

The case of Ella Waldstein reveals especially well how young women and their parents became entangled in escalating disputes over questions of sexual virtue and filial obedience. In the summer of 1916 sixteen-year-old Ella started "going around with a bad crowd of girls," often staying away from her Brooklyn home until one or two o'clock in the morning. Ella, also the daughter of Russian Jews, had never before given her parents any trouble; in fact, for two years she had worked without complaint as a factory operative, helping to support a family of six. But now Ella rebelled against her insular life and began to adopt the imprudent manners of young women she saw at work and on the street. Ella's parents could not understand or accept their daughter's conduct or her wish for an identity separate from the family, and, fearing for her safety and sexual virtue, her mother and father "talked to her and begged and pleaded with her to come home earlier." Ella listened to their pleas in stony silence. "When they asked her where she had been she would say she had been with a girlfriend or simply would not answer. No matter how they scolded her she never talked back."

Throughout the following year, tension within the Waldstein home mounted. Ella's relatives learned that she was spending her evenings on Coney Island, usually at a concession stand run by a handsome married Irishman who "was not of our kind . . . and not very respectable." The man gave Ella expensive gifts, and her parents suspected that she was prostituting for him. Mrs. Waldstein begged her daughter to stay at home in the evenings. But Ella refused to give up her evenings on the town or her gentile boyfriend. By this time the girl's relationship with her family was near the breaking point.[42]

Yet often conflict with family members began even before the girls showed any definite interest in heterosexual romance or sex. They aroused the anger or disapproval of parents and older siblings simply by looking for friends and recreation outside the family setting or by seeking changes in employment without their parents' approval. Parents or guardians resented their daughters' interest in the dress, language, and amusements of urban youth and their desire to find more congenial work. Fathers especially interpreted any social independence as a threat to their authority and the cohesion of the family and tried to prohibit many activities. Thus Louisa Parsons, the seventeen-year-old daughter of a Utica, New York, house-painter-turned-insurance-agent, frequently clashed with her father because "she changed her works without I or wife knowing of it, she would be started to Sunday school meeting & would not go ther but to some other girls home." Mr. Parsons was an excitable man with a serious drinking problem, and every attempt to escape his supervision met with threats and verbal abuse.[43] Consumed by discontent and anger, Louisa refused to back down or give in to her father's demands regardless of the painful repurcussions.

Young women's commitment to autonomy sometimes took on even more intensity and risk when outraged kin resorted to physical violence. Rae Rabinowitz, a seventeen-year-old girl who initially threatened familial norms merely by looking for friends among her coworkers in Brooklyn, could see no harm in what she was doing and complained that her siblings and mother were "sticks" who wanted to sit in the house all evening while "the neighbors sit on their front stoops and visit." But her brother David had fashioned himself the household patriarch after his father deserted the family, and he refused to condone Rae's social agenda, complaining that her girlfriends made a bad impression. For months the two wrangled, and Rae suffered harsh words or beatings whenever she returned home after spending time with her peers. Although Rae's other siblings were unhappy about David's severe treatment, they could see little in the way of an alternative. According to one brother, "All of the kind talk and advice had no more effect on her than they would have on a piece of wood." Finally, when David told Rae in a "moment of exasperation" that "if she was going to run the streets and not come in at night she could leave home," the teenager took off for Coney Island with a girlfriend, willing to sever all family ties if she could gain freedom and physical safety. Rae had no money, no plans, and no place to stay, but she was past caring and impulsively ran away from home, believing that she would somehow figure out how to survive on her own.[44]

In the Waldstein, Parsons, and Rabinowitz households, adults and daughters were sharply at odds over the girls' quests for new identities. Unwilling to compromise seemingly essential moral values or patterns of authority, the parents refused to accommodate their daughters' demands; in turn, having decided that obdurate parents or siblings deserved little of their good will or respect, the young women acted in ways that accentuated their alienation.

Yet young women's persistent efforts to establish autonomous social identities did not always provoke anger or bitterness. Some parents were simply too exhausted or demoralized by their own problems, or too confused by their girls' conduct, to respond angrily. Eleanor Hamlisch's mother simply looked the other way when, in her late teens, Eleanor began to frequent cabarets, use heroin, and engage in occasional prostitution. Mrs. Hamlisch had raised five children alone, working as a practical nurse after her husband deserted her, and she had neither the interest nor strength of will to try to guide her daughter. Other parents became apathetic, but only after a prolonged period of futile strife. For example, when eighteen-year-old Cecilia Tomasi disappeared from her Rochester home in 1928, the girl's parents did not bother to look for her. In fact, Cecilia's father, an Italian baker, told a social worker that "they were glad to see her go. She had bad associates, and conducted herself vulgarly and was a bad example to the other children in the home." Cecilia had been ungovernable for years, and earlier efforts to manage her and meet "all her needs and requests" had not changed her behavior.[45] Whether parents reacted to rebellion with anger or indifference, the young women in my sample learned that they could not expect their families either to endorse or to guide their participation in youth subcultures.

Although New York's delinquent young women intentionally engaged in unorthodox conduct to establish themselves as different from and unac-countable to kin, prior experience had not taught them to view the world beyond their families' doors with a critical eye. Indeed, they were often unprepared to defend themselves against abuse or exploitation or to support themselves with the returns of legal employment. These young women participated in the life of the street with little thought and with little ability to resist the dangers it presented.

Certainly, rebellious resolve did not help to guide these young women in their relations with men. The delinquents had little understanding of gender dynamics and limited access to information about sex, venereal disease, or pregnancy. Many of them showed poor judgment in their encounters with the opposite sex. When eighteen-year-old Louise Peffley ran away from her parents' home in Gloversville, New York, she joined a traveling stage troupe called the Chinese Cabaret and immediately married one of its young members. Louise did not care for her husband; indeed, she had known him for only a few days. She simply wanted "to show her father she could leave home."[46]

In a somewhat different case, when controversy between Ella Waldstein and her Russian Jewish parents spiraled out of control, the young woman was left on her own to decipher her Irish boyfriend's intentions. Ella was already used to hiding her social affairs and troubles from her family. She had not told her parents about the neighborhood boy who sexually molested her when she was fifteen, nor had she asked for their advice when she later contracted venereal disease from another young man and needed help secur-ing medical treatment. Now, the lack of trust between parents and daughter left Ella without useful guidance or protection, and as she continued to go to Coney Island every evening to visit her boyfriend, she could only hope that he was telling the truth when he said that he would someday divorce his wife to marry her.[47]

Ella's boyfriend was probably not being entirely truthful, but he did not otherwise treat her badly. However, Ella had been molested in the past, and she was one of thirty three young women in this study who claimed to have been raped, molested, coerced into sexual relations, or subjected to physical abuse by a male partner or acquaintance. Rae Rabinowitz was one of them. When Rae ran away to Coney Island to escape her brother's abuse, she was forced to have sex with two sailors. Rae accepted their seemingly generous offer to obtain a hotel room for her, not understanding that they expected sexual favors in return. As she later told Bedford's psychiatrist, Dr. Cornelia Shorer, "I will never forget that day. . . . You never want to do such a thing only I did not want to stay on the street all night. . . . [The sailor said,] 'If you don't let us do it you won't have no place to sleep tonight.' . . . That's when I gave myself away. . . . I didn't think they would do such a thing. You know some fellows have pity."[48]

Sometimes poor judgment also led these young women into relationships with men who persuaded them to engage in criminal activity. Thus Emily Carrington participated in forgery at her husband's request. Emily had been raped by her father while she was in her mid-teens and, for her own protection, was sent to a reformatory for young girls. Shortly after her release at seventeen she married a paroled convict whom her father had befriended while he was imprisoned for raping Emily. Following her husband's direction, Emily forged endorsements on checks that he had stolen from a shirt-factory owner. In another such case, seventeen-year-old Almira Danvers moved away from her family in Ithaca, New York and, after a brief attempt to support herself, became entirely dependent on her lover. When he asked her to act as a decoy in an assault and robbery he had planned, the young woman agreed. Similarly, Myra Henning, married at sixteen to a man she had known only two months, unwittingly became involved in passing forged checks for her husband. "She did not suspect her husband of wrongdoing until . . . she learned of his interests in other women and his attendance at wild parties." And at her boyfriend's urging, Doris Sugarman stole liberty bonds, insurance papers, and bankbooks from her mother. The two young people had run away from their homes after the boy's mother refused to give them permission to marry, but after three weeks their funds ran out and they had returned to Doris' mother's looking for money.[49]

Occasionally young women claimed that their male partners led them to prostitution. Louise Peffley told the staff at Albion that her husband pushed her into prostitution after he discovered that he could not make a decent living in the theater. Louise "kept on in this life because she was afraid of him as he would beat her and threatened her life."[50] Eileen McCarthy similarly claimed that she was forced into prostitution by her lover, a man who at first had impressed her and her abusive mother as unusually high-minded. Eileen told Bedford's psychiatrist that she had met her lover when she was sixteen:

> Both she and her mother were entirely fooled by this boy. They thought he was rich and refined and must come from a fine family. He found her with another man one day and brought her home to her mother saying she was not good and wouldn't marry her. He and her mother beat her till her head was covered with blood. They were both impressed with his high moral demands. She became pregnant by him and they tried to marry but could not get a certificate as they were too young. Eileen says that is one of the luckiest things that ever happened to her as he turned out to be a common crook and lead her a hard life and she would have been more in his power if married to him. She says he forced her into prostitution and both he and his mother took her money so earned.[51]

Of course, young women also became involved in illegal activities independently of men. Patricia O'Brien, the only delinquent in this sample from a genteel background, left her Boston home because of frequent clashes with her mother and took to shoplifting clothes from New York City department stores after she lost her job as a chorus girl. "She had nobody to borrow money from [and] did not want to ask her mother as this would mean returning to Boston."[52] And though Louise and Eileen may have been forced into prostitution, most girls who became involved in commercial sex probably did so voluntarily in a risky attempt to find money and adventurous independence.

Fifty-one of the young women in my sample were committed to New York's reformatories for prostitution or solicitation, and although Chapter 2 shows that some of them may have been wrongly convicted, it is nonetheless true that the potential financial rewards of prostitution made it a relatively appealing option for unskilled and uneducated women, at least occasionally. It was especially attractive to young women who no longer lived with their families and could not count on kin for economic support; only thirty-nine of the women had been living with their families prior to arrest or conviction. Those living on their own were unlikely to survive as waitresses, servants, actresses, dance instructors, factory workers, ushers, and sales-clerks, for the wages paid to working-class young women in the early twentieth century were intended for the dependents of husbands or fathers; they were not expected to provide a living wage.[53]

Prostitution also offered young women a way to pledge themselves to a life of moral defiance and insubordination. As Ruth Rosen has pointed out, prostitution was sometimes a form of rebellion against family. "If no one seemingly cared, or if family bonds were sufficiently torn by constant generational conflict, a daughter may have felt free to choose an illegitimate means of achieving upward mobility."[54] Moreover, a young woman's willingness to make sex a marketable activity was encouraged by urban youth subcultures that sanctioned the use of sexual expression as a social and economic strategy. Joanne Meyerowitz notes that poorly-paid young women quickly discovered that access to companionship, pretty clothing, and recreation depended on the ability to attract male attention and a male pocketbook. "Through dating, pickups, gold digging, temporary alliances, and occasional prostitution, they sometimes found excitement, companionship, and, not least, some relief from poverty."[55]

Indeed, in trying to find positive meaning in commercial sex young women sometimes searched for distinctions between their conduct and "real" prostitution. Eleanor Hamlisch explained in an interview with Bedford's psychiatrist that she was not a prostitute though she "admits taking money from the men whom she knows well and with whom she has had sex relations. . . . She does not consider this prostitution; she says prostitution is going about with strange men whom one picks up on the street."[56]

Although the inmates at Bedford Hills and Albion generally divulged little to staff members about the reasons for their involvement in commercial sex, their abbreviated remarks on the subject strongly support historians' contention that financial need, alienation from kin, and involvement in urban youth subcultures all played a part. Sixteen-year-old Nanette Wilkins explained that occasional prostitution was a source of "money and pleasure" that helped to sharpen the social distinctions between herself and the overly strict aunt from whom she had run away. Nanette had a regular job as a domestic servant, but she "went with a few men twice a week who paid her" to earn money for clothes and the movies.[57] In contrast, Marian Jacoby constructed a narrative (hoping, perhaps, to gain sympathy from her keepers) in which prostitution was the outcome of family conflict and moral confusion. At the age of about sixteen Marian began to have sexual relations with her boyfriend but refused to marry him. That decision, motivated perhaps by an unwillingness to be tied down to someone she did not love, led to terrible disputes with her parents, and Marian's father eventually placed her in a private reformatory. After her release, Marian refused to live at home and moved to New York City, working occasionally as a salesgirl but earning most of her money through sexual commerce in hotels and apartments. Marian "says she didn't care what became of her—she started in the downward way & it had the best of her ever since." Yet she also admitted that the "downward way" was quite lucrative, allowing her to enjoy New York's nightclubs and theaters: she "made over $100 week—had over $1000 saved—was not on street much—was kept most time."[58]

Whatever the young women gained from their involvement in prostitution, sex work was still a perilous business. Both Nanette and Marian managed to avoid the disease, violence, and drug addiction that were often a part of that trade; in speaking of their involvement in it, they stressed the money and their access to entertainment. They could not, however, avoid the surveillance and condemnation of the state.

The inmates at Albion and Bedford Hills during the early twentieth century shared important characteristics. They were, for the most part, from the lower rungs of society. Insecurity and hardship tended to make their homes depressing and unpleasant, and they looked for amusement and companionship elsewhere. Along streets pulsing with life, and in dazzling amusement parks, movie theaters, and dance halls, these young women hoped to shed their worries, to indulge their dreams. They declared their loyalty to peer cultures, endured conflict with kin, and struck out on their own when life at home became intolerable. But city streets often failed to sustain the young women's search for autonomy and security. Pleasure balanced uneasily with danger and constraint. Many of these adolescents were ill equipped for self-sufficiency and independence. Inexperience and social constructions of gender, class, and race had severely limited their options and powers of self-preservation; consequently they often failed to defend themselves against poverty, manipulation, and sexual exploitation. Moreover, as we shall see, in repudiating familial and societal norms, these troubled rebels unwittingly invited governmental intervention, exchanging restrictive norms and harsh family discipline for the unwelcome correction of the state.

CHAPTER TWO

"The Confusion of Standard among Adolescent Girls":
Reformers Confront the Girl Problem

Disadvantaged young women's reinvention of female adolescence produced controversy not only in their own homes but in society at large. Throughout the Progressive Era, America's cities rang with the alarmed voices of vice reformers, settlement workers, and sex educators who saw this rebellion against conventional morality as an ominous development. These champions of reform were not without sympathy for working-class, immigrant, and African American young women who sought to shed the burdens of Victorian or Old World girlhood by exploring new opportunities for work, recreation, education, and community service. However, they could neither sympathize with nor trust disadvantaged females' explorations of heterosexuality, believing that most attempts to defy nineteenth-century sexual prohibitions would inevitably lead to prostitution and the defilement of American homes and communities. Her voice rising in alarm, the sex educator Dr. Mabel Ulrich told a Manhattan audience in 1915, "The great menace of the American city life today was not the man who was going around trying to lure young people into horrible lives, but was the young girl . . . who was perfectly free to roam the streets morning, noon, and night, who apparently had no moral outlook at all and who was constantly corrupting the young men and boys of large cities." Seeing shades of harlotry in lower-class young women's bold manners and casual sexual affairs, Ulrich and other Progressive reformers urged Americans to resist the sexualization of female adolescence and thus to save disadvantaged young women and their communities from the "living death" of prostitution.[1]

Adolescent girls from middle-class homes did not escape criticism for their rebellious conduct and erotic interests, but, as we shall see, they were usually too much a part of mainstream society to be suspected of behavior analogous to that of the ultimate female outsider, the prostitute. Moreover, by the 1920s when public concern over the rebellion of middle-class daughters was at its peak, some middle-class parents were themselves abandoning Victorian "prudery" for a new ethic of sexual fulfillment, prompted by the popularization of the ideas of Sigmund Freud and Havelock Ellis and the growing availabilty of birth control. Unwilling to equate the sexual fumbling of their own daughters with prostitution, privileged Americans made noticeable efforts to accommodate young women's efforts to reinvent adolescence; they listened attentively to experts in the emerging field of "mental hygiene" who endorsed "normal" adolescent sex play and denounced "outdated" efforts to repress young women's psychosexual development.

Many parents, especially the relatively poor and uneducated, were never exposed to the modern thinking of mental-health experts. They had neither the skills nor time to read advice literature and did not join parent-education programs or seek advice from experts at child-guidance clinics. Equally important, mental hygiene's permissive reformulation of female adolescence had little impact on state agencies that had already launched a deliberate campaign to contain the so-called girl problem. The young women who became inmates in New York's state reformatories between 1900 and 1930 found themselves at the receiving end of a spate of new laws and legal procedures that deliberately cast a wide net around female adolescent rebellion. In an attempt to interrupt disadvantaged girls' careless descent into corruption and vice, New York criminalized disobedience and sexual rebellion, inviting working-class parents to place "incorrigible" and "wayward" daughters who were too old to be charged as juvenile delinquents under the temporary tutelage of the state. New York also widened the legal definition of prostitution to include both casual and commercial sex and gave police license to engage in aggressive surveillance and deliberate deception while searching for immoral young women.

Undoubtedly the majority of young women in working-class, immigrant, or black communities, whatever their conduct, never saw the inside of a court or a state reformatory. Some young women, however, were bound to be caught. Those who became inmates at New York's state reformatories were not necessarily the most "disorderly" or "promiscuous" females on city streets; after all, Bedford Hills and Albion were designed for women and girls who were not yet "hardened" to lives of crime and immorality. Rather, these were young women who struggled against formidable odds to carve a new sense of self out of America's urban landscape. Alienated from kin, lacking financial resources, and dependent on their own inadequate powers of judgment and self-preservation, they were unable to elude the interventionist strategies of the state.

The sexualization of working-class female adolescence began to provoke public debate and organized resistance during the second half of the nineteenth century. Observing young women's growing participation in the work force and fearing the consequences of their exposure to harsh working conditions, tawdry amusements, and vice-ridden city streets, thousands of respectable Victorian women joined together to shield working girls from moral trespass. The reformers worried especially about the increasing numbers of self-supporting "women adrift" who lived apart from kin or domestic employers, bereft of solicitude or Christian oversight.[2]

The reform women of the late nineteenth century were primarily middle-class volunteers of profound Christian faith who believed in women's essential virtue and stressed the external pressures that caused working girls to "fall." Generally ignoring the possibility that some of these wage earners might take pleasure in confounding Victorian standards of female respectability, the reformers depicted young women as guileless victims of urbanization and industrialization: shop girls and factory workers prized virtue but lost their moral fortitude because of material and social deprivation. Overwork, poverty, and the absence of family weakened their ability to withstand the debauched pleasures of the theater or dance hall and left them vulnerable to the seductions of men and to the temptations of an "easy" life in prostitution. Desperate and forlorn, they tried, foolishly, to mitigate their suffering by responding to the entreaties of "a certain class of men who will pay vice largely, while virtue starves." Once having "fallen," they faced a cruel double standard that prevented them from retrieving their lost reputations; in contrast, their male partners easily eluded societal condemnation. In the eyes of the moral reformers, working girls were victims, not instruments, of sexual passion.[3]

Hoping to divert young women from concert saloons and cheap theaters where licentious men and prostitutes were a constant presence, the reformers tried to offer "rational" amusements, "strong, sensible teaching," and good Christian homes to the "orphaned" wage earners. They organized boarding homes, vacation societies, and social clubs for working girls in cities around the nation, cooperating with the newly organized Young Women's Christian Association and other church-affiliated organizations. In contrast to an earlier generation of women who joined antebellum reform societies to "rescue" female alcoholics and prostitutes, these reformers hoped to render rescue unnecessary by devoting much of their energy to prevention. Rescue work was not abandoned, however, and Gilded Age reform women also promoted the establishment of mission homes and reformatories where "fallen" young women and girls might be restored to "paths of rectitude and right."[4]

New York was the site of particularly vigorous female activism. By the mid 1880s, the Young Women's Christian Association of the City of New York operated thirty-three lodging and boardinghouses for self-supporting working girls in the metropolitian area, as well as a circulating library and free classes in bookkeeping, typewriting, and commercial photography. The city also boasted an active Working Girls' Society, which offered to its several hundred members low-cost housing, classes, employment services, inexpensive country vacations, and one-day excursions to nearby Yonkers, Staten Island, and Glen Island. The preventive network was similarly active in New York's smaller cities. The YWCA, for example, organized services for young women and girls in Albany, Buffalo, Hudson, Poughkeepsie, Rochester, Syracuse, and Utica. And seventeen branches of the Girls' Friendly Society, an affiliate of the Episcopal church, offered classes, library facilities, employment assistance, and recreational opportunities to young working women in Albany, New York City, Rochester, Utica, and Yonkers. For working-class girls who had already succumbed to the temptations of immorality, private charities in cities throughout the state opened small group "homes" that promised "reformation and protection." Finally, with support from the New York State Board of Charities and the New York State legislature, reformers affiliated with the Women's Prison Association established three large state reformatories capable of redeeming hundreds of "fallen" young women in their late teens and twenties: the Hudson House of Refuge in 1887 (reorganized to serve delinquent girls under the age of sixteen in 1903), the Western House of Refuge at Albion in 1893, and the New York State Reformatory for Women at Bedford Hills in 1901.[5]

Over time, however, nineteenth-century women activists began to question their moral assumptions, reevaluating working girls' moral character and the efficacy of their own programs. Engaged as they were in preventive work, the reformers pondered the reasons for female immorality, analyzing the likely moment of young women's "fall" so that timely action might avert a fateful plunge into iniquity. But as their exposure to working girls grew, they were dismayed to find that the objects of their charity often seemed intentionally ill mannered, vain, and careless about their virtue. The girls wore suggestive clothing, stayed out on the streets and in dance halls late at night, and flirted indiscriminately with men, rebuffing all forms of moral uplift and any sign of patronage or charity.

Certainly, it was possible to explain this behavior. Grace Hoadley Dodge, chair of New York's Committee on the Elevation of the Poor in Their Homes and director of the New York Association of Working Girls' Societies, had no doubt but that young women's "defects" of character could be attributed to industrial toil and material privation; these forces acted "directly upon the nervous system . . . preparing an easy victory for the army of temptations that assail from without." Still, whatever the source of their defects, vain and pleasure-seeking working girls were agents as well as victims of immorality. The theme of victimization continued to dominate preventive work for the remainder of the nineteenth century, but women active in preventive organizations could not entirely ignore the willful defiance and moral indifference of those they endeavored to protect and improve. Unexpectedly, and with deep bewilderment, female reformers encountered young women who challenged the merit of Victorian constructions of womanhood.[6]

In the early twentieth century worry about young women's potential for wrongdoing increased as a new generation of Progressive reformers sought to "save" working girls from immorality and vice. Many Progressive reformers were college-educated women and men who hoped to resolve a host of urban problems by the forceful deployment of civic virtue and social-scientific method. Prostitution captured their special attention—as it seemed to symbolize modern America's moral declension—to demonstrate in especially stark terms the tragic consequences of rampant commercialization, unchecked immigration, and unrestrained industrial exploitation. But even as they revived the language of victimization and spoke in anguished tones of impoverished virgins forced into prostitution by the duplicity of profit-seeking foreign-born "white slavers," Progressive reformers "discovered" thousands of young women who appeared to engage voluntarily, even happily, in immoral activities that ranged from suggestive dancing to commercial sex. More so than the reform activists of the 1870s and 1880s, Progressive reformers felt compelled to acknowledge and interrogate working-class female adolescents' rebellion against Victorian morality. Labeling their discovery the "girl problem," the reformers called for an aggressive season of intervention. Without it, "thrill-seeking" young women and girls would continue to corrupt community health and morality, even as they wrecked their own chances for happiness.[7]

The Progressive interpretation of the girl problem was presented with unusual clarity in *Young Working Girls*, a 1913 publication written by Robert A. Woods and Albert J. Kennedy, officers of the National Federation of Settlements. Based on evidence submitted by two thousand settlement workers employed in cities around the nation, *Young Working Girls* became an important resource for urban reformers. In the words of Harriet McDoual Daniels, one of the settlement-house researchers for the book and the author of a separate volume on urban girlhood, "[for] those of us who have sought in vain for literature on the girl problem, this book, with its wealth of material and its sane broad point of view, gives a comprehensive understanding of this most difficult of all problems."[8]

Woods and Kennedy defined the girl problem as that "confusion of standard among adolescent girls, which is everywhere noticed and commented upon." In poor neighborhoods, young women and girls had little desire "to stand well in the eyes" of their elders; neither tradition nor family claimed their affections. Rather, individual pleasure was their goal; casual and promiscuous sexual relations the route they traveled to obtain it.[9]

In the authors' estimation, the girl problem was caused largely by imperfections in modern society, among them "the reorganization of [girls'] sphere of life through its invasion by modern industry, . . . ill-regulated work [that forced girls] to spend their strength beyond reason, . . . the disintegration of neighborhood life in towns and cities, . . . [and finally] a vast system of commercialized amusements . . . radically in need of regulation." But while the authors took pains (as had the reformers who preceded them) to enumerate defects in the urban environment, they identified for the first time "causes within" adolescent girls that made them highly susceptible to immoral stimuli, namely "the physical changes and the mental excitation which characterize adolescence."[10]

Here, Woods and Kennedy drew on the recent work of G. Stanley Hall, president and senior professor of psychology at Clark University and the nation's leading authority on adolescence. Synthesizing the research of dozens of physicians and psychologists and employing the evolutionary and psychoanalytic theories of Charles Darwin and Sigmund Freud, Hall characterized adolescence as a developmental stage of unusual intensity and danger. During adolescence boys and girls broke out of the narrow consciousness of childhood to engage in a "long pilgrimage of the soul from its old level to a higher maturity." Most adolescents experienced confusion and intense emotion as they began to consider their place in the larger world; though capable of noble action, improperly supervised adolescents were likely to plunge recklessly into delinquency and vice.[11]

The sex instinct in female adolescents was especially strong and, like adolescence itself, extraordinarily problematic. According to Hall, the sex instinct had a "boundless plasticity. . . . nothing is so educable, so easily exalted or debased." Properly channeled sexual impulses could make female adolescence "the culminating stage of life with its . . . enthusiasm and zest for all that is good, beautiful, true, and heroic." However, when adolescent girls were denied moral guidance, their passion tragically became the "psychic foundation and background upon which the colossal and . . . ever more youthful evil of prostitution is built."[12]

Eager to apply Hall's findings to urban experience, Woods and Kennedy used the evidence gathered by their colleagues to show precisely how the girl problem grew out of the everyday circumstances of the nation's working girls. The typical adolescent girl, whatever her social class, was a creature "acutely conscious of her individuality" who craved both independence and admiration. She experienced "a practically overwhelming consciousness of sex combined with a growing desire for companionship. . . . Driven to self-expression, she wavers between day-dreams and sudden spurts of energy which drive her to endeavor to do everything and to be everything."[13]

The desires and impulses of adolescence were not, the authors admitted, necessarily wicked. Indeed, when spirited girls were offered protection and guidance, they often demonstrated "exceptional sympathy and leadership" and a fine religious and ethical sensibility. But in poor industrial neighborhoods thoughtful supervision was in short supply. Factory and store managers made no effort to protect the girls they employed, while ill-regulated dance halls and public amusements exposed them to moral license and the enticements of pimps and procurers. Most important, Woods and Kennedy noted, parents in immigrant and working-class homes abdicated responsibility for their daughters' moral development and failed to channel adolescent passions into nonsexual activities:

Little effort is made to prepare the daughter for the opportunities and dangers of her work in life, and the girl has constantly to face situations unfamiliar to herself, and even to her mother, at a time when her judgment is unformed, and her emotions least controlled. Training and knowledge, which should be given in the home, have to be picked up in the street. Only infrequently do parents consciously organize the home to protect the daughter from herself and others, to minister wisely to her physical and recreative needs, and to sustain in her those vague reachings out after a larger and fuller life which are characteristic of adolescence.[14]

Woods and Kennedy claimed that working girls, deprived of the direction they needed, tried to satisfy their yearnings for independence and admiration by rebelling against their elders and indulging in "showy dressing" and "loud talk." Similarly, their awareness of sex and desire for companionship often led them "into short-lived and cliquey alliances with those of [their] own sex, and into various forms of adventure with members of the other sex." Tragically, most young working women failed to recognize how short was the distance between "moral lapse" and prostitution; at once headstrong and naive, they did not realize that "the girl who falls finds it almost impossible to regain her self-respect in communities where she is known." Moreover, many girls mistakenly believed that "if they do not accept money they keep themselves without the sphere of prostitution."[15]

Similar representations of the girl problem appeared in the reports and tracts issued by urban vice commissions, although here the sympathetic tone of the settlement workers was often supplanted by alarmism, a tendency to stress disadvantaged young women's selfish individualism, their disregard for hard work, and their enthusiastic participation in immoral relations. Organized and directed by prominent figures in business, medicine, the law, organized religion, and academics, the common task of the nation's twenty-seven state and local vice commissions was to reveal the myriad ways in which sexual indecency and prostitution threatened America's physical well-being and moral order; not surprisingly, the commissions tended to arouse hostility rather than compassion toward girls with "loose morals."[16]

Thus New York's Committee of Fifteen, an association of prominent business and professional men (and predecessor to the better-known Committee of Fourteen), complained that many young girls were drawn to "experiment with immorality" because they could not stand "tedious and irksome labor . . . [and] are impregnated with the view that individual happiness is the end of life." In an even more condemning tone the Massachusetts vice commission protested that young working girls "profess utter lack of respect for their parents and contempt for their home life. . . . [Many of these same girls] habitually have immoral relations with boys and men without expecting or accepting financial reward or gain. . . . Some of them are already willing and anxious to begin a life of professional immorality."[17]

In contrast to settlement workers, numerous vice commissions also emphasized "feeblemindedness," preferring to link female immorality to mental defect rather than to the typical, albeit misdirected, urges of adolescence. By the second decade of the twentieth century, intelligence testing was widespread in penal institutions, hospitals, and asylums, and the results appeared to disclose high rates of inferior intellectual capability among inmates, especially prostitutes. With such data at hand, many vice reformers in the 1910s were quick to infer that feeblemindedness must be the primary "cause" of female delinquency.[18] Relying on this facile explanation, the Pittsburgh vice commission claimed that "underlying all other causes [of immorality], perhaps a predisposition for the life of the prostitute must exist." Clearly, feeblemindedness was that predisposition. "Born with defective intelligence and shiftless tendencies, they are predestined to become criminaloids. Without much resistance they enter upon and follow the easiest way."[19] The Wisconsin commission elaborated on this subject: "Not only does the mental defect often take the form of sexual perversion and abnormal sex impulses, but the feeble-minded girl, not able to take results into consideration, not keen enough to foresee the consequences of immoral acts, and too ignorant of her own body to understand the meaning of her feelings and the results which attend relaxation from a normal standard, falls an easy prey in the hands of a seducer."[20]

Whether they highlighted feeblemindedness or not, by the early twentieth century America's Progressive reformers were aware of a daunting girl problem. Convinced that undisciplined working girls presented the nation with a grave and vexing problem, and certain that parents were ill equipped to manage them, settlement workers and vice reformers joined with club leaders, probation officers, social workers, and sex educators in New York and other states to devise practical means to bring young women under control.

Significantly, outright repression or punishment was not their principal object. Many of the individuals involved in this work were themselves avowed "New Women"; having defied gender conventions to pursue careers or an active public life, they expressed compassion for adolescent girls from impoverished or immigrant homes who wanted to loosen and redefine the ties that bound them to their families. Harriet McDoual Daniels declared that women settlement workers wanted to prepare adolescent girls "not for the older type of womanhood but for the new and responsible position of woman in the world." And Mary Simkhovitch of New York City's Greenwich House claimed that her goal was to foster "the freeing of woman that she may become the master of her own life."[21] The reformers accepted adolescent girls' impassioned search for self as appropriate to their life stage, dismissing the traditional Victorian demand that girls behave in a submissive and undemonstrative manner. They acknowledged too that female adolescents were sexual beings, rejecting the Victorian belief in girls' essential passionlessness. Their updated picture of girlhood showed the female adolescent "in all her pleasure-loving, drifting adventures . . . hunting steadily for the deeper and stronger forces of life . . . [feeling] for the first time the insistent needs and desires of her womanhood."[22]

Still, Progressive reformers refused to forswear female chastity as a behavioral ideal, convinced that the only alternative for working girls was prostitution. Invisible in privileged communities (though it was surely an indulgence of many middle-class men), prostitution appeared to be pervasive in urban entertainment districts and in the neighborhoods of the transient poor. To the reformers and officials who endorsed the campaign against the girl problem, the traffic in women was a business conducted for profit, and unscrupulous police officers, saloon keepers, dance-hall operators, tenement owners, and young men on the make did not hesitate to gain by it, indifferent to the suffering and disease it caused. Even more important, prostitution's ubiquity demonstrated that young women of low social status erred tragically in trying to throw off Victorian and Old World sexual conventions. In urban ghettos the sexualization of female adolescence served to simplify the work of pimps and other immoral business operators, providing them with a steady supply of young women foolish enough to believe in false promises of ease, luxury, and excitement. Reform activists could not but conclude that the sexualization of female adolescence was a spurious and dangerous route to happiness. Unable to discern any essential difference between the sexually adventurous girl of low social status and the prostitute, convinced that every act of flirtation was a step "on the road to destruction," they recast virtue as a goal to be achieved by deliberate effort and searched for ways to reconcile this aim with young women's legitimate quest for self-expression.[23]

Over time, Progressive reformers, most of them women, endorsed a variety of practical reforms, expanding and revitalizing the field of preventive work. First, claiming that impulsive young working girls could not dedicate themselves to virtue if they were prey to immoral temptations, manipulation, and coercion, reformers around the nation endorsed an array of protective policy initiatives. As leader of the Committee on Amusements and Vacation Resources of Working Girls, Belle Lindner Israels lobbied unceasingly for protective reforms in New York City, while other women and men worked in Chicago, San Francisco, and elsewhere to regulate dance halls, local hotels, and tenements through laws that restricted the sale of alcohol and prohibited "tough dancing," prostitution, and pandering in commercial properties. The reformers also urged the passage of laws outlawing white slavery or "compulsory prostitution." In New York the new laws made it illegal for a man to compel his wife or any other woman by "force, fraud, intimidation, or threats" to enter into prostitution.[24]

Under the banner of protection, Progressive reformers also tried to enlist working girls in moral "self-defense," urging them to join "protective leagues" that engaged in community surveillance. This facet of protective work developed first in New York City, where Maude Miner, a graduate of Smith College and Columbia University and a tireless advocate of preventive and protective reforms, founded the Girls' Protective League in 1910. The adolescent members of the league investigated and reported immoral conditions at dance halls, amusement parks, and moving picture theaters and compiled a "black list" of workshops and employers who subjected young women to insults and harrassment. They were also expected to encourage one another in "right thinking" and moral behavior; as *The Survey* magazine reported, "Each girl is expected to become to some extent, her sister's keeper." By 1915 the league in New York City had 2,039 members organized in twenty-seven neighborhoods. During the 1910s and 1920s girls' protective associations also formed in Cleveland, Detroit, Minneapolis, New Haven, and many other cities, and a national agency, the Girls' Protective Council, was established in 1925.[25]

Closely related to their support for protective measures, Progressive reformers sought to bring working girls into closer association with ethical and educated women, stepping up sponsorship of girls' clubs in New York and other states. During the 1910s and 1920s most of the clubs were led by professional female social workers and college-educated volunteers, that is, women whose training allowed them to understood and "sympathize" with the needs and interests of adolescent girls in a modern urban society and thus to compensate for the deficiencies of working-class, black, or immigrant parents. The YWCA and Girls' Friendly Society of the Episcopal church took a leading role in organizing club activities for young women in New

York's smaller cities and towns. In New York City the YWCA and Girls' Friendly Society were joined by dozens of settlement houses, the Girls' Athletic Club, the New York Association of Women Workers, the Girls' Protective League, and the Vacation Savings Fund Association in organizing clubs for young women and girls. Many settlement houses made a special effort to reach out to immigrant young women from Catholic and Jewish households; the Educational Alliance, Hebrew Educational Society of Brooklyn, Young Women's Hebrew Association, and the Council of Jewish Women also organized girls' clubs for the Jewish community. The clubs gave adolescent girls opportunities to hold public dances in "wholesome" settings, attend concerts and museums, participate in literary debates, study dramatics, meet with labor leaders and consumer activists, engage in homemaking and handicraft projects, and take part in community service, charitable, and fund-raising acitivities.[26]

Similarly, the National Urban League and other black organizations and churches organized recreational, educational, and religious programs for adolescent girls of African American descent, hoping to keep them away from dangerous amusements and protect them from immoral landlords and employers. For example, New York City's Association for the Protection of Colored Girls helped new migrants from the South find suitable employment and wholesome recreation and directed them to housing provided by the White Rose Home, the Colored Mission, and the black YWCA of Brooklyn. St. Cyprian's Parish, located in a poor black district on Manhattan's West Side, sponsored public dances and an athletic club for girls with the help of a paid social worker and two volunteers from Columbia University. And with the cooperation and prodding of black reformers, the Henry Street Settlement in Manhattan opened a separate "colored" branch to meet the recreational and educational needs of New York City's burgeoning African American population, male and female.[27]

Progressive reformers pursued a third line of defense against female adolescent immorality by developing sex education programs for adolescent girls, especially girls from disadvantaged and working-class homes. The reformers' investigations showed that most parents completely ignored their daughters' need for sex education; young women growing up in poor and vice-ridden neighborhoods consequently took direction from peers who knew little about meaningful love relationships but a great deal about "romance" and the immediate gratification of erotic impulses. This was a tragic state of affairs, for those girls who had "strong desires for the experience of love" and who would have made "the most valuable wives and mothers" were instead driven to "immature and dangerous love affairs" and "conspicuous conduct on the streets." Physician sex educators, settlement workers, vice reformers, and girls' club leaders hoped to strengthen working girls' loyalty to a strict standard of sexual virtue, not by insisting that the sexual impulse was wicked but rather by teaching that it was an instrument of beauty and spiritual power when restricted to the marital relationship. As Woods and Kennedy pointed out, "The definite problem is building up a sound coherent attitude toward life and human nature . . . [and] awakening loyalty to the present and the future self, to the home, and to the neighborhood."[28]

Realizing that long-held taboos discouraged candid discussions about sexuality between parents and daughters, Progressive reformers urged club leaders and settlement workers to make sex education a common topic of conversation in girls' clubs. At the same time, Progressive reformers worked to legitimize sex education by organizing at the national level. Here, the YWCA became the undisputed leader in the field, hiring female physicians to give lectures on sex to schoolgirls and working girls, mothers, college women, normal-school students, social workers, and girls' club leaders in cities and towns around the nation. The YWCA's level of activity intensified dramatically during World War I as it cooperated with the federal government's efforts to discourage promiscuous relations between reckless young women and khaki-clad soldiers and sent more than 149 women lecturers, all of them trained physicians, around the country to tell audiences of young women and mothers that they must treat "square conduct as an expression of loyalty to the cause for which America was fighting."[29]

Opposed to the old double standard, wartime sex educators nonetheless urged young women to acknowledge the differences between male and female sexuality, most important, to appreciate men's inability to stop at flirtation. Thus Dr. Rachelle Yarros, one of the most noted wartime lecturers, told her female audiences that they must understand the dangers of "coquetting" and "leading on." These forms of behavior gave girls "a good deal of satisfaction" but were viewed by men as "an open invitation to take liberties." Katharine Bement Davis, director of the Social Hygiene Division of the Commission on Training Camp Activities, similarly stressed the importance of feminine restraint. Her message to the adolescent girl was that it was wrong to "play with love."[30]

As a final preventive strategy, Progressive reformers strongly endorsed intervention by professional social workers to keep girls who were already in "moral danger" from embarking on "careers" in delinquency. In New York

City a number of social service organizations—the Jewish Board of Guardians, Catholic Charities, the (Episcopal) Church Mission of Help, Big Sisters, and the New York Probation and Protective Association (later the Girls' Service League)—worked with rebellious or sexually delinquent adolescent females who had been referred to them by parents, teachers, or community leaders. Organized by Maude Miner in 1908, the New York Probation and Protective Association also operated a home for delinquent girls called Waverly House. In Upstate New York, similar work was undertaken by groups such as the State Charities Aid Association. Hoping to interrupt young women's descent into delinquency, the agencies adopted the "individualized" and "scientific" methods of the emerging social-work profession: trained social workers and volunteers carefully investigated each girl's circumstances, then attempted to "adjust" parental expectations, schooling, vocational training, employment, and recreation to suit her needs and interests. Over the years, most of these agencies also hired staff psychiatrists and psychologists who conducted mental examinations and studied the "emotional factors" and "mental defects," including "feeblemindedness," that contributed to girls' rebellion and delinquency.[31]

Female police officers also participated in delinquency prevention and intervention. During the Progressive Era, advocates of prevention lobbied hard for women police to patrol and supervise young women in parks and in dance halls and other commercial amusements. The city of Rochester established the precedent of using female law-enforcement agents to prevent female sexual delinquency when it hired its first woman officer in 1913. Other cities around the nation rapidly followed Rochester's example, with the greatest proliferation in hiring occurring during World War I, when young girls flocked to military camps to meet men in uniform. Taking direction from the federal government, local communities hired hundreds of women to patrol military training camps and nearby places of amusement and to prevent or stop illicit trysts between young women and soldiers. The women saw themselves as both professional social workers and surrogate mothers, providing guidance to young girls who might be tempted to stray from the paths of virtue. Specifically, they tried to protect young women both from their own poor judgment and impulsivity and from the influence of prostitutes and immoral or duplicitous men. Much of their time was spent working with runaway girls, returning them to their homes and trying to forge some sort of reconciliation between parents and daughters. By 1925 Binghamton, Ithaca, Poughkeepsie, Rochester, Syracuse, and Utica were among the many cities in New York with one or two policewomen on staff.

New York City appointed its first woman police officer in 1918 and by 1925 had a force of sixty-one policewomen.[32]

Women and men involved in Progressive reform realized that the preventive network could never fully contain the girl problem. Many young women escaped the notice of club leaders, sex educators, social workers, and female police officers. As reformer Belle Lindner Israels noted in 1909 after visting summer amusement places in New York City, "One is struck by the absence of the settlement girl. Of many hundreds of girls spoken to only nine had ever heard of a settlement or a church society."[33] Other young women deliberately avoided the preventive network, wary of the service providers' moral intent.[34] And parents, especially the alcoholic or abusive, were often inclined to look askance at intrusive social workers or other "do-gooders." For example, although young Julia Kramer, an inmate at Bedford Hills, had at various times been referred to the Henry Meinhart Settlement Club, Big Sisters, the Girls' Service League, and the Jewish Board of Guardians by schoolteachers who complained of her poor scholarship and "vile stories to other girls in her class," Julia's father, a dry-goods store owner who "disciplined his children by inflicting severe beatings and giving them little recreation," refused to accept agency advice or supervision, even after Julia ran away from home.[35]

The preventive network may have served as a useful, albeit flawed, agent of support and socialization for thousands of adolescent girls, but others were untouched by its efforts. Fewer than ten of the one hundred inmates in this study had any contact with a preventive agency prior to their arrest and conviction.

Acknowledging the limitations of preventive and protective work, reformers in New York and elsewhere called upon the state to take direct control of young women and girls whose treacherous descent into immorality could not otherwise be halted.[36] Lawrence Veiller, a member of New York's Committee of Fourteen and described as a "hard-boiled realist" who "harbored little faith in the inherent goodness of his fellow men," played a leading role in these efforts.[37] He was supported by the other members of the committee, including Maude Miner and Belle Israels, who had long worked to obtain protective and preventive reforms for working girls. The committee acted on the belief that disadvantaged adolescent girls felt the power of their sexuality but lacked the ability to judge or control their conduct; absent effective familial or community controls, only state action could prevent these unruly young women from harming themselves and their neighbors. By persistent lobbying, Veiller and the Committee of Fourteen won in 1923 the passage of a state law that superseded a number of inadequate local statutes and made it easier for frustrated working-class parents to use courts, probation officers, and reformatories to extract obedience and sexual virtue from "wayward" adolescent daughters. The committee also obtained legal reforms that expanded the definition of prostitution and dramatically enhanced the state's powers of surveillance, allowing undercover police to entrap and arrest disorderly young women who lived apart from and beyond the oversight of kin.[38]

It was in hopes of preserving her home that in June 1917 Alice Sterling took her seventeen-year-old daughter Ilene to the Rockland County Court in Suffern, New York, and asked that the girl be sent to the New York State Reformatory for Women at Bedford Hills. Ilene and her mother brought to the court a tempestuous and intensely personal conflict over the meaning of female adolescence. While Ilene took behavioral and moral clues from her working-class peers, Mrs. Sterling demanded filial obedience and adherence to nineteenth-century standards of girlhood decorum. As a working-class woman who had only recently settled into a stable marriage (her third), Ilene's mother did not want her good fortune and hard-won respectability destroyed by a wayward teenage girl. She complained that her daughter was disobedient and sexually promiscuous and that she "could do nothing with her." Lately, Ilene "had been associating with a railroad man," and Mrs. Sterling feared that the girl was pregnant again, for the second time in two years.

Ilene had a different story to tell. In court, and later as an inmate at Bedford Hills, the teenager reported that her home life was unbearable. Her first stepfather had been abusive and alcoholic, and following the stillborn birth of her child, she became the victim of her mother's unreasonably strict supervision and constant "nagging." Ilene "felt all the time that her people were talking about her having the child and felt that they were above her." Twice she ran away from home to escape her mother's rebukes. Ilene had some good times living on her own, but the various jobs she found were ill paying and physically exhausting, and she was raped one evening by a man who took her and two girlfriends for an automobile ride. If she was indeed pregnant for a second time, the man responsible was her rapist. Ilene could not understand why her quest for independence and her unfortunate pregnancies need cost her her mother's affection and understanding. But cost her they did, and the older woman begged for state assistance after deciding that the girl was completely beyond her control.[39]

Ilene's case was neither unusual nor isolated. Seeking to protect their homes from conflict and disorder, and fearful of the loss of social standing that might come from having an "immoral" daughter, many desperate parents made recourse to the courts during the early twentieth century; twenty-two of the one hundred young women in this study were given reformatory sentences at the request of family members. Thus, just days after Rae Rabinowitz ran away to Coney Island to escape her brother's violent methods of control, her family located her, took her to court, and asked that she be committed to Bedford Hills as an "incorrigible girl." And Rosa Covello, the seventeen-year-old daughter of an Italian peddler, was charged as a "wayward minor" after trying to protect her boyfriend from prosecution for rape. Rosa's father had forced her to sign a complaint against the young man, hoping to disguise his daughter's sexual misconduct and to protect his family's reputation; in protest, Rosa ran away from home, attended her lover's arraignment, and cleared his name. For her outrageous disobedience, Rosa's parents had their daughter sentenced to Bedford Hills.[40]

African American parents made use of the courts as deliberately as did immigrant and Anglo-American parents. When twenty-year-old Evelyn Blackwell became pregnant "after running about nights with different men," her father, a respected African American mechanic, "absolutely refused to have the girl at home." Relations between Evelyn and her parents had been severely strained by two earlier pregnancies, and the girl had been pushed into a hasty and disastrous marriage while awaiting the birth of her second child. Now, Evelyn's father, a recent widower, could not stand the dishonor (and perhaps the expense) of yet a third illegitimate child. If Evelyn's mother had been alive, the matter might have been handled differently, but Evelyn's father took his daughter to court and "asked to have the girl sent away." Similarly, when Deborah Herman's hardworking black mother found out that her unruly daughter was pregnant, she "did not care to have her home without being married so asked to have her sent away where she'd learn better."[41]

Parents who had struggled for months or more to control a disobedient daughter usually went to court in reponse to a sign or act of defiance—an out-of-wedlock pregnancy, running away from home, or testifying on behalf of a boyfriend—that signaled unequivocally a daughter's refusal to submit to family discipline. So too, a love affair that violated racial, religious, or ethnic boundaries might be interpreted as the "final straw." Ella Waldstein was taken to court by her Russian Jewish parents, charged with "wilful disobedience," and sent to Bedford Hills when she refused to stop seeing her married Irish boyfriend. And Lena Meyerhoff's Russian immigrant parents, though reluctant to act, finally took their girl to court on the advice of the Jewish Board of Guardians after her illicit romance with a black chauffeur produced a bastard child. Mrs. Meyerhoff asked for a reformatory sentence on the grounds that the girl "habitually associates with dissolute persons, . . . left her home in Woodbridge [N.Y.] . . . and came to New York City where she lived with J. Smith to whom she is not married and bore an illegitimate child to him."42

In requesting state assistance, the parents of disobedient and sexually rebellious girls took advantage of a novel provision of New York's penal law, one that permitted a legal partnership between families and the criminal justice system. That partnership began in 1886, when, responding to public pressure, New York City amended a municipal statute to allow parents or the police to request a reformatory commitment for any girl over the age of twelve who is "found in a reputed house of prostitution or assignation; or is willfully disobedient to parent or guardian and is in danger of becoming morally depraved." The 1886 law was amended several times, and under the so-called incorrigible girl statutes, disobedient and immoral young women were sent to various private reformatories, including the Protestant Episcopal House of Mercy, the Roman Catholic House of Good Shepherd, and the New York Magdalen House (later Inwood House). After it opened in 1901, the state reformatory at Bedford Hills also accepted "incorrigible" and "ungovernable" young women. The statutes were especially useful to parents and guardians whose girls were over fifteen years of age and therefore too old to be disciplined as juvenile delinquents.43

The laws did not apply to adolescent females beyond the boundaries of New York City, but by the late nineteenth and early twentieth centuries, Upstate families occasionally made creative use of local and state laws on vagrancy, disorderly conduct, and petit larceny to secure the commitment of rebellious girls to the state's reformatories.44 Thus Millicent Potter was committed to Albion after her father, a carpenter, went to court complaining that "for six months past, [she] has been frequenting disorderly houses against the wishes of her parents and becoming an inmate of such houses." Penelope Jaros's mother, the wife of a truck and cart driver, asked for her daughter's commitment to Albion on the grounds that the girl "idles her time around the city." And eighteen-year-old Eva Pomering, a farmer's daughter, was sent to Albion at the request of her older sister Susan after a Buffalo magistrate convicted the girl of stealing thirteen dollars from her Italian lover. Eva had been sexually promiscuous for some time and was infected with both syphillis and gonorrhea. Susan Pomering had tried to change her sister's habits and to find a job and medical treatment for her, but Eva had resisted her sister's care, and the arrest and conviction for petit larceny gave Susan an opportunity to ask the state for help.[45]

In 1923 New York passed the Wayward Minor Act, giving formal recognition to the legal rights of Upstate parents and guardians and precipitating a dramatic increase in the number of young women committed to the reformatories at Bedford Hills and Albion for defying the values and dictates of their kin.[46] Lawrence Veiller, the bill's principal author, asserted that the new law was an "urgent necessity in New York state. . . . Parental control of . . . youths is decreasing and there is no substitute for it." Indeed, Veiller remarked, "every day throughout the state mothers apply to the magistrates for aid in correcting wayward daughters who through evil companions are in danger of becoming morally depraved and leading a life of vice and crime." Hoping Veiller's measure would save many hundreds of young women from moral disaster, preventive associations and women's clubs strongly supported the bill; it also gained ready sponsorship in the state senate.[47] In addition, Veiller's proposal gained indirect support from the Court of Special Sessions of the City of New York when it issued a 1923 decision upholding the conviction and commitment of a nineteen-year-old girl under the old incorrigibility statute. Eschewing a narrow or merely technical argument in favor of conviction, the court offered sweeping validation of parents' right to demand obedience and virtue from their adolescent daughters:

> Under this statute [the defendant] is forbidden to do certain things because they are bad for her, and at this period of her mental and moral development, i.e. during her minority, the defendant is required to recognize not alone the proper exercise of parental authority, the commands and limitations of her parent or guardian, unless emancipated, but also, the fundamental principles of righteousness which underlie all human conduct, and which require obedience and demand respect to the parent and to the dictates of the moral law in its application to the family relation, tested by the distinction between right and wrong. This duty of the defendant rests on the fundamentals of protection of the family and its social welfare.[48]

With the passage of the Wayward Minor Law, the main provisions of the old "incorrigible girl" statutes were extended statewide to aid in the control of adolescent females.[49] The new law also eliminated some frustrating deficiencies in the old laws, the worst being that they failed to specify the upper age limit of defendants—that is, whether they applied to young women over the age of eighteen—and offered only vague guidelines as to the presentation of evidence in court.[50] Targeting young women in late adolescence, the Wayward Minor Law held that disobedient or immoral females between the ages of sixteen and twenty-one could be adjudged wayward minors solely on the testimony of their guardians.[51]

While New York's incorrigible-girl and wayward-minor laws upheld the principle of filial obedience, they simultaneously affirmed the state's obligation to compensate for the ineptitude of working-class, immigrant, and African American parents by devising measures to restore young women to lives of morality and obedience. State and private reformatories provided one site for behavioral reform. During the 1910s, however, probation had replaced the reformatory sentence as the preferred first option for inexperienced prostitutes and incorrigible girls. Validating that option, the Wayward Minor Act stipulated that parents might keep their daughters at home under the supervision of a probation officer rather than commit them immediately to a reformatory. Girls on probation avoided a punitive sentence; instead, taking direction from a trained probation officer, they were supposed to learn to cope with the demands of work and family and to resist the temptations of the street.

In New York City young women were often assigned to probation officers employed by the Jewish Board of Guardians, the (Episcopal) Church Mission of Help, Catholic Charities, or the New York Protective and Probation Society and its successor, the Girls' Service League. In Upstate New York, they were taken in hand by probation officers working directly for the courts or for the State Charities Aid Association. Ten of the young women in this study had been placed on probation by judges who thought them capable of change outside a reformatory setting.[52]

In theory, probation officers were to provide young women with regular supervision, helping them to resolve problems at home, school, or work which stood in the way of their good conduct. Probation officers were also supposed to provide advice to parents, telling them how to supervise their daughters without denying the girls leisure or "wholesome" amusement. As one probation officer remarked, "The girl who doesn't have the amusement that goes with her age in life has been deprived of what ought to be her's."[53] In practice, however, probation was a flawed and often ineffective system. In the early twentieth century most cities in New York suffered from a chronic shortage of probation officers; indeed, Edwin Cooley's 1927 state survey concluded that most probationers were visited fewer than eight times a year, with each visit lasting only ten to fifteen minutes. Moreover, Cooley found that only five courts in the state had probation bureaus that "utilize a definite plan of constructive treatment"; consequently in many cases "there is no assurance that the supervision is not . . . lacking in constructive imagination and sound guidance."[54]

Not surprisingly, when probation officers did make their infrequent visits, they discovered, in the words of probation officer Alice C. Smith, that "to adjust the difficulty in the home that has driven [the girl] away . . . is a difficult thing to do."[55] Probation officers rarely spoke the language of immigrant parents who were not yet fluent in English; even when language was not a barrier, parents resisted the meddlesome questions and guidance of probation officers. According to Katharine Bement Davis, Bedford Hill's first superintendent and an outspoken critic of probation, "incorrigible" young women who were sent back to their own homes by the courts inevitably encountered conditions "exactly what they were when the relationship was such as to drive the girl to go out. . . . The mother is just the nag that she always was; the father is just as severe if she is out late nights."[56]

Returned to her parents after being convicted of incorrigibility for staying away from home over a weekend, Anna Levinson's experience clearly illustrates the weaknesses of probation. The probation officer assigned to Anna's case by the Jewish Board of Guardians found that the girl's parents were unresponsive to her suggestions and that nothing she could do would make them change. They were unwilling to grant Anna any freedom or recreation, believing that it was enough to wait for the girl "to become older and settle down and be contented with her home, as are the other children in the family." Hostilities in the Levinson household escalated, yet they were hidden for some time from the probation officer by Anna's mother. Anna later told staff members at Bedford Hills that her mother "was always telling the Probation Officers and Social Workers how good and kind they [the parents] were to her, but in reality the mother and father were continually quarrelling and the home life was anything but peaceful and she for one was anxious to break away. . . . The mother would not hesitate to tell neighbors and relatives the details of her daughter's incorrigibility." Unable to get along with her family, Anna was back in court within six months; this time she was sent to the House of Good Shepherd, a private reformatory, for a year. At the end of the year she was once again returned to her parents but ran away after less than two months at home. Eight weeks later she was arrested for prostitution and committed to Bedford Hills.[57]

Although she was atypical of the reformatory inmates in this study for having experienced probation, once Anna ran away from home she became much like the seventy-eight young women who were sent to Bedford Hills or Albion after a police arrest and court conviction (fifty-one for solicitation or prostitution, twenty-seven for offenses ranging from disorderly conduct to petty larceny and assault). These young women shared with the wayward minors and incorrigible girls histories of domestic dissatisfaction and family conflict. But most of them were no longer living with their families, having fled the poverty, strict supervision, and onerous filial obligations of their adolescence. Living without kin, they confronted formidable obstacles to economic survival, frequently using casual sex and occasional prostitution as routes to upward mobility and social autonomy, sometimes resorting to petty theft or other criminal activity. And denied the aura of social respectability that family membership conferred, sooner or later they came face-to-face with the heavy-handed machinery of urban police surveillance.

Young women's vulnerablity to police arrest was most dramatically elevated by New York State's amending of the vagrancy law in 1915. The amended law became New York's principal weapon against female sexual delinquents of all ages, and it continued to fulfill that function, virtually unchanged, until the state's sweeping revision of its penal and criminal codes in 1967.[58] Before it was amended, the state vagrancy law, passed in 1881 as part of the Code of Criminal Procedure, included among its definitions of a vagrant "a common prostitute who has no lawful employment whereby to maintain herself." But New York City refused to prosecute under this law because it was too burdensome to prove both the absence of lawful employment and the fact of having engaged in illicit sex. In 1882 the city devised as an alternative a disorderly conduct law, allowing the police to arrest women who annoyed city residents by loitering or soliciting in a "public thoroughfare."[59]

For two decades, this law satisfied public authorities. Drawing on the premises of the common law, New York City's prohibition against disorderly conduct protected the "innocent" public from being accosted by "fallen women" without preventing interested men from seeking their company.[60] Police tolerated the presence of brothels so long as they operated in entertainment districts and working-class or immigrant neighborhoods, away from respectable residential areas. According to Willoughby Cyrus Waterman, an early-twentieth-century authority on prostitution, "The disorderly elements of society are thus herded together, and other citizens by avoiding contact with the district would not have their sensibilities outraged by being forced to be spectators of obscenity and disorder."[61] Occasionally political pressures prompted the police to raid or shut down brothels and "disorderly houses," but prostitutes were most often arrested after police or detectives observed them loitering on the streets, approaching passing men, or soliciting from the windows of disorderly houses. Once arrested, they usually paid a bribe to the arresting officer or a small fine in court and quickly returned to the streets.[62]

However, by the early twentieth century, the disorderly-conduct statute was deemed woefully inadequate. Solicitation and prostitution were spreading quickly from segregated "disorderly houses" to tenement houses, dance halls, saloons, hotels, and massage parlors, but in all of these places, immoral young women were beyond the legal or effective reach of the police. Indeed, the passage of a 1901 law prohibiting solicitation or prostitution in tenement houses had done little to suppress vice because police lacked the authority to conduct surveillance operations against women prostituting indoors.[63] And, in the meantime, tenement-house prostitution exposed innocent families and children to a continuous pall of immorality and corruption. Tenement-house prostitutes bribed small children to run errands for them, and they relied on older boys and girls to direct male passersby to their rooms. The Committee of Fourteen's investigations showed that most families were too "terror stricken by their immoral neighbors" to dare to complain to the police.[64]

Complaints about inadequacies in the law also began to be heard in other parts of the state. The reform citizens of Syracuse, for example, still dependent on the 1881 vagrancy statute, complained in 1913 that they lacked the legal means to counter street solicitation and occasional prostitution. These were increasingly common forms of immorality, but they were not covered by the outdated state law.[65]

By the 1910s New York City's Committee of Fourteen was convinced that efforts to suppress prostitution must target young women who were indifferent to questions of sexual control and lived in circumstances that accentuated their moral disabilities. If the state was to contain or discourage the sex trade, it must follow these young women into their homes, their places of work, and their places of amusement, just as would pimps, procurers, and customers.

After intensive legislative lobbying, the Committee of Fourteen secured the passage of an amended state vagrancy law in 1915. Under the amended law, the definition of a vagrant was expanded to include (1) any person "who offers to commit prostitution," (2) any person "who loiters in or near any thoroughfare or public or private place for the purpose of enticing . . . another to commit lewdness [or] . . . unlawful sexual intercourse," and 3) any person "who in any manner induces . . . [another] to commit any such acts."[66]

Arrests in New York City under the new vagrancy law quickly outpaced arrests under the older disorderly-conduct and tenement-house statutes.[67] The amended law relieved New York's courts of having to prove both the absence of lawful employment and participation in illicit sex before they convicted women of vagrancy. At the same time, it overturned the prior legal assumption, embedded in New York City's disorderly conduct law, that solicitation was an offense only when it was committed in public. The new law substituted the idea that women willing to engage in nonmarital sex were a threat wherever they went and to whomever they came in contact. Moreover, it expanded the definition of prostitution to include sexual favors that were not rewarded with a monetary payment.

Finally, the amended statute sanctioned police entrapment, enjoining municipal police to assume the guise of lovers or potential customers to find young women who might be "tempted" to participate in illicit sex. Undercover police officers and paid informers looked for young women who lived alone or without kin in poor and minority neighborhoods, noting style of dress or demeanor. After striking up an acquaintance, the undercover officers or their accomplices indicated that they were eager to accompany their prey to a hotel room or private residence, and they might also suggest that they were happy to pay for sex. Detectives and decoys entered these rooms without warrants or witnesses. Not trusting sexually adventurous working girls' ability to steer clear of prostitution, indeed, unable to distinguish between casual consensual sex and prostitution, New York's legal system worked to uncover and punish sexual desire. During the 1910s and 1920s New York entered the business of testing young women's willingness to engage in sex, and it made arrests based on police officers' personal assessment of young women's inclinations.[68]

The women who became inmates at Bedford Hills and Albion offered a number of accounts of "unfair" arrests and convictions. Although Nellie Roberts, the young woman introduced at the start of Chapter 1, was not set up by a "stool pigeon," she claimed that she had been mistakenly convicted of prostitution, never having taken money for sex. Speaking more directly to the issue of entrapment, nineteen-year-old Frances Brewer told the Bedford Hills intake officer that she had been arrested by a man who pretended to be a friend and turned out to be a member of the New York City vice squad. The intake officer at Bedford Hills wrote this abbreviated account of Frances's self-defense: "Went to movies with fellow, then another night 'stood him up,' met him again and he asked her to go to movies. She went home to mend rip in dress. Outside door does not lock so good—he went in. Followed her to her room, put $20 on bureau, tried to kiss her. She would not allow it, rebuffed him—he tapped on window, called in detective—She was arrested."[69]

Even women who admitted to prostitution complained that their arrests occurred under contrived and unfair circumstances. Marian Jacoby, a successful call girl who rarely solicited clients on the street, told the intake officer at Bedford Hills that she was arrested as she stood outside a theater, hailing a taxi to take her home. "An officer slipped up to the taxi and told her to step out or he would drag her. She did so and he took her to the police station and swore she had solicited him and he had offered her $10."[70]

The female delinquents at New York's reformatories further suggested that the darkness of one's skin could put a young woman at particular risk for arrest. Caroline Browning, a young black woman, claimed that she had a perfectly respectable job as a waitress and was set up by two white police officers. One engaged her in conversation as she stood on the street with a friend and her landlady's child. The other officer "came across, wanted to know what she was doing talking to a white man. Told her she was under arrest. Told in court he saw her 'idling along the st., at 10 p.m.'"[71] Similarly, Yvonne Waters reported that she was arrested in a Harlem flat where she had just rented a room, unaware that some of the other occupants in the flat were prostitutes. For health reasons, Yvonne had recently quit her job as a live-in domestic servant and was living on her own for the first time. The white undercover officers who came to the apartment questioned Yvonne "about her employment and when she told them that she had no steady job . . . they arrested her. They swore on the stand that both [Yvonne and her landlady] had offered to commit an act of prostitution with them. Yvonne denies this emphatically."[72]

Certainly, one might expect women who were arrested for solicitation to deny the charges against them. But a number of reformers and public officials who investigated criminal procedure also condemned the excessive liberties taken by police and the courts in seeking arrests and convictions of immoral women. Thus in 1917 and again in 1930 and 1932 the procedures used to capture prostitutes provoked sharp criticism. The muckraker Frank

Harris published a three-part exposé of New York City's legal response to prostitution in *Pearson's Magazine* in 1917. The well-known author Malcolm Cowley wrote a series of articles critical of New York City's vice squad for the *New Republic* in 1930; that same year Samuel Seabury, a prestigious former justice on the New York Court of Appeals, directed an official investigation into New York City's magistrate's courts. All three men reported that undercover officers made widespread use of frame-ups and rackets to arrest innocent females. They complained too that judges unjustly discounted the testimony of the accused, did not challenge the perjured testimony of police officers, and deliberately used high rates of conviction to further their own careers.[73]

Although generally sympathetic to New York City's policy of repression, the political scientist Willoughby Cyrus Waterman, in his 1932 study of municipal vice reform, challenged law-enforcement agents' treatment of African American women. Waterman did not dispute the high incidence of prostitution among blacks in Harlem, attributing it to industrial and social discrimination and to the migration from the rural South of young women "ill-equipped to make satisfactory adjustments to city living." Nor was he suprised to find that African American women were arrested at a rate far exceeding their proportion in the city's general population. Nevertheless, he could not help but question their high rate of conviction compared to white women's, blaming it on their helplessness in dealings with the police and the courts.[74]

None of these criticisms altered New York's laws or police procedures. Harris's criticism was undoubtedly muffled by the federal government's wartime crusade against female immorality. During the war, new federal policies led to the swift closure of red-light districts in cities and towns near military camps and to the detention of approximately thirty thousand women and girls for promiscuity, prostitution, or infection with venereal disease, often without due process, trial, or legal counsel.[75] And in the decade following the war, the use of entrapment in prostitution cases was fully sanctioned by New York's higher courts. According to jurist and legal scholar W. Bruce Cobb, in at least four separate prostitution cases the decisions of the courts' judges revealed adherence to the "underlying theory . . . that it is proper by entrapment to take advantage of criminal inclination." The Seabury investigation of 1930 prompted the dismissal of two of New York City's most active magistrates on charges of corruption, but neither Seabury nor Malcolm Cowley nor Willoughby Waterman was able to provoke fundamental changes in New York's legal campaign against the girl problem. New York's vagrancy statute had been fully accepted as a useful weapon against female immorality, and entrapment remained a fixture of the criminal court system.[76]

Ironically, New York's campaign against the girl problem reached full development at the same time that professionals in the new field of mental hygiene began to reject the alarmist mentality of Progressive reformers in favor of a more permissive moral standard for adolescent girls. By the late 1910s and 1920s the girl problem was spreading into the middle class, and even the most "respectable" parents found themselves unable to thwart their teenagers' participation in sexualized youth cultures or their patronage of popular amusements. Affluent mothers and fathers lamented their daughters' exhibitionist tastes in dress, verbal facility with regard to sexual matters, and enthusiasm for unchaperoned dating. They worried about where their daughters' behavior would lead and where they, as parents, should "draw the line."[77]

A few Progressive vice reformers insisted that these young women were on the same "road to destruction" as their less affluent sisters. For example, in 1914 George Kneeland, a nationally prominent vice investigator, told a New York audience of delegates from the General Federation of Women's Clubs that a "startling minority" of young prostitutes were middle-class young women who had rebelled against "home control." These "misguided" girls came "from homes such as yours," Kneeland declared, and "are typical American girls, daughters of respectable and prosperous parents." Similarly, in a 1917 investigation of respectable white-collar workers in Baltimore, Winthrop Lane claimed that he found pretty young stenographers, clerks, and telephone operators involved in "every kind of compromising relation," from affairs with their married bosses to commercial prostitution.[78]

Yet there is little evidence to suggest that middle-class parents took claims of this sort seriously; their own daughters could not be desperate or foolish enough to resort to prostitution. Moreover, by the 1920s they were just as likely to hear from the popularizers of Sigmund Freud and Havelock Ellis that Americans repressed sexual desire at their peril and to encounter popular writers who defended young women's sexual independence, proclaiming it a welcome repudiation of the false morality and repression that had been tolerated by bourgeois Victorians. Deeply troubled by the latest version of the girl problem, but unwilling to assume the worst of their daughters or to consider involvement with probation agencies and criminal courts, middle-class mothers and fathers looked for alternative ways to think about and handle their adolescent girls.

They were aided by professionals in the emerging field of mental hygiene. During the 1920s psychiatric social workers, psychiatrists, and psychologists were hired by hundreds of new mental-hygiene and child-guidance clinics around the country to help youths and parents, both middle- and working-class, adapt to a world of rapidly changing morals and expectations. Many mental hygienists also published widely, writing advice books and articles for parents and adolescents. Although some practitioners worked with delinquents in court clinics, increasingly, during the 1920s, they devoted themselves to intervention with young people who had not yet attracted the attention of the law.[79] Mental hygienists brought to their work the belief that both delinquency and mental illness resulted from the "mental conflicts" of the individual, conflicts that often originated in the unwise or repressive attitudes and actions of parents.[80] But they also shared an optimistic faith in parents' and youths' capacity for change and "adjustment"; in their view the human personality was a social construct, a set of emotions, habits, and conscious perceptions that responded readily to social interaction and therapeutic intervention.[81]

The new practitioners reasoned that troubled or "maladjusted" girls might be intercepted while their antisocial behavior was still minor; with diagnosis and counseling for parents and youths, "hampering tendencies" might be prevented from turning into serious delinquencies.[82] More specifically, they sought to promote constructive "adjustments" to female adolescents' modern quest for autonomy, teaching girls and parents that rebellion against home rule and heightened sexual curiosity were ordinary occurrences in the "normal" psychosexual development of the female adolescent. By promoting a "scientific" understanding of female adolescence, mental hygienists hoped to avert self-destructive and delinquent conduct and to spare girls the heavy expense of searching for a new sexual ethic "by the costly method of trial and error."[83]

There can be no doubt that mental hygienists, many of them women, endorsed a striking departure from the moral views and protective strategies of Gilded Age and Progressive reformers. Responding to psychoanalytic theories of human sexuality, as well as to girls' observable and seemingly inextinguishable interest in autonomy and sex, they overturned the longstanding call for close supervision by real or surrogate parents. Jessie Taft, one of the most prominent psychiatric social workers of the 1920s, claimed that female adolescents must "emancipate" themselves from their families and turn "steadily, frankly, courageously, toward the world of independence and responsibility." The foremost developmental task of "all young people" was "to leave behind the comfortable protection of the family and maternal solicitude."[84] Similarly, though female adolescence was undoubtedly a period of stress and confusion, Gerald Pearson, a psychiatrist with the Philadelphia Child Guidance clinic, called upon the adolescent girl to liberate herself from family ties and "make her own place through her own efforts."[85] Mental hyienists thus cast aside the nineteenth-century dictum that innocent and vulnerable girls required careful familial protection. So too, they boldly discarded Progressive reformers' demand for the rigorous societal regulation of female adolescents who had rebelled against "home rule."

Nowhere was freedom from parental oversight more important than in the realm of sexuality. According to the mental hygienists, the adolescent girl who made awkward attempts to win male favor was moving beyond the "immature" homosexual attachments of late childhood; if overprotective parents discouraged her interaction with male peers, she faced the prospect of remaining "stranded somewhere along the line" of psychosexual development, unable to attain adult heterosexuality.[86] Young girls who were warned only of the "pitfalls of sex" were likely to develop the "indelible impression of sex as something abhorrent."[87] Other young women, subject to "harsh and domineering" fathers, were likely to exaggerate the "masculine element" in their own personalities as a protection against abuse.[88] Jessie Taft reasoned that the adolescent girl must be afforded the freedom "to experiment and even to make mistakes." Similarly, Phyllis Blanchard, chief psychologist at the Philadelphia Child Guidance Clinic, contended that "the striving for independence, even though it may lead the girl into direct disobedience and cause her to display exaggerated patterns of behavior, is in many ways more wholesome than an opposite type of reaction. The girl who yields passively to the parental domination has much less chance of making her life adjustments at a grown up level."[89]

Convinced of the significance of the developmental tasks confronting the adolescent girl and sensitive to the obstacles intruding upon her success, professionals in mental hygiene came out strongly in favor of the "new girl's" assertiveness, her marked curiosity about sex, and her social independence. Moreover, hoping to prevent bitter familial strife, the experts urged parents to abandon inflexible rules of conduct and obsolete values and to encourage rather than forbid the unstructured socializing popular among teenage girls and boys.[90] Significantly, however, they asked parents not to refrain from all oversight or guidance. Underneath adolescents' bravado, the mental hygienists averred, even the most outspoken "new girls" were absorbed in a personal struggle that was essentially conformist in goal; despite their antisocial demeanor, they wanted direction, wanted to figure out how to fit in to their homes and communities.[91] As Phyllis Blanchard pointed out, "The true picture is not one of an insurrectionist younger generation, all following the same line of conduct, as modern journalism would have us believe; it is rather that of distinct individuals struggling with very human problems and desirous of making some endurable adjustments to the demands of living."[92]

Extending this line of thinking to the troublesome matter of sexual conduct, mental hygienists took particular care to explain that parents should discourage adolescent girls from engaging in heterosexual intercourse. Blanchard suspected that the controversial practice of petting was probably harmless and perhaps even constructive because "the girl who makes use of the new sex freedom . . . may be better prepared for marriage than if she had clung to a passive role of waiting for marriage before giving any expression to her sex impulses." She did not believe, however, that "normal" girls would benefit from premarital intercourse. Fear of physical pain, pregnancy, and gossip would persuade most adolescent females to avoid sex and "draw a distinct line between the exploratory activities of the petting party and complete yielding of sexual favors to men," but Blanchard and other mental hygienists did not want parents to leave their girls alone to ponder this difficult subject. Rather, parents would do well to offer their offspring sympathetic and informed counsel.[93]

Mental hygienists' message to parents was that they should adopt the role of informed and supportive mentors while steering clear of moral righteousness and stringent regulation. To do otherwise was to invite dire consequences. Unhappy girls would become sexually promiscuous, using erotic encounters to "escape" an intolerable home life. According to Blanchard, "the girl who enters upon unsanctioned love affairs is neither 'oversexed' nor a 'prostitute type,' but rather the victim of her family situation and of emotional conflicts caused thereby." Affirming this argument, Gerald Pearson noted that sexual promiscuity served the adolescent girl from a strife-filled home as a flight from reality and a "regression" into the "subjective satisfactions" of childhood, giving her the feeling that "she was wanted by somebody." And Jessie Taft, describing a young woman with an abusive father and an overly indulgent mother, suggested that promiscuous relationships were a desperate bid for love and protection. In this particular case, the young woman had "all of the repressions which her mother's hatred of men, her father's behavior, and conventional sex taboos could produce"; sex was "disgusting" to her but she knew of no other way to try to satisfy her "childish cravings."[94]

To the early experts in mental hygiene, promiscuity and prostitution were extraordinary behaviors, the result not so much of inadequate familial control but of excessive meddling, discipline, and protection. Moreover, sexual misconduct was interpreted as a "symptom" of past mistreatment rather than as a serious infraction of moral standards. Because adolescent females were at an impressionable age, professionals in mental hygiene argued that sexually delinquent girls could be helped to face and overcome their difficulties. But if this was to happen, the parents of delinquent girls needed to refrain from punishment. Instead, with their daughters, they needed to seek professional counsel, learning to "adjust" their own needs to those of the troubled adolescents in their midst. Mental hygienists did not deny parents the right to judge their daughters' behavior, but they urged them not to act punitively or without "expert" guidance.[95]

Undeniably, the new mental-health experts were agents of social control. They constructed a model of female adolescence that designated as "normal" the girl who engaged in unchaperoned dating, kissing, and fondling while they labeled as "abnormal" the girl who participated in premarital coitus, took the initiative with a male partner, or expressed sexual interest in other women. Appropriating the languages of psychology, psychoanalysis, and social work, the new professionals created a powerful set of social and moral expectations for "modern" female adolescents. Still, despite these biases and limitations, the work of mental hygienists represented a liberal effort to accommodate rather than repress young women's efforts to give new meaning to female adolescence. Certainly, it called into question the Progressive campaign to control and repress the sexualization of female adolescence.

Mental hygiene was firmly institutionalized during the twenties as psychiatric clinics were established throughout the nation. By 1928 there were over 470 of these facilities. At least 102 were "child guidance clinics," generally established under the auspices of the Commonwealth Fund, which treated maladjusted children and adolescents on an outpatient basis. Fewer than one-quarter of the child-guidance facilities were open full-time, but all of them offered the professional services of at least one psychiatrist, one psychologist, and several psychiatric social workers. Their clients included adolescent females who were referred by their parents or teachers for sexual misconduct. And in addition to the special mental-hygiene and child-guidance clinics, many high schools and colleges began to employ mental-hygiene professionals to examine their female students and identify those in need of psychiatric attention.[96]

However, the "liberal" message of mental hygiene probably reached few of the families whose daughters eventually came before the courts at the request of parents or following a police arrest. The parents of New York's delinquent females generally had rudimentary reading skills and little time for education; their exposure to the new thinking and the new treatment modality could have been only minimal at best. Mental-hygiene clinics in New York City and Upstate New York accepted working-class clients, but none of the parents in my sample sought help from a facility of this type.

Rather, by the 1920s the parents of New York's delinquent girls were likely to be exposed to a pyschological and psychiatric idiom that selectively combined the ideas of mental hygiene with Progressive views on female sexual delinquency. New York's law-enforcement system was not deaf to the mental-hygiene movement; indeed, by the 1920s the Jewish Board of Guardians (JBG) and the Girls' Service League (GSL) had on staff social workers trained in psychiatry who fully accepted the notion that "mental conflict" of some kind was the source of young women's delinquency; in these agencies probation often involved not just demands for moral reform but attempts (albeit inadequate) to investigate and resolve social and emotional disputes in the families of probationers. Alice Menken, the head of the probation department at the JBG, pointed out that the "keynote of service to a probationer is to understand her personality and interpret her needs." The GSL and JBG also offered professional psychological testing and psychiatric counseling to probationers, although on an irregular basis. Finally, the GSL cooperated with the New York City Women's Court, where most prostitution and incorrigibility cases were tried, conducting occasional mental examinations and psychiatric interviews with convicted "incorrigible" girls and prostitutes who were waiting to begin probation or a sentence in a reformatory.[97]

Operating within the criminal-justice system, however, the ideas of mental hygiene served to reinforce rather than supersede the state's tendency to view female adolescent disobedience and sexual expression as dangerous behaviors. New York's criminal court system was committed to a Progressive rather than a liberal standard, a standard that affirmed sexual purity as the norm to which young women must be held. Moreover, the court system was highly responsive to the "scientific" argument of the 1910s that young women's deviance from purity was frequently caused by feeblemindedness or some other mental defect. The fixation with feeblemindedness declined by the 1920s, but the state's alarmist view of female adolescence, its exceedingly broad definitions of sexual delinquency and prostitution, and its commitment to sexual control were never challenged in a substantive way by court-affiliated psychiatric social workers and psychologists.[98]

Indeed, mental hygienists working within court settings generally concluded that the young women who attracted the attention of the law were of a distinctly different type than the girls referred to clinics by parents or teachers, that is, far more "maladjusted," far less amenable to therapeutic intervention or reform. Thus Naomi Gorstein, examined by mental hygienists working for the New York Probation Department following her arrest for petty larceny and complaints of sexual promiscuity, was found to be of "inferior mentality and emotionally unstable; she acts in a childlike manner and fails to appreciate the morality of her acts."[99]

Augusta Scott, a psychiatrist who conducted examinations for New York City's Women's Court, confirmed and publicized this very pessimistic view of delinquent young women's mental and emotional traits when she published a study in 1923 of three hundred women who had been recently convicted by the court. The 114 incorrigible girls in the group were "unstable, neurotic, and mentally subnormal." Scott judged the 160 women convicted of prostitution to be less "neuropathic" than the incorrigibles, but they tended to be "exceedingly shallow and empty emotionally." In the entire group, only thirty-three could be described as "normal"; the great majority suffered from some combination of mental defect, personality disorder, and mental disease. Viewing these young women in terms of their impact on society rather than as adolescents "struggling with very human problems and desirous of making some endurable adjustments to the demands of living," Scott stressed their multiple handicaps and inability to adapt to societal norms. Working within the criminal-justice system, Scott was compelled to uphold the notion that disobedience and overt sexual expression in adolescent girls were grounds for state control.[100]

In an era in which Americans expressed great perplexity over changes in the behavior and values of female adolescents, the parents of New York's delinquent girls responded by demanding obedience and repentance from their rebellious daughters. When the girls failed to cooperate, parental action combined with state policy and legal procedure in important ways. Increasingly after 1900, New York's law-enforcement apparatus was receptive to working-class, immigrant, and black parents who agreed with Progressive reformers that the girl problem was a grave threat to home and society. The state, by granting parents access to the lower courts, affirmed the right of guardians to the obedience of adolescent daughters. And with its amending of the vagrancy law in 1915, New York State committed itself to the apprehension of disadvantaged young women who, in the process of breaking free of parental authority, showed signs of responsiveness to male sexual desire.

In effect, New York State supported a class- and race-linked response to female adolescent rebellion. By the 1920s, the criminalization of prostitution and incorrigibility was so well entrenched that police, judges, social workers, and probation officers could not abandon their search for sexually "delinquent" young women in poor urban neighborhoods or adjust to the permissive code of conduct that was being developed for more privileged adolescent girls. In fact, when psychiatrists and psychologists employed by the courts applied the lessons and principles of mental hygiene to the girl problem, they created and supported an image of wayward girls and prostitutes that tended to emphasize the young women's abnormalities and their harmful maladjustment to familial and community standards. Convinced that these young women were too dangerous to be at large, the state assigned the reformatories at Albion and Bedford Hills the daunting task of restoring them to lives of virtue and obedience.

PART TWO
Going Straight

CHAPTER THREE

"Every Minute Is to Me like Eternity":
Inmates at Albion and Bedford Hills

The female "delinquents" given over to the care of Albion and Bedford Hills had gravely offended the normative expectations of family members, reformers, and magistrates. Now the state denounced their "misguided" attempts to obtain autonomy and, without fully comprehending either the reasons for their pursuit of freedom or the confusion and hazard that attended their quest, demanded that they forfeit their former associates and amusements. Seeking no less than the delinquents' social and moral transformation, the criminal-justice system placed them in the custody of reformatory personnel—almost exclusively female—who were to instruct them in habits of deference, chastity, and respectable toil. At both Albion and Bedford Hills the expressed aim of matrons, teachers, and superintendents was "to strengthen [female delinquents'] character and awaken within [them] the desire to go back out into the world and live a good and useful life."[1]

The reformatories' task was not easy. Social historians familiar with the many recuperative institutions (public and private) that emerged in the United States during the late nineteenth and early twentieth centuries know that the individuals who came in contact with welfare, correctional, and therapeutic personnel frequently tried to resist or modify official definitions of aid and reform. Of course, the volunteers and trained professionals who operated mission homes, social-welfare agencies, and mental-hygiene clinics wielded considerable authority over their charges and could penalize or withhold assistance from those who refused to cooperate with established programs and policies. And as Estelle Freedman, Nicole Hahn Rafter, and Barbara Brenzel have shown, officials at women's prisons and reformatories possessed an especially great capacity for social control: retaining the legal authority to "reform" women who had not voluntarily sought their aid, they regulated inmates' day-to-day lives and denied them all but the slightest contact with the outside world. Nonetheless, in correctional facilities as in less closely controlled settings, the recipients of care often disappointed their guardians, challenging rules and expectations they found repressive or alienating. Rather than simply buckle under to the dictates of their middle-class superiors, more than a few inmates, clients, and patients tried to resist or manipulate institutional agendas.[2]

At Bedford Hills and Albion, young inmates challenged the authority of their keepers with ingenuity and zeal. Often unimpressed by the reformatories' attempts to restore them to "noble womanhood," inmates used vulgar language, traded stories about sex, and refused to tolerate the work assignments or punishments meted out by reformatory personnel. They rioted, hatched plots to escape, and participated in interracial homosexual romances that violated fundamental cultural taboos. Even inmates who were not openly defiant expressed resentment over their loss of liberty and the demands and evaluations of matrons and classroom instructors. Refusing definition as the tractable objects of reform, some inmates tried to resist correction altogether; others tried to negotiate with their keepers, hoping to make the reform process reflect their own interests.

But what, in the long run, did such resistance achieve? Did inmates, in fact, provoke changes in reformatory programs, lessen the authority of their keepers, or advance their own interests? How did confinement in a reformatory affect young women who were struggling, simultaneously, with the label of "delinquency" and with an ongoing search for social identity?

At the time of their commitment, most young women knew little about the goals and methods of the reformatories in which they were to spend up to three years of their lives.[3] Certain, however, that their liberty would be sharply curtailed, the female delinquents often grew belligerent and anxious as they traveled to the institutions under the watchful eyes of a taciturn female marshall. Acknowledging the poor disposition of inmates newly arrived at Albion, Flora P. Daniels, superintendent from 1916 to 1929, remarked that "in most cases the girl did not want to come, she resents the action of the court which sent her, and it is perfectly natural that she should have an attitude of distrust and suspicion toward those whose duty it is to care for her." In a similar vein, Amos Baker, Bedford Hill's first male superintendent, who served from 1921 to 1926, commented that the reformatory's new inmates were of two types, either "timid and in fear" or "antagonistic and uncooperative."[4]

Realizing that they could not hope to reform young women who remained apprehensive or hostile, both Daniels and Baker tried to win the confidence of their newest inmates. In personal interviews with each fresh arrival to Albion, Daniels attempted to "divert the girl's mind from the idea that this institution is a place of punishment and to show her instead that it is a home where she may receive many opportunities for development that have been denied her before." Baker conducted similar meetings at Bedford Hills, wanting to give new inmates "an opportunity to ask questions about the life in the institution." Baker was convinced that most girls left his office "in a more hopeful and better frame of mind than when they entered," but one wonders how long their optimism lasted.[5] Throughout the years from 1900 to 1930, and regardless of any individual superintendent's efforts, the initial weeks and months at the reformatories tended to be disorienting and stressful. Indeed, as young women became acquainted with the reformatories, many were likely to feel that their initial fear or belligerence had been amply justified.

All new inmates spent several weeks (sometimes months) in specially designated reception buildings. Here, on their first day, the young women were relieved of their personal clothing and valuables, given uniforms, bathed and examined by a physician or nurse, and assigned to individual isolation rooms, where they remained in medical quarantine for at least two weeks. The reformatories wanted to make sure that all cases of venereal disease were diagnosed and that no infectious or contagious diseases were introduced to the reformatory population.[6]

But quarantine was also likely to upset whatever composure the new inmates still possessed. It stripped young women of belongings that gave them a sense of personal identity, severed them from nearly all human contact, deprived them of any opportunity for independent action, and impressed on them the gravity of their new situation. So unpleasant was this period of medical isolation that it occasionally spurred timorous inmates to abandon any thought of rebellion or self-assertion. Deborah Herman, for example, told a staff member at Bedford Hills that, having been sent to the reformatory by her mother to learn a lesson, it "only took her a day to learn better."[7] Reformatory personnel, however, worried that isolation more often had the opposite effect, provoking young women to brood about their unhappy circumstances and grow more rather than less resentful of their keepers. Sophie Polentz found the experience so distasteful that she ran away from Bedford Hills, accompanied by another inmate, just hours after her release from isolation. "A search was made for them all night but without success"; five months later Bedford Hills finally located Sophie and returned her to the institution.[8] Unable to ignore the disadvantages of quarantine, Amos Baker remarked, "No doubt this isolation is a good practice, but I realize from my own observation and from the statements of inmates how irksome and depressing this period is."[9]

Exceptional cases such as Sophie's notwithstanding, when new inmates were finally released from quarantine their intensive initiation into the goals and methods of the reformatories got under way. Still living in the reception buildings, but now participating in the life of the reformatory, the new inmates began to learn about the two basic strategies that Albion and Bedford Hills used to transform delinquent females into "good" and "useful" women: an array of "opportunities" for "self-improvement" buttressed by a coercive program of rules, penalties, and censorship.

The "opportunities" provided by Bedford Hills and Albion were supposed to approximate those afforded adolescent girls growing up in white middle-class homes. Both institutions were established in large part because of the tireless work of Josephine Shaw Lowell and Abby Hopper Gibbons, nineteenth-century activists whose concern for the "fallen" members of their sex stemmed from an assumption that moral degradation was unnatural and accidental in women, regardless of class or social rank. Subscribing to the gender-essentialist values of white middle-class domesticity, and believing that principled women could not honestly deny the bonds linking them to their hapless sisters, Lowell and Gibbons called on society to help "ruined" women discover the "natural" virtue that lay hidden in their hearts. As prominent figures, respectively, in the New York State Board of Charities and the Women's Prison Association of New York, Lowell and Gibbons championed the creation of special institutions for the redemption of immoral women, institutions that would convert these "unfortunate" creatures to the social and moral precepts of "true womanhood." Unlike existing men's prisons and reformatories where inmates' compliance and reform was obtained through strict regimentation and punishment, the women's reformatories would, as in the middle-class family, achieve discipline and rectitude through bonds of affection and sympathy. Protected and cared for as though they were the daughters of reformatory personnel, "fallen" young women and girls would unaffectedly embrace womanly habits of domesticity, chastity, generosity, and piety.[10]

With Lowell's and Gibbons's vision guiding them, Albion and Bedford Hills resisted the values of the new sexual order and institutionalized Victorian standards of middle-class womanhood. Most important, the reformatories developed a so-called family system whose central feature was the cottage housing plan. New inmates learned that if they behaved well in reception they would be "promoted" to one of numerous "homelike" cottages that clustered on the reformatories' unfenced rural property. At Bedford Hills and Albion each cottage housed approximately thirty young women who lived with two matrons as members of a single "family," imitating the standards of privacy, order, and feminine decorum found in prosperous Victorian households. Although the level of material abundance in the reformatories was below that of most middle-class homes, each cottage inmate was given a comfortably furnished room of her own, and every cottage had its own dining room, living room, and kitchen. Inmates who were pregnant and those who arrived at the reformatory with infants were housed in a special cottage with its own modern nursery. Supervised by their matrons, cottage residents learned to perform the housekeeping duties necessary for the upkeep and comfort of the cottages. At the same time, through work, play, and cooperative living, cottagers actively pursued character reformation. As Albion's Superintendent Daniels noted, "If our methods are successful, [the girls] will soon have a genuine regret for [their] former mode of living, and realizing [their] weakness will look to us for advice, or at least will be in a receptive mood for the help which we wish to give."[11] Inmates who advanced the furthest in this project, abandoning self-indulgence and insolence for cooperation and diligence, earned the "opportunity" to become "self-governing"; graduating to an "honors cottage," they helped set rules for their own household and monitored one another's conduct.[12]

The reformatory staff knew, of course, that most of its inmates would not become full-time homemakers after their release. The great majority were poor and single, and they would have to work for wages, at least until they married. So that they might support themselves without resort to prostitution or crime, reception-hall inmates learned that they would have the "opportunity" to pursue academic and vocational training. At Albion and Bedford Hills most inmates attended academic classes for one-half of each weekday, receiving instruction in the same broad range of academic subjects covered in the state's public schools. The reformatories (like the public schools) sought to provide young women of the working classes—whether white and native-born, African American, or immigrant—with the literacy skills, national values, and habits of self-discipline and deference that would ensure their development as "helpful and honorable members of society."[13]

Building on the foundation developed in academic classrooms, the reformatories' vocational classes trained inmates in the practical skills needed for lawful employment. Both institutions emphasized the traditional trades of "respectable" wage-earning women: domestic service, commercial laundering, industrial sewing, and dressmaking. Almost from the time that it opened in 1901, however, Bedford's superintendent Katharine Bement Davis, a university-educated "new woman," sought to broaden the opportunities of her charges by supplementing training in the traditional fields with instruction in hat making, machine knitting, chair caning, cobbling, bookbinding, painting, and some carpentry. Albion added instruction in chair caning, basketry, and weaving gradually during the late 1910s and early 1920s. In addition, in response to the growing interest of America's working-class women in office work, a select minority of inmates had the opportunity to train in this field. From as early as 1904, Bedford inmates who were thought to be exceptionally capable were allowed to study stenography, typing, or bookkeeping, and, by the 1920s, Albion also offered instruction in office skills to a few select inmates. During their first few weeks at the reformatories, women wishing to train in these fields were asked to declare their interest to their keepers.[14]

When not occupied in classes or housework, the inmates were encouraged to take advantage of a variety of social and recreational activities. As Flora Daniels explained, through opportunities for leisure "we try to make them happy and to induce on their part a receptive attitude to influences for good."[15] At both institutions, inmates engaged in farming and gardening and attended classes in gymnastics, dance, arts and crafts, and music appreciation. Perhaps more to the liking of most inmates, by the 1910s each cottage at Bedford had a piano and the cottages at both reformatories were equipped with record players. Phonograph records, books, and magazines could be borrowed from the reformatories' libraries, where newspapers were also available. In addition, at Bedford and Albion inmates attended motion-picture shows on a regular basis and both institutions encouraged them to participate in the pageants, plays, and community sings that were produced on holidays and on special occasions throughout the year. Both reformatories also brought in college faculty, noteworthy public figures, musicians, and performers to edify and entertain the inmates.[16]

Finally, inmates were given the "opportunity" to partake of regular religious worship and spiritual instruction. Albion offered Catholic and Protestant services in its chapel; Bedford provided services for Jewish as well as Christian inmates. The reformatory chaplains also gave informal talks on topics such as friendship, honor, and loyalty. The spiritual component was considered essential to inmates' moral reformation, as Albion's board of managers made clear in 1903, when it remarked that "young women even more than young men are susceptible to religious influences, and to neglect, or not properly to provide, for such influence in a place where the chief aim is to build character is a serious mistake." Two decades later the commitment to spiritual growth and religious instruction remained strong, though American society was increasingly under the sway of secular values. Bedford Hills dedicated two new chapels in 1922, one for Protestant and Catholic services, the other for Jewish observances. In his annual report for that year Amos Baker noted, "The setting aside of particular places for religious worship has proved very beneficial to the general morale of the Institution."[17]

Although staff members and administrators hoped that inmates would take full advantage of the reformatories' rich opportunities for self-improvement, young women in reception learned from their keepers that Albion and Bedford Hills relied on a parallel system of coercive measures to guide the bewildered and prod the recalcitrant. The first of these measures was a set of normative standards or rules governing daily conduct: inmates were required to complete lessons and work assignments diligently, treat their superiors and peers with respect, and refrain from profanity, obscenity, discourtesy, and violence of any kind.[18] Both institutions kept inmates under constant surveillance to make sure that they complied with reformatory expectations, and almost from its founding, Albion's matrons and teachers registered their appraisal of inmates through a formal "marking" or "merit" system. Ten thousand demerits were placed against the name of each new arrival, and the inmate had to work these off by good conduct before being considered for parole.[19]

The reformatories also relied on a formidable array of sanctions—including the loss of full meals, postponement of parole, and solitary confinement in one's room or in special "disciplinary" or "prison" buildings—to compel unruly inmates to appreciate the importance of good conduct.[20] And although no matron would have admitted it, young women in reception at Bedford Hills during the 1910s may well have heard rumors that the reformatory occasionally resorted to brutal physical punishment to control its most severe disciplinary cases. Cruel forms of physical punishment, especially the "stringing up" of handcuffed inmates, were used until public scandal forced the institution to abandon them in 1920.[21]

Last, all inmates at Albion and Bedford Hills were required to sign a statement indicating that they acceded to the reformatories' censoring of all personal mail. The reformatories did not want inmates to hear from friends or associates who might undermine or discourage their reform and thus categorically prohibited correspondence with, or visits from, individuals who were not in the inmates' immediate families. Letters from lovers or admirers were never passed to the inmates. Similarly, correspondence from men who claimed to be cousins, uncles, or even brothers was held by reformatory administrators while they investigated the writers' identities and backgrounds. Even correspondence between inmates and parents or siblings was carefully read, usually by the assistant superintendent. Reformatory censors used their discretion in refusing to pass many letters to and from family members, especially letters that harshly criticized the inmates or the reformatories.[22]

By the time they had spent several weeks in reception, the new inmates at Albion and Bedford Hills were supposed to understand both the new social identity the reformatory expected them to work toward and the various opportunities and coercive measures that would be used to spur them toward their goal. But this initial period of orientation probably aroused anxiety or fueled resentment at least as much as it restored calm and confidence. Ester Bromwell, a Bedford Hills inmate, apparently developed a "disagreeable" attitude while in reception, telling the matrons, "I am not going to stand for people watching and picking on me all the time."[23]

Young women recently arrived at the reformatories could not be sure that class work and industrial training would provide them with valuable goals and skills rather than with tiresome and demeaning lessons. Nor could they know whether pageants, plays, and other recreational activities would provide genuine pleasure or be a nuisance and a bore. Finally, they could not yet tell how intrusive the institutions' surveillance would be or how severe the punishments. Ultimately, all these concerns and ambiguities dissolved into one pressing question: was it in the inmates' self-interest to conform to the reformatories' demands and expectations, or was it better to rebel against them?

There was no simple or immediate answer to their query. Rather, experience was the inmates' only guide. And as the young women confined to

Bedford Hills and Albion labored to turn experience into understanding, they spent much of their time engaged in struggle, both overt and veiled, with reformatory personnel. While staff members strove to make sure that the young women in their charge "profited" from the reformatory setting, the inmates disputed the merit of the reformatories' "opportunities" and contested the efficacy of their coercive strategies. The reformatories filled with tension and distrust, as inmates introduced their own values into the institutional setting and staff members struggled to retain practical and ideological dominance. Indeed, inmate resistance gravely taxed staff members' sympathy and spirit of self-sacrifice, threatening to destroy the foundation on which the reformatories had been built.

There were, to be sure, inmates who usually behaved well throughout their commitment to Bedford Hills or Albion. In my sample of one hundred women, approximately forty were generally "good" or even "excellent" while at the reformatories.[24] Susan Rivington, a former prostitute, was "always good" while at Albion from 1901 to 1904. The conduct of Nellie Weston, an eighteen-year-old committed to Albion in 1915, "was all that could be desired. She gave no trouble and was helpful." Nora Patterson, another former prostitute, was "exceptionally good" during her commitment to Bedford Hills just after World War I. And Merced Borja was "excellent" in work, conduct, and effort while at Bedford in the late 1920s.[25]

But good behavior did not necessarily signal contentment or willingness to admit a need for correction. In fact, "good" inmates often expressed the view that they did not deserve the label "prostitute" or "female delinquent" and should not have been sent to an institution filled with "bad" women. They conformed to reformatory rules and accepted the moral oversight of matrons and teachers not because they agreed with the reformatories' estimation of their character or conduct but because they were desperate to get away from institutions that had the power to withhold their freedom, mar their reputations, and damage their self-esteem.

Nora Patterson was one of these anxious, albeit obedient, inmates. Nora had run away from her home in Allentown, Pennsylvania, in 1917 at the age of seventeen after arguing with her parents over the young man she wanted to marry. She worked as a waitress in Akron, Ohio, for several months and then quit her job to marry a new boyfriend. The marriage was stormy, and when her husband was drafted in July 1918, Nora moved to New York City, where she became a prostitute and worked for a pimp who provided her with a fairly decent standard of living.

Nora rarely worked on the streets and was probably able to sustain an image of respectability. Her mother and father undoubtedly knew nothing of their daughter's involvement in commercialized sex until Nora was arrested, just two months after arriving in New York. At first she was sent to Inwood House, a facility for minor female offenders operated by the New York Magdalen Benevolent Society, but after eight months she escaped, was caught, and was taken to jail. In a letter written from the city jail while waiting to hear if she was to be returned to Inwood or sent elsewhere, Nora pleaded for her mother's help and forgiveness. She did not try to defend her past conduct or claim that she had a right to live as she pleased. She did not denounce the police or the courts. Instead, as she faced what it meant to be judged and treated as a prostitute, Nora begged for the assurance that she might be allowed to live down her recent past and regain her social standing as a "good girl": "I am down here at the court again. I think I am getting transferred to another place. Write a letter to Mrs. Douglass [probably the woman in charge at Inwood] and see what she has to say and Oh, Mother plead for me for you know I wasn't bad at home. Mother I want to see you so bad I hardly know what to do, My heart is broken, a visit from you would make me so happy."[26]

Nora was sent to Bedford rather than back to Inwood, and once there the young woman behaved well because she desperately wanted to prove to her mother that she was not as bad as the label "convicted prostitute" implied. She did not find it difficult to be good but hated being at the reformatory because she was constantly reminded that she was not good enough.

Merced Borja, a young Puerto Rican woman, betrayed even more conclusively than Nora the discontentedness that "good" women felt at Bedford or Albion. Merced was convicted of pickpocketing and was sentenced to Bedford when, lacking a Spanish translator, she misunderstood the judge who presided over her trial and nodded in the affirmative when he asked if she was having sexual relations with the man who employed her as a private-duty nurse. Merced's behavior at Bedford was exemplary and she won special notice for "very beautiful drawn work and embroidery." Trying hard not to fault the institution, Merced insisted in a (censored) letter to her friend Maria that the reformatory was a "wonderful place . . . [where] we go to school just as on the outside." Yet at the same time Merced complained that "I am suffering and every minute is to me like Eternity." Believing that she should never have been committed to Bedford, Merced lived in fear that her former friends would desert her. She pleaded with Maria, "Don't be afraid, come to see me, don't be afraid, I am not in a bad place at all. . . . I still have many years to live and I will show you then that I am always the same and that I will do anything I can for you although your and my ideas are very much apart."[27]

The discontent of the institutions' "good" inmates surfaced over the details of their confinement as well as over the fact of commitment itself. And while "good" inmates' discontent might be expressed in an occasional letter to someone outside the institution, it was also expressed within the reformatory setting. Grace Demerest, committed to Bedford Hills in 1917 for vagrancy, was depressed rather than disobedient during her first year while undergoing regular (and probably unpleasant) treatment for a stubborn case of gonorrhea. Noting that she "never wants to go out . . . [and] has no interest in class room work," staff members asked Grace to explain herself. Her reply: "I don't want to learn anything new, I would rather sleep."[28]

Other "good" inmates frankly declared their dissatisfaction over work assignments or disciplinary decisions in notes to the superintendent. Thus, upset about being removed from Bedford's industrial sewing room because of poor health, Merced Borja tried, unsuccessfully, to plead her case with Superintendent Amos Baker. She wrote, "I don't see Dr. Baker any reason why you don't want me to work there any more as I feel perfectly alright to do the work and I like it very much. I don't feel sick at all the only thing I worry too much and that make me look very bad."[29] In a somewhat different case, Patricia O'Brien, one of the rare upper-middle-class inmates at Bedford Hills, wrote to Dr. Baker about a fight she had had with another inmate. Profoundly alienated from the other women at the reformatory, and feeling that she had been unfairly blamed and punished for the recent altercation, Patricia wrote to Baker to inform him of the "true" facts: "This girl . . . Tillie . . . took an instinctive dislike to me from the first. . . . [The fight started] over some trivial thing. she struck the first blow and I couldn't keep my self respect if I didn't strike back." Because of the fight Patricia had been removed from a position she enjoyed in the kitchen at Stafford House, a residence for staff members, and was confined to her cottage. There, she was "very lonely as no one speaks to me, they are afraid of offending Tillie." Viewing Baker as a "court of last appeal," Patricia asked "for another chance to work in the kitchen."[30]

Merced and Patricia made the superintendent at Bedford Hills aware of their discontent; however, neither inmate obtained from Baker the reaction she wanted. Merced was not allowed to return to the sewing room; Patricia was not released from punishment and did not regain her position in the kitchen at Stafford. And believing that they could not bear the reformatory experience or gain early parole unless they retained the good will and sympathy of the reformatory staff, Nora and Patricia abandoned their campaigns and made the best of their unhappy situations. Ultimately, the discontent of the "good" inmates lacked coercive force.

In contrast, the generally troublesome inmates (sixty out of one hundred) were openly resentful of the reformatories' expectations and defiant of their rules. At least initially, becoming "good and useful" had so little appeal that they were willing to risk frequent punishment and the postponement of parole. These young women expressed their contempt for the reformatories' goals in innumerable ways, including insulting staff members or other inmates, fighting, breaking things, using "bad" language, telling "low" stories about their prior sexual experience, smoking, refusing to work, engaging in lesbian romances, and trying to escape.

No doubt the "troublesome" young women disrupted order and "progress" in the reformatories. In fact, faced with these and hundreds of other inmates who refused to become the docile and repentant young women for whom the reformatories had been founded, Bedford Hills and Albion were compelled to alter their programs and procedures. It would be foolish to suggest that the resulting modifications necessarily marked a triumph for inmate resistance; the reformatories' innovations were meant to enhance, not diminish, institutional controls. Nonetheless, inmates forced the reformatories into a defensive position, unable to count on the positive appeal of their programs.

Most important, Albion and (to a greater extent) Bedford Hills turned to increasingly segregative procedures—along behavioral, psychiatric, psychological, and racial lines—to support and preserve their established programs of reform. Developed and modified over the years, superintendents and staff members came to view inmate classification and differential treatment as "scientific" measures essential to the success and internal order of the reformatories.

Albion had begun to classify inmates shortly after it opened its doors in 1893. Already committed, of course, to the segregation of inmates by sex, Superintendent Mary K. Boyd followed the advice of contemporary penologists and further separated inmates by age, "criminal history," and general conduct.[31] By the turn of the century, the standard practice during reception was for officers to observe new inmates carefully, assigning to cottages the youngest girls and those who were "easily influenced for good and anxious

Young female defendant with female probation officer during sentencing to the Western House of Refuge, Albion, New York, circa 1910. Courtesy of the New York State Archives, Albany, New York.

Rules Governing Girls
of the
Western House of Refuge,
Albion, N. Y.

my love to [crossed out] dearest mother & pa. and you dear[?]

I.   Promt obedience to officers; courtesy to all. ✝

II.   Always rise when spoken to by an officer. ✝

III.   Refrain from discussing the events of your past life; beginning this rule from the day of entrance and while in quarantine: mention to no one the offence for which you were committed.

IV. Falsehood, profanity, obscene language and actions strictly forbidden. ✝

V.   Personal cleanliness required.

VI.   Reverent attitude and conduct always required at prayers. ✝

VII.   Lounging or loafing in recreation-room not allowed; keep your feet on the floor and your hands off your companions; treat one another kindly and considerately. ✝

VIII. Writing or receiving notes, or passing them for others is forbidden; also calling from windows, or trying in any way to communicate from one building to another is prohibited. ✝

IX   Any damage to walls or woodwork, or furnishings, or destroying clothing or any State property; writing in Bible or defacing it, or other books, in any way, will be severely punished ✝

X.   Girls are never allowed to go from one part of the building to another, nor into one another's rooms, without permission. ✝

The ones I put a cross are the ones I brake and got punished. I did it once to other But punishing me did not[?]

"Rules Governing Girls of the Western House of Refuge, Albion, N.Y." This list was given to inmate Eva Pomering in 1918. Courtesy of the New York State Archives.

Calisthenics in the gymnasium at the Western House of Refuge, Albion, New York, circa 1895. Courtesy of the New York State Archives.

Classroom at the Western House of Refuge, Albion, New York, circa 1920. Courtesy of the New York State Archives.

Young inmates with their babies at the Western House of Refuge, Albion, New York, circa 1905. Courtesy of the New York State Archives.

```
Name                                    Western House of Refuge for Women

Heart lesions  none                     Deformities  Lordosis.

Gonorrhoea  Negative.  Syphilis  Wass.positive.  Other diseases
                                                 Diphtheria.
                                                 Pertussis.
                                                 Measles.
                                                 Typhoid in childhood.
Social and moral traits                          Nasal obstruction.

Judgment  some.                         Temper  controlled.

Industry  good worker.                  Moral sense  fair.


Mental traits

Concentration  is good.                 Reasoning -yes


Association of ideas  good.

Memory,  Auditory  normal               Visual good.

Motor coordination  balanced.           Muscular strength  reduced.


Summary    Normal mentality.

Physical   Her physical condition is below par and syphilis is also
           present. Was not well as a child. Respiratory system is de-
           fective.

Mental     Physical age: 21 7/12.  Mental age:XIV.
              This gives her a normal intelligence quotient.  Reasons
           to some extent. Able to initiate and carry out a plan. A
           good case for reformation as she has normal mentality,is
           attentive and adaptable.

Delinquencies
      Sex.



Diagnosis          Feeble-Minded      Imbecile     Moron

Normal             Subnormal          Psychopathic

Insane             Hysterical         Epileptic

Prostitute         Alcoholic          Criminalistic
```

Record of psychological examination of Louise Peffley at the Western House of
Refuge, Albion, New York, circa 1915. Courtesy of the New York State Archives.

Name ~~████████~~   Western House of Refuge for Women

Heart lesions None   Deformities   Post nasal.

Gonorrhoea   No data.   Syphilis Wasserman   Other diseases
    Pregnancy,3 months duration   negative.   Chicken pox
         on entering.   Measles
                                    mumps
Social and moral traits   pertussis.

Judgment   She placed her baby under   Temper ugly,defient,uncontrolled.
         the faucet and left it.
Industry   None,lazy.   Moral sense   None.

Mental traits

Concentration   Very poor.   Reasoning Does not plan yet.

Association of ideas Very poor.

Memory,   Auditory Very poor.   Visual   Very poor.

Motor coordination   Very poor.   Muscular strength Reduced.

Summary Feeble-minded.

Physical Presents no sensory defects.Well nourished.Musculo-nerve
    coordination defective.Looks mentally deficient.History of chicken-
    pox,measles,mumps and whooping cough. *Unmarried, one pregnan-*
    immoral since age 15
Mental   Physical age 19-2. Mental age 9-6. Visual and auditory memory
    still that of early childhood. Compares objects but does not draw
    conclusions.Will always need supervision and segregation as she has
    reached her mental limit.Physically will improve and continue to do
    a few household tasks,

Delinquencies   Sex

Diagnosis   <u>Feeble-Minded</u>   <u>Imbecile</u>   Moron

Normal   Subnormal   Psychopathic

Insane   Hysterical   Epileptic

<u>Prostitute</u>   Alcoholic   Criminalistic
    for money.

Record of psychological examination of Polly Overton at the Western House of
Refuge, Albion, New York, circa 1915. Courtesy of the New York State Archives.

PAROLE CONDITIONS

Girl's Name _____

Address ... Knowlesville ... N. Y.

I, Mrs. _____ do hereby agree to the conditions imposed upon me

by assuming charge of _____

s. baby paroled to my custody of the Western House of Refuge.

That said _____ is to be required to keep the terms of parole placed upon her when conditionally discharged from the Institution.

1. That she shall be obedient, respectful and courteous.
2. Shall accept the wages agreed upon between the Superintendent of the Western House of Refuge and her employer, and her wages to be retained by employer, excepting such amount as the latter thinks necessary for girl. To be saving and careful in her expenditures, buying under supervision of someone designated to accompany her.
3. She is to consult employer as to her amusements, recreation, and social diversions. To form no friendships, not to visit or receive visits from members of her own family unless approved by the Superintendent. Is not to go out nights excepting when accompanied by a responsible person, and to go very seldom at night. To have one afternoon a week and go to church at least once in two weeks.
4. She is to write her monthly reports regularly, these to be signed by employer and mailed in time to be received before the first of the following month. The monthly reports to be made on report blanks furnished by Superintendent. Employer is authorized and requested to open and read all mail sent and received by girl. Also parcels by post or express.
5. She may write private letters to Superintendent.

I also agree to guard her morals, language and actions, and aid her as much as possible by advice as to her present and future conduct, and as far as may be possible, to uplift and strengthen her in all things that tend to her future well being.

(Signed)

Girl's name _____

Date ... 9-15-20 ....

"Parole Conditions" as signed by guardian and inmate; found in the file of Sallie Poster, who departed from the Western House of Refuge, Albion, New York in 1920. Courtesy of the New York State Archives.

for help in the path toward reform." In contrast to these "promising" cases, inmates found "entirely wanting in all womanly instincts, coarse and vulgar in manner," were confined to private rooms in the Reception Hall until they understood that "to be an accepted member of the family implied respectful manner, proper language and prompt obedience to the rules."[32] The temper of the times was decidely racist, but because virtually no African American inmates were sent to the institution from the predominantly white cities and rural villages of Upstate New York, Albion did not bother to institute a policy of racial segregation.

Bedford had adopted a similar scheme as soon as it opened in 1901, separating the youngest and most cooperative inmates from older and "hardened" offenders.[33] Unlike Albion, however, Bedford Hills received numerous black inmates from New York City, and Katharine Bement Davis, Bedford's first superintendent, made a deliberate decision to place them in cottages and classrooms along with their white peers. Davis was proud of her maternal grandmother's activism in the antislavery cause and had herself worked with African Americans in a Philadelphia settlement house. Impatient with the Jim Crow sentiment that dominated her era, she forthrightly rejected racial segregation at Bedford Hills.[34]

Within a few years, however, the initial classification schemes were found inadequate to the needs of the reformatories. Severe overcrowding made a shambles of the existing classification systems. Officers at Bedford Hills found that, because of overcrowding, they could not "promote" girls from the "lowest grade" into the cottages and corridors set aside for "middle" and "high grade" inmates. Similarly, Albion's second superintendent, Alice Curtin, lamented that "the comparatively innocent must room next to the thoroughly depraved" in the reformatory's reception hall. "There is no isolation, no question of classification, but simply finding a place for the last-comer to sleep."[35] To make matters worse, the courts kept sending to the reformatories young women who seemed incapable of benefiting from their programs.[36] At first, the superintendents at Albion and Bedford Hills blamed the dearth of "good" inmates on newly established probation programs that gave novice offenders a chance to reform in their own communities, leaving the reformatories with women "who have . . . gone so far in lives of dissipation and crime as to be unable to profit" from "training and discipline."[37] But as their frustration deepened, reformatory officials began to ascribe the conduct of unruly or impassive inmates to "mental defectiveness," an elastic designation that encompassed "feeblemindedness," "psychopathy" and other vaguely understood mental disorders. Even early on, just after the turn of the century, Susan Rivington's inability to make substantial progress at Albion was attributed to a mental condition. "Susan was a nervous wreck. She was in school one year but made little progress. She could scarcely hold the pen steady enough to write her own name."[38]

During the first two decades of the century, "feeblemindedness" and "psychopathy" became popular explanations for female criminality among Progressive penologists and antiprostitution activists; these explanations presumed a medicalized view of women offenders, defining them as diseased and defective rather than merely ill behaved. Significantly, in reformatory settings psychopathy and feeblemindedness came to be seen not only as precipitating causes of immorality but as serious impediments to reform.[39] At Albion, for example, Superintendent Alice Curtin complained frequently during the early 1910s of "feebleminded" inmates and girls "not rightly balanced" who undermined the discipline of the reformatory and made little progress toward reform. Similarly, at Bedford Hills staff and members of the board of managers lamented "the heavy drag of the mentally defective who seldom appreciate what is being done for them and are generally incapable of entering into the spirit of cooperation" that prevailed among "normal" inmates.[40]

Unwilling to let the reformatories be destroyed by the misconduct and incompetence of "mental defectives," administrators at Albion and Bedford Hills tried to graft new scientific remedies onto old programs for moral uplift. At Albion, shortly after taking over as superintendent in 1916, Flora P. Daniels arranged for diagnostic examinations of the most troublesome inmates through the State Board of Charities.[41] Polly Overton, for example, was tested in 1916 or 1917. The examination confirmed that she was decidedly feebleminded, being deficient in good judgment, reasoning, and concentration; Polly also had an "ugly, defiant, and uncontrolled temper." But Albion lacked the resources to segregate Polly or provide her with special treatment; she remained a regular member of the inmate population, adding to the burdens of her keepers.[42]

In contrast, Bedford Hills aggressively pursued an internal program of classification and differential treatment for mentally defective inmates. In 1910 Superintendent Katharine Davis began to invite promising young female social scientists to the reformatory to investigate the mental status of her inmates. Preliminary studies in 1911 by Reed College psychologist Dr. Eleanor Rowland suggested that perhaps a third of the inmates were feebleminded and incapable of understanding the moral significance of their actions. Other mental defects were also present in the inmate population.

According to Rowland, some girls evinced "mental imbalance which amounted to almost insanity, and . . . still others . . . a nervous hysteria which prevents anything like progress."[43] The following year, tests conducted by Jean Weidensall, a psychologist who had trained at the University of Chicago and worked at the (Chicago) Juvenile Psychopathic Institute, disclosed persistently low IQ scores among Bedford's inmates. But Weidensall hesitated to interpret the results as either an accurate measure of mental capability or a full explanation of delinquency and called for further investigation.[44]

Convinced that mental defectiveness was a serious problem but realizing that it was probably neither the sole cause of female immorality nor the only handicap thwarting inmates' reform, Davis decided to make Bedford Hills a center for the scientific study of prostitutes and other female delinquents. In 1911 Davis made arrangements with the millionaire John D. Rockefeller, Jr., an outspoken opponent of prostitution, to establish the Laboratory of Social Hygiene at Bedford Hills on land adjoining the reformatory. Operational by 1913, the laboratory's professional staff evaluated each new inmate from social, familial, psychological, psychiatric, and medical standpoints over a three-month period. With the data thus gathered on each inmate, staff members assessed the causes of delinquency, established a prognosis for reform, and recommended a suitable program of treatment within the reformatory setting.[45] Responsive to theories linking mental defect to delinquency, the laboratory's methods also reflected the ideas of the emerging mental-hygiene movement which downplayed the role of inherited defects but nonetheless considered female delinquents to be mentally abnormal, that is, "individual personalities, maladjusted to life, for each one of whom an individual plan of treatment should be made."[46]

In the case of Ilene Sterling, who had been committed to Bedford Hills by her mother, the laboratory staff concluded that the girl's "waywardness" had been caused by a combination of factors: first, an impoverished home further darkened by maternal immorality, alcoholism, and paternal abuse; second, emotional immaturity and an unwillingness to "control herself." Ilene showed no signs of mental defect but she "wants to be a child . . . [and] has a tremendous streak of stubbornness in her." At Bedford Hills, Ilene would need "very firm management" and would have to be kept "away from the lively girls."[47] Ester Bromwell, a young black woman convicted of prostitution, had been raised with little home discipline in Harlem and was likely to be an even greater problem than Ilene. The laboratory found that "she is the hyperkinetic type which craves continually activity and amusement. She has never learned to take responsibility and look at life from the adult standpoint." Ester would have to be carefully controlled because "she is the sort of a girl who would not hesitate to smash out."[48]

Following the laboratory's "expert" recommendations, in 1916 and 1917 Bedford Hills implemented a new scheme for classifying inmates and reformatory cottages. The institution placed the "low and medium grade morons" and the "psychopathic group" in newly constructed cottages, where they would be preventing from disrupting inmates who were merely "maladjusted" and would obtain care and supervision specific to their needs and disabilities. Thus the Frances Bement cottage for "psychopathic" girls operated as an experimental hospital in which staff members working under the direction of psychiatrist Edith R. Spaulding tried to control and rehabilitate inmates who suffered from extreme "emotional instability" and violent tempers. Experience and careful study had shown that the "psychopaths" were the most disruptive girls in the reformatory, far worse than the "feebleminded" inmates, who were simply slow or unable to learn. The hospital's plan of treatment combined recreation, rest, and occupational therapy with "various negative forms of discipline such as wet packs, hydrotherapy, isolation, restricted diet, and deprivation of privileges."[49]

In the midst of the innovations in psychiatric and psychological diagnosis and treatment, Bedford Hills also decided to abandon racial integration and place African American young women in cottages separate from white women. The shift in policy occurred after Katharine Davis resigned from the reformatory in 1914 to accept an appointment as New York City's commissioner of corrections. Without Davis at its helm, staff morale at Bedford slipped, as did public confidence in the institution's methods of operation.[50] An investigation conducted in 1914 and 1915 by the State Board of Charities revealed severe disciplinary problems at the reformatory (despite the innovative work of the laboratory), among them a disquieting pattern of "unfortunate attachments" between white and black women in the reformatory.[51]

Of course, lesbian relationships also occurred between women of the same race at Bedford Hills. Assistant Superintendent Julia A. Minogue, one of the key witnesses in the investigation, testified that "there is as much of this romantic attachment between white girls as there is between white and colored girls. But, as Minogue pointed out, "there is no denying that the colored girls are extremely attractive to certain white girls and the feeling is apt to be more intense than between white girls alone." Ultimately the state investigators concluded that the interracial attachments were to blame for "a very considerable part of the disciplinary problems" at the reformatory.[52]

Significantly, the Board of Charities constructed an interpretation of lesbianism at Bedford Hills that was conspicuous in its reference to only one of several prevailing representations of deviant female sexuality. There were no assertions here that African American women, oft described by whites as unnaturally libidinous and licentious, were "seducing" "innocent" white girls; rather, the black inmates were portrayed as the recipients of white affection. Nor was there talk of the inmates' "character inversion" (i.e., masculinity) or their "deviant" sexual object choice; in fact, staff members from the Laboratory of Social Hygiene who might have referred to the latest sexological theory were not invited to testify.[53]

Instead, speaking to white middle-class fears that the Caucasian race was not sufficiently invested in its own preservation, reformatory staff members and Board of Charities' investigators represented lesbianism as a portent of race "degeneration" or amalgamation: they predicted that white girls involved in romantic attachments with African American inmates would forfeit the privileges and obligations of their race and "take up living in colored neighborhoods" after their release from the reformatory.[54] Borrowing and modifying the ideas of eugenicists and antifeminists who criticized white college-educated women for "selfishly" declining marriage and motherhood, investigators at Bedford Hills accused white homosexual inmates of actions promoting "race suicide." On this basis, the investigators "earnestly" recommended racial segregation, and the new superintendent, Helen A. Cobb (1914–20) hastened to follow their advice.[55] Black and white inmates were henceforth housed in separate cottages, and, informally, black inmates were denied access to the reformatory's courses in stenography and bookkeeping.[56] During the Board of Charities' investigation former superintendent Katharine Davis had defended the old policy of racial integration in the popular press, but she could not prevent its demise.[57]

Classification, differential treatment, and segregation did not end the reformatories' difficulties. In the midst of the institutional upheavals of the 1910s, both institutions reported difficulty hiring and retaining matrons and teachers devoted to the reformatory cause.[58] Moreover, as we have seen, Albion was never able to pursue "scientific" remedies to the extent it would have liked. Thus, although inmates at Albion in the 1920s continued to be tested periodically by the State Board of Charities, Superintendent Daniels could not segregate mentally defective inmates into separate cottages;

rather, she assigned feebleminded inmates to classes and domestic tasks she thought appropriate to their limited abilities.[59] Moreover, in 1918 Bedford Hills was forced to close its Laboratory of Social Hygiene and psychopathic hospital when Rockefeller declined to renew funding for these projects and New York State, contrary to his wishes, declined to "take up and continue" the work. Like Albion, the reformatory henceforth depended on the State Board of Charities for occasional mental examinations of inmates.[60]

Bedford Hills' commitment to differential treatment was given a small boost in 1920 when New York's legislators revised the laws governing the institution, requiring it to hire a psychiatrist as superintendent. As the first superintendent hired under the new law, Dr. Amos Baker, previously a psychiatrist at New York's Sing Sing Prison, presided over the reopening of a "psychopathic" cottage, but it was soon closed again for lack of funds. After its closing, Bedford's most seriously disturbed inmates were transferred to New York State's Hospital for the Criminally Insane at Mattaewan. Similarly, Baker lacked the resources to invest in mental-hygiene case work with the more typical "maladjusted" delinquents so that their personal conflicts might be understood and worked out. Only with regard to the severely feebleminded was Baker able to take special action. In his second year at Bedford Hills the reformatory opened a Division for Mentally Defective Women on the site of the Laboratory for Social Hygiene to provide indefinite custodial care for feebleminded delinquent females. Women could be sent directly to the division by the courts or could be transferred there from Bedford's regular facility.[61]

Most important, the reformatories' control remained far from absolute as inmates continued to rebel against their keepers. Often, defiant young women acted as individuals, but they also misbehaved together. Thus in 1920 the inmates at Bedford rioted, "fighting with knives, flatirons, stones, and clubs, back and forth over the institution grounds for an hour holding twenty-five State Troopers and the police force of Bedford at bay." The riot was considered a racial incident—it began over a fight between a white and a black inmate—and the participants in the riot took sides according to race. Racial tensions at segregated Bedford, as elsewhere in the postwar nation, remained undeniably high.[62]

The riot also marked the end of a nearly five-year dispute (since Davis's departure) among staff members, inmates, and state officials over the meaning of "reasonable discipline" within the reformatory setting. Convinced that the inmate population was dominated by psychopaths and the mentally enfeebled, but never able (even while the Laboratory of Social Hygiene was

in operation) to build sufficient facilities or hire enough specialized personnel for the "defective" inmates, reformatory officials and staff at Bedford
Hills resorted instead to severe punishment to subdue unruly "defectives."

Complaints by inmates about harsh and brutal discipline precipitated
three investigations into the reformatory. In 1915 the State Board of
Charities exonerated the reformatory of all charges of "intentional cruelty."[63] A second investigation in 1918 by the State Commission of Prisons
took the inmates' charges more seriously and deplored prevailing disciplinary practices in the reformatory, especially the lengthy confinement of
"disturbed" inmates and runaways in Bedford's prison and disciplinary buildings, the latter a dungeon-like structure without toilet facilities or natural
light. Still, the commission refused to criticize either the superintendent,
Helen Cobb, or her assistant, Julia Minogue. "[It] should be said that they
assumed their duties at a time when discipline was bad, that they have been
obliged to carry on a system not of their initiation and that the records show
that they have consistently and continuously endeavored to improve
discipline and lessen the severity of punishment."[64]

By the next year, however, the inmates' complaints were too loud and too
public to ignore. During December 1919 and January 1920 the State Commission of Prisons conducted another investigation, on one visit witnessing
a spontaneous inmate rebellion that

> afforded the examiners opportunities to get a first hand glimpse of reformatory
> discipline. An incipient revolt started among twenty-five negro girls in Lowell
> Cottage when they were told they would forfeit their recreation privileges and
> would be sent to bed at 6 o'clock unless some one produced a dress yoke one of
> the cottagers said had been stolen from her. . . . Some of the girls were found to
> be attacking the attendants with strips of carpet, all were screaming, and some
> were devoting their attentions to the glass window panes with great success. In
> a half hour the girls were quieted and persuaded to "be good" without resort to
> any of the disciplinary measures as to which complaint has been made.[65]

Although it found much to criticize in the inmates' conduct and some
evidence of appropriate forms of discipline, in the end the commission
determined that reformatory staff often relied on unnecessarily brutal and
degrading forms of punishment to control their most unruly inmates: "Young
women, many of them admitted to be psychopaths, who had transgressed
the rules . . . were handcuffed with their hands behind their backs and
fastened to the cell grating by another pair of handcuffs attached to those on
their wrists so that, in some cases, their toes, or the balls of the feet, only

touched the floor; and while thus suspended, their faces were dipped into pails of water until subdued."[66]

The investigators ordered the modification of disciplinary measures at the reformatory, but in doing so they incurred the bitter resentment of the newly appointed superintendent, Florence Jones, who believed she had been deprived of power to govern the institution. Jones chose to leave Bedford rather than submit to the commission's order, and, in this context, the race riot occurring just three days after Jones announced her resignation might best be interpreted as both a racial incident and a show of the inmates' disrespect for their departing keeper. The inmates knew that their claims had been been vindicated, knew that public sympathies were on the side of girls who had been "strung up" and subjected to "water treatment," knew that Bedford's staff had been told that it could no longer resort to brutal punishment.[67]

Indeed, in accepting appointment as the next superintendent of Bedford Hills, Amos Baker spoke carefully of his obligation to use humane and "modern" methods of control. He was not only the first psychiatrist but also the first man to oversee the reformatory, the state having decided that a male doctor was better equipped than a woman (with or without medical credentials) to handle the reformatory's inmates without resort to excessive punishments.

> I am going to run the institution on a humane plan. I will not allow any harsh or barbaric punishment. I believe a lot of the inmates are psychopathic cases. I will use whatever scientific methods can be provided to help this class of girls. I shall enforce discipline. This is necessary in any institution. I am not afraid of having any trouble with the inmates. I believe a doctor would not be as apt to have trouble as a layman. I am going to concern myself with the mental side to the question, but I will also try to improve the education and deportment of the girls. I believe a man can run the institution. I am going to try.[68]

Amos Baker did, in fact, prove to be a relatively sympathetic and humane superintendent.[69] But although there were no riots under his watch, inmates continued to engage in acts of rebellion and resistance as they had before he was hired. Acting in pairs or groups, reformatory inmates before and after 1920 announced their identification with distinctive inmate subcultures, subcultures that legitimated the right of young women to define their own values and to oppose as irrelevant the genteel model of womanhood upheld by their keepers.

The interracial lesbian relationships between inmates were a particularly significant form of inmate subculture. Although no record exists of lesbian attachments at Albion, they were, as already noted, a well-recognized problem at Bedford Hills. And not surprisingly, racial segregation did not put an end to interracial homoerotic relationships. Rae Rabinowitz, the seventeen-year-old who was sent to Bedford as an "incorrigible girl" in 1917 after being beaten by her brother and raped by two sailors was "more or less trouble about colored girls all the time." She was "interested in some colored girl every few weeks" and was frequently punished for sending notes to one or another of her black girlfriends. Similarly, Melanie Burkis, a wayward minor who began her sentence at Bedford in 1924, was much criticized for her "distasteful and demoralizing . . . obsession" with a "colored" inmate.[70]

The homoerotic relationships between inmates signified young women's interest in creating scandal and disapproval. The relationships were a form of behavior through which young inmates tried to give evidence of their own power; that is, they used their capacity to shock and offend to deny their defenselessness against the demands of the reformatory staff. Melanie Burkis thus made it a point to make her "obsession" for Valerie Revere very obvious to others. Indeed, one of the Bedford schoolteachers complained that "if thwarted in any undesirable action toward Valerie Revere she showed plainly that her affection for her teacher or desire to improve was assumed in order to continue her obsession for the colored pupil."[71]

Of course, the lesbian romances at Bedford Hills also revealed young women's interest in bending and testing prevailing definitions of gender and race. Impatient with the Victorian norms of their keepers, Bedford's lesbians similarly defied conventions within urban youth cultures that privileged heterosexuality and racial segregation. Bedford's lesbians transgressed the boundaries of masculinity and femininity and deliberately crossed the "color line," even pretending membership in the race of the "other."

Thus, when Jewel Foster, one of Rae's black girlfriends, wrote Rae a love letter, she adopted the personna of a white woman and became "Mama Blondie," addressing Rae as "My own loving Daddy." "Mama Blondie" devoted much of her letter to showing that she was worthy of her "Daddy's" love and intended "to be a good true mama to you now and out in the big world." Jewel emphasized the seductive and aggressive masculinity of her lover and reveled in fantasies of her "beautiful daddy . . . teasing and trying to fuck me and do everything that goes with. . . . I bet you'd make me ask for more, for I am glad to say that I cant get enough jazz." Unable to maintain this fiction with perfect consistency, Jewel at one point referred to Rae (5'2" tall, 101 pounds) as a "pretty doll" with "cute little arms," but then returned to calling Rae her "pop" and "dear dad." In closing, Jewel declared, "I am your little Mama Blondie Indeed I love my daddy I scream I do."[72]

Through individual and collective acts of rebellion, the inmates at Bedford Hills and Albion let staff members know that they cared little for the reformatories' "opportunities" and were unwilling to tolerate their regulations and sanctions. Resenting the state's intrusion into their lives, the young women compelled instructors and matrons to acknowledge their ability to frustrate the reform process. The reformatories' "good" girls had little success in prodding reformatory personnel to modify "unfair" disciplinary decisions; in contrast, through a campaign of prolonged defiance and displays of utter disrespect the worst inmates at Bedford forced the institution to abandon hated forms of punishment and to close the disciplinary building.

Nonetheless, over time, the reformatories powerfully affected inmates' behavior and their sense of self. By withholding freedom and placing about the inmates' heads a cloud of dishonor, they compelled young women to reexamine the behavior that led to their incarceration, to reconsider the merit of self-assertion and sexual expression. And by penalizing inmates who defied reformatory expectations and rules, Albion and Bedford Hills taught delinquent young women to appreciate the value of caution and calculated conformity. Indeed, the institutions' officers held before their most disorderly inmates the unpleasant possibility of being classed not merely as "delinquent" but as "mentally defective" or "psychopathic," thereby becoming subject to further restraint and social stigma. The rebellious subculture of inmates offered an important alternative to the behavioral paradigm of the reformatory staff, but it was often left behind as inmates realized that timely parole required compliance with the reformatories' demands. The institutions hoped that punishment would deter future offenses and in many cases this tactic clearly was effective. Unfortunately the surviving documentation does not tell us whether inmates found the outdated model of Victorian womanhood of their keepers inspiring or compelling; it is likely that many young women left the reformatories, as they entered them, in search of a satisfying social identity. But though they might not identify with the reformatories' behavioral ideal, most of the young women at Bedford and Albion began to appreciate that "staying out of trouble" had its advantages. There was something to be said for adaptive behavior.

For example, Ella Waldstein was "childish" and somewhat defiant only during her first year at Bedford. After that, her behavior showed "marked improvement." Numerous minor punishments and confinement for eight days in the reformatory's dilapidated prison building were unpleasant enough to cure Ella of her disobedient outbursts.[73] Similarly, Florence Pirelli, another Bedford inmate, tried twice to escape from the reformatory, but after her parole was postponed for three months, she gave no further trouble.[74] Even Rae Rabinowitz showed a definite improvement in behavior. Rae was at various times punished for passing love letters, "being impertinent," and calling others "vile names." She lost recreational privileges, had her parole date postponed, and was at least once placed for two weeks in Bedford's disciplinary building. The weight of these punishments may have eventually induced Rae to heed the reformatory's rules, for when Rae came up for parole consideration she was judged a good and obedient inmate. She had even "given up colored girls."[75]

There were, to be sure, inmates who remained defiant despite repeated punishments and chastisement. Melanie Burkis, for example, was disruptive throughout her commitment to Bedford in the mid-twenties. In addition to her "obsession" for Valerie Revere, Melanie caused trouble by defying her cottage matron, quarreling with other inmates, refusing to work, throwing notes out of her window, and telling stories about the sexual habits of her former lover, a black man, to her cottage mates. She was frequently punished, and on at least one occasion was transferred from her regular cottage to the segregation cottage, which had recently replaced the disciplinary building.[76]

It is impossible to say for certain why some young women could not be prevailed on to reform, how they managed to face, again and again, punishments meted out by outraged or disgusted staff members. We can, however, use the available evidence to speculate about their feelings and perceptions. Marian Jacoby, a Bedford inmate, may have been too angry to accept Bedford's demands for reform, despite the costs. Having previously spent nearly two years at New York's Magdalen Home on charges of waywardness and solicitation, Marian was already familiar with the unpleasant routines of a reformatory. Moreover, she insisted that her committment to Bedford Hills was the consequence of entrapment by members of New York City's vice squad. Unwilling to participate in her own reform or to control her temper, Marian escaped three times from the reformatory, was three times recaptured, and spent nearly all of her time while at Bedford Hills in its disciplinary and prison buildings, where she joined with the other women confined there in shaking her cell grate, screaming, whistling, and pounding on the floor. On numerous occasions she struck and kicked reformatory matrons, and then had to be subdued and handcuffed to her cell.[77]

Other inmates may have been too uncertain of their own sense of self to have known how to weigh the relative merits of misconduct and conformity. Eva Pomering was "a great deal of trouble" at Albion, spending four months in the institution's prison building and suffering a five-month postponement of parole and frequent loss of recreation and meal privileges. Yet despite her miserable record, Eva's feelings about the reform process were actually ambivalent and contradictory, as she revealed in (censored) correspondence. Thus, on one occasion, Eva displayed a spirit of proud defiance as she wrote across the top of a printed copy of Albion's rules of conduct that she planned to send to her older sister Susan: "Here are the rules [we] are compelled to obey, image me obeying all these rules. me obey them, well I should say not. here are all the rules I broke. The one I have put a little cross [next to]."[78] In the same correspondence Eva also tried to win Susan's sympathy and provoke outrage against the reformatory, explaining on the back of the rules sheet that the punishments meted out at Albion were unjust: "if I am caught it will mean That I'll lose my record, recreation, and my full meals. . . . That's where they starve a girl half to death." Finally, however, Eva revealed a distinctly different set of emotions and admitted that she wanted to be good and needed encouragement from her family. "please Susan dear, write more often, it will help me to be better you no if you don't write I think you don't care what becomes of me so that is why I don't care and get into punishment, this is an awful place girls are here for all kinds of things, its awful But I should worry I'm not like them."[79]

Some of the reformatories' most unruly inmates may also have discovered that there were actual advantages to being labeled feebleminded or psychopathic. Eugenia Lekkerkerker pointed out in her 1931 study of American women's reformatories that the "psychopathic" women at Bedford Hills discovered that "they could not be held responsible for their acts." If a woman did not mind being considered "crazy," she could "do as [she] pleased" and incite others to follow her example.[80] Moreover, the application of psychiatric and psychological nosologies amounted to little more than a thin veneer on the basic structure of the reformatory, and "defective" inmates were not incapable of discerning the shallowness of the reformatories' segregative controls. Renate Friedman spent five months in Bedford's psychopathic hospital in 1917 and over a year in Huntington cottage, a unit for "troublesome" inmates. In both places Renate was a constant trial to her keepers; in particular, she liked to talk to other girls about her "fast life" and tried to encourage a spirit of insubordination, once telling another inmate "that when she was in the Magdalen home & other places . . . the girls stuck together & when they wanted a riot they had one for all the girls joined in." Yet despite her poor record and unfavorable classification, Renate's parole was not delayed, and she was allowed to leave Bedford having shown "only slight improvement" at the institution.[81]

Gertrude Leavitt, sentenced to Bedford Hills as a wayward minor in 1922, the same year that the Division for Mentally Defective Delinquents opened, similarly discovered the imperfections in Bedford's handling of its "feeble-minded" inmates. Gertrude was "a troublesome, quarrelsome girl, frequently in punishment. Exhibitionistic, profane, and vulgar." But despite her bad behavior, it took Bedford Hills two years to conduct mental tests and recommitt Gertrude as a mentally defective delinquent to the new division. There Gertrude confronted the theoretical possibility of an indefinite sentence. Instead, she was released on parole after only one month.[82] Relatively few feebleminded women (usually with IQs of 65 or less) were recommitted to the Division for Mentally Defective Delinquents from Bedford's regular division, and in most cases they still followed the basic reformatory program and were discharged on parole well before the end of three years, even without evidence of good behavior. Bedford tried to provide "mentally defective" inmates with closer supervision than the regular girls, but it could not afford to keep them indefinitely and did not have the specialized staff to offer them individualized therapy or counseling.[83]

Finally, some "normal" young women may have felt that the reformatories' authority was simply unequal to their own powers of resistance. By the 1920s Bedford released nearly all of its inmates, whatever their behavior, within one year, and Albion within a year and eight months. Faced, on the one hand, with badly damaged reputations after the scandals of the late 1910s and, on the other, by judges who were increasingly in favor of non-institutional forms of treatment for novice and petty offenders, officials at Bedford Hills and Albion believed that the reformatories could not survive unless they shortened the period of incarceration.[84] But, of course, shortened incarceration carried the risk that some young women would feel that they had no incentive to reform. Sophie Polentz's parole officer complained that on the train ride from Bedford to New York City with several other new parolees the young woman "boasted that no girl had been more disorderly that she and that she had been given her parole in eight months. Even though she ran away, was impudent and saucy to the matrons and never hesitated to tell an officer just what she thought of her in impolite language."[85]

Though she was proud of her ability to escape Bedford unreformed and unrepentent, Sophie's boasting was, in fact, premature. Sophie and other young women who delighted in exploiting the reformatories' weaknesses exaggerated their ability to act with impunity. On parole, New York's delinquent females would discover that the reformatories continued to be a nagging presence in their lives, demanding that they remain chaste, deferential, and hard-working even in the midst of circumstances, personalities, and amusements foreign to the reformatory setting. They would be subject to the judgment of the reformatories while newly exposed to the competing demands and appeals of employers, family members, and peers.

Few young women would find parole easy, even those who had learned to cultivate caution within the reformatories. The reformatories did not prepare them to contend with rival or dissimilar claims and values; rather, it promoted a working-class version of Victorian womanhood in isolation. Moreover, as the next chapter shows, the reformatories did not offer inmates the implements with which to repair the broken familial relationships that cluttered their pasts. In visits and correspondence with relatives, inmates had a chance to reinvestigate the family claim, but reformatory rules and conventions prevented them from communicating openly. These young women needed to come to terms with the values and sentiments of their families but were given limited opportunity to do so. As they left the reformatories to begin parole, young inmates were likely to be reunited with parents who had not themselves made any attempt to "reform" and were still ill prepared to understand or cope with their daughters.

CHAPTER FOUR

"I Live in Hopes of Her Come from There a Better Daughter":
Families and the Reformatories

Although we might think of the dynamic of reform as one that exclusively involved the inmates and their keepers, it was actually a three-way affair, bringing young women, reformatory officials, and family members together to wrestle over goals and methods. Inmates at Bedford Hills and Albion were decisively cut off from the friends and lovers they had known in the outside world, yet they were permitted some contact with their immediate families. In fact, with the exception of the wayward minors, most young women were probably in closer touch with kin while confined in the reformatories than they had been for some time before their commitment. Family members received letters from their girls about life in the reformatories, in return sending them news from home and advice on how to conduct themselves in the institutions. Less frequently, parents, siblings or other relatives visited the young women at Albion and Bedford Hills. Some families also kept up an active correspondence with reformatory superintendents, hoping to obtain accurate reports of the inmates' progress or news of their pending release on parole.[1]

In letters and visits most family members expressed acute exasperation and humiliation over their girls' misconduct and incarceration, all the while showing that they intended neither to disown the delinquents nor to abandon them to the state's care. It was the rare parent or guardian who claimed that he or she would have "nothing more to do" with a delinquent young woman.[2] Instead, most evinced genuine interest in the inmates' welfare, training, and reform. Alva Burrows's mother reacted to the news of her daughter's reformatory commitment and out-of-wedlock pregnancy with great dismay, exclaiming to Albion's Flora Daniels, "It seemed I could hardly Stand the Blow," but she did not wash her hands of the eighteen-year-old girl.[3] Rather, Mrs. Burrows corresponded regularly with Alva and wrote many letters to the superintendent, hoping to be kept informed of her daughter's activities and conduct. Six months after Alva's commitment, she asked Daniels for a frank assessment of the girl's achievements, revealing at the same time her own aspirations for her daughter. "Now Please tell me candily what you think about her, Has she Improved in her ways and is she Lirning too do House work for she was Determined she would not do housework no matter what I tryed to say . . . I do want her to be a nice girl and Obedient, I really think this is doing her good. but oh the Sorrow it brings tears to our eyes."[4]

Yet no matter how sincere their interest, nor how closely their definitions of "improvement" seemed to match those of the reformatories, the inmates' families never earned the trust of the superintendents and staff at Bedford Hills and Albion. Too many parents wrote disheartening or disparaging letters to their daughters, rather than uplifting ones. Moreover, reformatory authorities knew from experience that some families would eventually challenge the institutions' authority and try to inscribe competing demands on the reform agenda. Mrs. Burrows, initially so supportive of Albion's efforts to "improve" her daughter, became "Disgusted" and "red Hot" with anger when she learned that Albion would continue to "claim jurisdiction" over Alva while she was on parole. "During that time she cant Do anything without writing back there For permission and then you people have to Investigate things." That Albion had allowed Alva to keep her new infant but declined to make the father of the child "settle for what he has done" only further infuriated Mrs. Burrows. Convinced that Albion was misusing its power, she declared, "People think they always know more than Parents do about their own, *its a sad mistake*."[5] Though Mrs. Burrows's open hostility was remarkable, she shared with other parents a willingness to contest the wisdom and fairness of reformatory policies.

Of course, the reformatories were far from helpless in dealing with the inmates' families. Acting as censors, the superintendents and assistant superintendents at Albion and Bedford Hills carefully read all correspondence written by or sent to the inmates, removing letters and erasing passages that might "upset" delinquent young women or family members and provoke contempt for the reformatories' authority. And in most cases the reformatories' administrators were able to deflect both outright criticism and requests for changes in institutional procedures by claiming that parents or other relatives "had a wrong understanding of the aims and purposes" of the reformatories.[6] Contests between families and the state over the right of kin to participate in the correction of delinquent females usually resulted in a victory for the reformatories.[7]

Yet even as they successfully controlled the inmates' families, reformatory administrators and staff demonstrated the limits of their own power. Specifically, they proved unable and unwilling to help inmates and kin resolve the differences that reinforced young women's quests for autonomy and contributed to their sometimes reckless investment in urban street life. Bedford's and Albion's established task was not to change the inmates' homes or neighborhoods but to reform delinquent females by removing them from the "ignorance" and "moral contagion" that inspired or induced their "ruin." Insulated from probation officers, psychologists, and psychiatrists who worked in court and clinic settings and tried, albeit without great success, to "readjust" relations between delinquents and their families, and having little faith anyway in the integrity of inmates' parents and siblings, reformatory personnel stressed restraint and interdiction rather than mediation. Meanwhile, family members looked forward to improvements in the young women's deportment but gave few signs that they planned to modify their own conduct and expectations. Excused by the reformatories' skepticism from reexamining well-entrenched habits and values, family members let themselves believe that the "lessons" to be learned were all on the inmates' side.

Families initially became involved in the reform process because the reformatories invited them to do so. Matrons and teachers hoped that the fictive family ties binding inmates and staff would prove strong enough to transform disorderly females into righteous young women. But to their puzzlement and disappointment, experience proved that lessons in modesty, diligence, and self-sacrifice were likely to remain abstract unless inmates received support from members of their "real" families. Despite inmates' complaints about their home life, staff members found that delinquent young women tended to be unresponsive to the reformatories' programs when they were oppressed by fears of familial indifference or rejection.

Bedford Hills and Albion thus depended on close kin to relieve inmates' anxieties and to mitigate their resistance to reform. In fact, when correspondence was not forthcoming, the reformatories' superintendents sometimes wrote to family members to chastise them for their neglect. In 1923 Bedford's superintendent Amos Baker wrote to ask Nanette Wilkins's aunt, the person responsible for the wayward-minor charge against the sixteen-year-old black girl, to correspond with her niece. Baker did not mention Nanette's frequent misconduct, but he did point out that "your niece, Nanette Wilkins, tells me that she has not heard from any of her people in some time and she is somewhat discouraged and anxious. I think a line from you would cheer her up and encourage her."[8] Similarly, in 1911 Albion's superintendent Alice Curtin wrote to Margaret Daly, urging her to correspond with her sister, Edith Parnell, who had been sent to Albion five months earlier for prostitution. Although Margaret had written to Superintendent Curtin to find out how Edith was "getting along" and to ask if Curtin thought the girl was feebleminded—for how else, she mused, could one explain why Edith "would have ackted the way she did?"—neither Margaret nor her siblings (both parents were deceased) had written to the inmate herself. Curtin felt certain that their negligence was undermining Edith's reform.

> It is rather discouraging to a girl, even a bad one, if she never hears anything from her people. . . . Edith was very good the first few weeks she came, and was then promoted to a cottage; since that time she has behaved very badly. . . . I think Edith is brighter than she appears to be. She is not so foolish but she knows better than to behave as she does. I think however, it might help matters if you could write to her, and possibly, if you can afford to do so, send her a box for Christmas.[9]

Though reformatory personnel realized that they could not singlehandedly turn disobedient girls into compliant inmates, their dependence on kin carried heavy traces of ambivalence and mistrust. Appreciative of relatives who tried to uplift the spirits of oft-disgruntled inmates, reformatory officials and staff nonetheless lacked confidence in family members' ability to serve as reliable advocates of behavioral reform. Simply put, they doubted the "good sense" of the inmates' "real" families and fully expected kin to obstruct as often as facilitate reform. Despite their dedication to a model of womanhood that honored obedience to the family, authorities at Bedford Hills and Albion could not be certain that parents and other relatives deserved inmates' deference and respect.

This distrust of inmates' families was based on middle-class reform traditions and trends in contemporary social science, as well as on practical

observation and experience. During the nineteenth century, moral reformers and charity officers who visited the homes of the urban and immigrant poor often came away from their work appalled by the intemperance,
abuse, and depravity they had seen. Though prejudice and misunderstanding undoubtedly colored their perceptions, domestic distress may well have
been on the rise in working-class neighborhoods, thanks to the pressures and
pitfalls of early industrial capitalism. In any case, organizations such as the
Society for the Reformation of Juvenile Delinquents, the Children's Aid
Society, and the Society for the Protection of Children worked simultaneously to save children and youths from domestic disorder and to convince
the middle-class public that immigrants and the poor made unfit parents.[10]

The critical attitudes of Victorian charity workers were reinforced during
the early twentieth century by Progressive activists and social workers who
"discovered" through professional and scientific investigations that
working-class, immigrant, and African American parents often failed to
shield adolescent daughters from the moral dangers of modern city life;
tragically, some of these parents also transmitted inheritable "defects" to
their offspring.[11] So too, by the 1910s and 1920s, professional social workers
and mental hygienists advanced the idea that female immorality was usually
a response to adverse psychological and emotional family dynamics; especially among the disadvantaged, unresolved domestic conflicts prompted
young women to indulge in antisocial behavior.[12]

Reformers and social scientists who uncovered grave "irregularities" in
working-class, immigrant, and African American family life affirmed the
findings of personnel at Bedford Hills and Albion. Through intake interviews with inmates, background investigations, correspondence, and occasional face-to-face meetings with kin, reformatory authorities concluded
that the parents of inmates were often woefully ill prepared to guide their
daughters through the perils of adolescence to young womanhood. Few of
the inmates' parents evinced outright criminality or immorality, but they
seemed to know nothing about protecting or controlling their daughters in a
complex urban society.[13] The staff at Bedford Hill's Laboratory of Social
Hygiene found, for example, that Eleanor Hamlisch's mother was respectable "but weak and without force. She was quite unable to control Eleanor."[14] So convinced was Superintendent Flora Daniels of the inferior
character of Albion's inmate families that she complained about their inferior "standards of living," "low grade mentality," and "lack of discipline" in
her annual reports to the New York State legislature. Having little reason to
hope that the inmates' families would surmount their assorted flaws, Daniels

drew the obvious inference. "The social background of most of our inmates is so poor that we wonder how any good can come of it."[15]

Faced with families scarcely worthy of the name, the reformatories essayed to circumscribe their involvement in the inmates' reform, intercepting letters containing family news or personal remarks that might upset the inmates or cause them to resist reformatory discipline. In addition, censors retained letters to the inmates that openly defied the reformatories' moral authority and social control. Occasionally, a single letter proved objectionable on both counts, as Albion's censor discovered on reading a letter sent to Alice Arlington from her mother. Mrs. Arlington lashed out at both Alice and Albion, having learned that her "troublesome" daughter would probably be required to stay at the reformatory for another full year:

> how do you think I am agoing to live with out you all of another year to come. I feel sure it will shorten my life, so if you *Like* the Place there better than to come home to Live with your old mother and Father time will tell all. . . . I know the matron there that time we were to see you last . . . complained of you not being good I ask her to tell me of what you done that was so bad all she could say was that you was Disagreable well perhaps she was just as bad so i dont believe all that I here.[16]

Some families sent not just one disruptive letter but a barrage of them. Albion's assistant superintendent thus censored Eva Pomering's incoming mail with scrupulous care, hoping that her family's persistent denunciations of the institution would not come to Eva's attention and make the disorderly young woman still more unmanageable. The problematic letters began to arrive after Eva complained bitterly, during a visit by her mother and older sister, of having been confined to a cell in the reception building's "prison corridor" for breaking her wash bowl and pitcher and inadvertently cutting her hands. Although the Pomerings had asked for Eva's commitment to Albion after she ran away from home, took an Italian lover, and contracted syphillis, their faith in the reformatory was destroyed by her complaints. With annoying frequency, letters arrived for Eva from her younger and older sisters condemning the reformatory's treatment of Eva. One from the younger sister read:

> My dear sister Appleblossom, Oh! Eva. How I do wish that you where safe at home with us. . . . I hope Dear that your hands are better. For shame of those that treat you like that. Oh! Eva I am so angry. What Darling mother said 'about the conditions that you are in.' Don't worry Honey. they who treat you

mean will suffer from the consequences. I no in my own heart that you never told a lie . . . I must say this much I certinally was shocked to here what mother said. I can't bear to listen to such awfull things. . . . I no in my heart that if you could write most anything you would not say the untruth. I no now that the head one says you can write only just a certain things. which are all lies of course. they are the ones who lie. Not you my dear sister. . . . And further more to think that you should get punished for such a little, nice baby thing as that. oh! Eva dear! I don't blame you one minute for . . . getting angry when you no you are innocent. . . . I hope the matrons who appeared real nice to both mother and sister will give this letter to you (ugh) go to the Dr. for your health *Please, oh!* thats my only wish.[17]

Realizing that inmates' remarks helped to shape families' opinions of the reformatories, authorities tried, although without complete success, to prevent their disparaging comments from reaching family members. Perhaps not wanting to provoke resentment, censors chose not to eavesdrop on conversations between inmates and visiting relatives. But the censors did read all correspondence written by the inmates, and they unhesitatingly retained letters that "misrepresented" the reformatories. For instance, finding that Rae Rabinowitz had written a letter critical of the reformatory to her older sister Yvonne, Bedford's superintendent Anna Talbot composed a note of her own, explaining that Rae's letter had been withheld because it "would give the wrong impression of things as they really are. . . . Rae has . . . little control over her tongue or temper."[18]

The censors also refused to pass letters in which inmates castigated family members. From their point of view decent young women were not supposed to speak disrespectfully to their elders; moreover, the reformatories did not want inmates to give families more reason to reproach their girls than they already had. Bedford Hills thus retained a letter that Blanche Preston had written to her aunt, the only family member with whom she was in close contact. Fearing rejection, Blanche had adopted a confrontational, accusatory tone that was unlikely to generate sympathy:

Dear Aunt, What on earth is the matter I haven't got any answere from my letters I wrote to you I guess you have forgotten me since I been in here Auntie Dear you know it make me feel very bad When I don't get any letter and the other girls do I want to know are you angry With me or not . . . you know that I havent forget you if you have forgotten me because I am in a place like this.[19]

As they read inmates' incoming and outgoing mail, the censors at Albion and Bedford Hills usually concluded that it was sufficient either to discard inappropriate letters or place them in the inmates' files. However, when reformatory authorities knew that a parent or relative was anxious for news from an inmate, they might, as was the case with Rae Rabinowitz's older sister, write a note to explain why a letter had been retained. And when reformatory superintendents had reason to worry that an inmate who had been deprived of expected correspondence might become more difficult to control, they sometimes wrote a didactic letter to the offending parent or relative. Rather than deny young women contact with their families, reformatory authorities in these infrequent cases tried to teach inmates' parents or guardians to model themselves after responsible middle-class mothers and fathers. For example, fearing that Polly Overton, a "feebleminded" girl, would react badly to a recent letter from her mother, Superintendent Daniels wrote to Mrs. Overton and explained that Polly should not be burdened with news that her mother was "heart Broek" over another daughter's tuberculosis: "We feel sure that it would make [Polly] feel very bad and as she cannot do anything to help you, I do not see what would be gained in knowing how discouraged you are over your daughter's illness. If I have an opportunity I will speak to Polly about it."[20]

Here, Daniels wanted to encourage Mrs. Overton to honor the ideal of parental protection, long esteemed by middle-class Americans. During the nineteenth century, prominent writers, ministers, and educators urged middle-class parents to shield their offspring, especially their daughters, from "harmful" ideas, "precocious" development, and "dangerous" associates. Of course, in an urbanizing nation with an expansive public press and a growing consumer market, parents fought an uphill battle and often were unable to fend off unsolicited ideas. Still, the ideal of parental protection persisted into the twentieth century. Social workers and settlement workers lamented parents' failure to shield girls from premature exposure to sexual desire and adult responsibility; popular authors also hammered away at the theme.[21] At Albion and Bedford Hills, reformatory censors upheld the ideal of parental protection by refusing to give inmates letters that conveyed disheartening family news or self-pity.

In other instances, authorities told parents that it would do no good to express anger or condemnation in letters to their daughters. Nineteenth-century middle-class Americans had believed that children successfully internalized the moral and social injunctions of parents only when those values were communicated with love and sympathy; in updating this tenet, twentieth-century educators, social workers, and mental hygienists argued that young women and adolescent girls were most likely to heed parental wishes when they were certain of their elders' understanding and respect. "[An] understanding demeanor rather than strict discipline could supply the control parents sought to impose on their adolescents."[22] Following the ideological tendencies of his professional colleagues, Superintendent Baker wrote to the mother of Lena Meyerhoff to urge her to be less critical of her daughter. The reformatory censor had already passed a disparaging letter to Lena, perhaps having failed to notice its bitter tone. Baker wanted to stop other letters of this sort: "[T]he statements which you made in your letter are true; nevertheless they were so upsetting to Lena that I doubt the wisdom of writing letters of this kind to her in her present situation. I know it is very difficult to decide just what course to pursue in regard to her, but I think encouraging letters would be better than those that tend to depress and discourage."[23]

Many families must have felt the impact of Albion and Bedford's censorship procedures, whether they received an admonishing letter from a superintendent or simply discovered that letters sent to or from the inmates "disappeared" in the mail. Occasionally a parent complained about the intrusiveness of the censors. Thus in 1917 Penelope Jaros's mother wrote to Albion's superintendent Daniels, greatly annoyed because Penelope had not received all the correspondence sent to her:

> i received a letter from her and she ask me what is the matter with me that i dont write to her, now I would like to know where her mail goes to and the time before that she told me in her letter that one sheet was gone no do you think that is Right to loose tho the Mail that way. if this is the way things go then there is no use of writing and wasting time and postage to. there was very importint news in the letter for her to know her father has ben hurt and some more. . . . I think it is verry hard for a girl not to hear from home now will you kindly say what was done with the mail.[24]

The dearth of such complaints, however, suggests that most families chose not to be offended by censorship or refused to run the risk of angering reformatory authorities by challenging their interceptions.

Censorship served Albion's and Bedfords interests, allowing staff to limit familial involvement in reform. In an ironic twist, however, censorship may also have worked to subvert Albion's and Bedford's reformist goals, preventing young women and their relatives from evaluating or mending their differences. Indeed, while censorship precluded inmates and their close relatives from receiving openly hostile or disheartening letters, by reading between the lines of their "approved" correspondence, inmates and kin may have readily identified signs of enduring misunderstanding or disapproval. Sophie Polentz received frequent missives from her father and probably realized that he felt victimized by his troublesome daughter. (Because Mr. Polentz wrote his letters in German, translations were always made before the letters were passed and those translations remain in Sophie's file.)

Mr. Polentz was disabled and had depended on his daughter's income until she became so disobedient that he was forced to send her to Bedford. In one letter, written from the sanatorium where he had been sent by a Jewish charity, Sophie's father wrote, "The Doctor of the Society has forbidden me to think too much and to worry, . . . but I cannot help it. So I want you to pray to God that I will be home again soon, but there is a strong doubt in my mind whether I will be able ever to feed my wife and children again. . . . I remain with best greetings as ever, your suffering father."[25]

In another letter, Mr. Polentz wrote of his sorrow that Bedford's parole board had refused to grant Sophie her parole, noting that Bedford's superintendent understood how badly Sophie's misconduct hurt her father, even if she did not. It read in part: "I can write you that Dr. Baker is one of the finest men that I ever met in my life, a true Gentleman. He feels sorry for you, and he also feels more bad for me than my own children. . . . Your Parole come up before the Parole of Manager [again] next month, and I hope that next month you surely will come home." Mr. Polentz wanted his daughter to recognize that she was partially responsible for his suffering, but rather than prompting her reform, his attitude may well have annoyed her and redoubled her rebellious intent. Certainly, she was a notorious troublemaker at Bedford Hills.[26]

Problematic as censorship may have been, it reflected the reformatories' abiding loyalty to nineteenth-century methods of reform. The almshouses, reformatories, penitentiaries, and insane asylums of the nineteenth century had relied on segregation from the outside world, surveillance, and moral discipline to convert dependent and deviant individuals into disciplined citizens of the republic. Although the various asylums failed fully to live up to their promise, according to David Rothman, "there were few attacks on the principle of institutionalization in the post-1850s decades."[27]

Bedford Hills and Albion tried to improve and "feminize" the methods of the earlier asylums but they did not reject the essential premises of institutional reform. Established to correct young women in isolation from immoral influences and associates, the two reformatories remained unprepared to help inmates and their families communicate their differences long after twentieth-century "experts" began to recommend deliberate arbitration of parent-child disputes. By the 1910s and 1920s social workers, probation officers, and mental hygienists all contended that antisocial behaviors were likely to persist unless skilled professionals helped parents and delinquents resolve their disagreements, especially those relating to changing patterns of work, recreation, and peer interaction. As we have seen, "experts" working in newly established mental-hygiene clinics and juvenile courts discovered that this task was far more easily identified than accomplished, and during the 1920s frustrated social workers and mental hygienists increasingly declined case work with delinquent youths and their parents in favor of clinical intervention with families whose children suffered from relatively minor personality, behavioral, and sexual disorders. Still, social-work and mental-hygiene professionals had at least realized that familial relations were often a source of ongoing conflict and provocation in the lives of young delinquents.

In contrast, the reformatories made little effort to adjust or resolve relations between young women and their kin, preferring instead to stifle potentially disruptive intra-familial dialogue. At Bedford Hills and Albion inmates learned that they must pay a price for their rebellion against social and familial norms, but the reformatories did not intentionally help young women and their relatives settle disputes or devise modes of communication and compromise that would lessen the likelihood of future rebellion and resistance. The reformatories simply tried, with little faith or success, to persuade young women and their relations to model middle-class norms in written communication. If inmates and their families managed to reconstruct or reforge the ties that bound them, they got little aid from Albion or Bedford Hills.

While censorship inhibited candid communication between inmates and their families, the implications of "one-sided" reform for New York's delinquent young women were most clearly spelled out not in the censored mail itself but rather in the correspondence between inmates' families and the superintendents of Bedford Hills and Albion. Here, family members appealed to the reformatories directly, hoping to jettison their truncated role in the reform process and to reclaim their authority as parents, guardians, older siblings, or (infrequently) husbands. Of the one hundred young women in my sample, sixty-five had relatives who tried to challenge the reformatories' control. The great majority asked for early release, but a few parents, like Mrs. Burrows, disputed the reformatories' supervision of parolees or the arrangements they made for young women's employment or residence on parole. And in at least one-third of these cases, family members tried to bolster the legitimacy of their claims by seeking the support of a social agency, lawyer, or public official.[28]

After 1920 extremely persistent or hostile intervention was most likely to come from the families or spouses of inmates at Albion. By 1921 Bedford had reduced the minimum time to be spent in the institution prior to parole to six months. The minimum time was increased to eight months in 1924, but that small increase was not enough to prompt familial intervention. When intervention for early release did occur in the 1920s by the families of Bedford inmates, it was generally not persistent. In contrast, throughout the 1920s the minimum term at Albion was still at least a year and a half, a period of time that seemed unduly long to many families and often prompted efforts to have inmates returned home. Comparable intervention at Bedford during the 1920s was unusual except from the families of inmates who had been committed or recommitted to the Division for Mentally Defective Delinquents.

It is perhaps surprising that family members who had been unable to control adolescent young women, sometimes going to court to ask for reformatory sentences, should request early parole or otherwise intrude in the reformatories' efforts to correct their errant offspring. Nonetheless, numerous mothers, fathers, and older siblings did just that, finding themselves loath to tolerate long separation from their daughters or sisters. Willing to set aside their anger and hostility, they wrote to the superintendents that they were eager to welcome their young women home or to participate in decisions surrounding parole. Of course, an absence of rancor did not imply their abandonment of long-held values or assumptions. Indeed, interventionist families fully expected paroled young women to demonstrate, at long last, sensible obedience to the family claim.

These high expectations usually led them to display temperate goodwill in their dealings with the reformatories. Most parents and relatives must have understood that it would be inexpedient to mount an overtly hostile or confrontational campaign against the reformatories. More to the point, their letters suggest prudent respect for the work of the institutions. Most interventionist families were certain that Bedford Hills and Albion performed a valuable service by training and disciplining delinquent girls; what they wanted was an authoritative part in the important enterprise at hand. They did not seek to displace the reformatories but to limit their power. In positive terms, interventionist families wanted superintendents and parole boards to yield to the their interests when assessing inmates' "readiness" for parole or deciding where parolees were to live and work. Almost always failing in their efforts, these families' letters and appeals offer clear proof of the institutions' substantial authority and enduring distrust. Just as significant, their campaigns reveal the unreconstructed attitudes that young women would encounter when they finally did return home.

Interventionist families asked for the early release of inmates for a variety of reasons. Perhaps the most explicit requests came from parents or other relatives who needed young women at home to help relieve acute economic or social distress. Suffering from dire poverty, illness, or the recent death of a spouse, sixteen families tried to assert their right to draw on a daughter's homemaking or wage-earning capabilities. Richard Oliver pleaded for his daughter Elizabeth's early parole from Albion, claiming that she was needed at home "to take care of my other three younger children and to do the house work owing to the death of my wife."[29] Similarly, an attorney for Alice Arlington's parents wrote to Albion to say that Alice was needed at home to look after her elderly mother "who is in dire need of care and comfort."[30] And Sophie Polentz's destitute and sickly father asked for the early parole of his girl, begging Superintendent Baker to show his family some mercy:

> Dear Dr. Baker, I fall to your feet and beg a favor. As you know I myself sent my daughter Sophie Polentz to Bedford Hills. . . . I beg of you to help a whole family from breaking up. I have only one daughter working now, and her earnings are but the small sum of thirteen dollars a week. I have seven small children and they cannot be supported on my daughter's earnings. Have pity on me and send my daughter Sophie out on parole so that she can help support the family and home.[31]

In one of the rare appeals from a hostile family, Eva Pomering's older sister Susan tried to arrange for early parole, claiming that Eva's mother was developing "mental trouble" and could not be adequately cared for by a fifteen-year-old daughter who remained at home. Susan's letters to Albion were always polite, but the reformatory's censors already knew from reading Eva's mail that her relatives believed the institution harshly mistreated its inmates, and subsequent letters sent to Eva by her younger sister showed that the family blamed Mrs. Pomering's mental difficulties on Albion: "Every since Mother went to see you why she can't rest to think that they treated you so meanly."[32]

The majority of interventionist families, unable to claim an economic or medical emergency, presented what they thought were other compelling reasons for early parole. Paula Brownell's stepfather wrote to Albion to say that Paula's mother would not move with him to Denver, where he had been offered a good job, unless "she can take her daughter with her."[33] Louise Peffley's mother wrote to Albion's board of managers to ask if her daughter, ill for several months, might be sent home to her mother's care. Louise's mother did not want the board to think that she was "finding fault" with the reformatory but felt that if Louise was home "we could have more done for her."[34] And Althea Davies's married sister asked for the early release of her sibling, recently delivered of a newborn infant, on the grounds that "the entire family is very interested in her and says that I should try her once again."[35]

Some families frankly admitted their desire to put an end to the emotional anguish caused by a young woman's incarceration. Thus Ella Waldstein's brother pleaded for early parole to relieve his parents' grief over Ella's long absence. Mr. and Mrs. Waldstein had not realized when they took Ella to court that the standard sentence to Bedford Hills was three long years rather than a few months. Now, after more than a year, burdened by worry and guilt, they desperately missed their daughter. Comparing his mother's situation to that of mothers eagerly awaiting the return of soldier sons from the recently concluded world war, Ella's brother wrote, "We have lived through the most historical period in the history of the world. Now the great world's conflict has come to an end and a great many mothers are longing for their dear ones to come home again. My mother is longing for her dear one too, and so I am appealing to you to help me in filling the vacant chair that has been standing at our table for the past 16 months."[36]

Expressing a rather different sort of anguish, Nora Patterson's young husband asked for early parole, hoping to salvage his precarious marriage and his prospects for worldly success. Richard Patterson had known Nora for only three weeks before they married and had been drafted into the army just a few months later. Deeply upset about Nora's involvement in prostitution while he was serving his country, but unwilling to admit that his marriage had been a mistake, Richard pleaded for sympathy from Bedford's superintendent: "Miss Cobb, can my wife be parroled in my hands. . . . It is hard to sit and think. Wondering when she is going to get out. I would free myself from her but now days it is taken a chance of geting some one worst. . . . I am a poor man working to get some think sone day but can not do it by myself. . . . Please give a chance for my sake."[37]

Whatever their motives for requesting early parole, families knew that their efforts would fail unless they convinced the reformatories that their girls were "ready" to be released and had a fair chance of succeeding "on the outside." Numerous parents and relatives claimed that they had proof, in the form of declarations of repentance, that the reformatories had successfully disabused their daughters of foolish notions of independence and sexual rebellion; with the state's obligations fulfilled, the families' job was to welcome the inmates home and test the authenticity of their so-called reform. Mr. Polentz thus included in his urgent plea to Dr. Baker a reminder that Sophie had recently "begged me to forgive her for everything she had done. She said she was young and innocent and did not know the way of the world."[38] Mr. Covello, another father in critical need of a daughter's assistance, wrote that "my dogther Rosa Covello . . . ask me forgive for the wrong she doing to me and my wife about 1000 time and she promise me she will be good and she tried to paid back . . . because she tasted the good correction in the reformatory."[39] And Mrs. Garrison, a mother who wrote to Albion to say that her daughter Molly was needed at home, claimed that the young woman "has learned . . . a good lesson about not listening to [her] parents and i think [she] will do better in the time to come for Molly was so willing to be punished for what she had done."[40] Althea Davies's sister noted in her request for early parole that, "Althea has promised with eyes of tears that she will amend her ways. She is very sorry of her deeds and promised me that she will not be found in any such trouble again."[41]

Even Susan Pomering, desperate to free her sister from Albion's "mean" treatment, tried to convince the reformatory that Eva was ready to be a good and obedient parolee: "Its the first time that Eva has ever done a thing like that and I know my younger sister Eva will never do it again." To the reformatory staff Susan must have seemed unrealistically optimistic, but there is no reason to doubt the sincerity of her hope for Eva's reform. Writing to Eva some months after pleading for her early parole, Susan told her sister, "I do hope and prey yo will never land in an nother place like that gain keep away from bad girls and boys be by yourself and save your money. . . . I do hope you realize what that all means now dear."[42]

Relatives also tried to convince Bedford Hills or Albion that they could provide "good homes" and were willing to try, once again, to hold young women to high standards of conduct. Thus, when Ella's brother got no satisfactory reply to his poignant letter to Bedford Hills, he and his parents restated their appeal, turning for help to the Educational Alliance, a Jewish settlement house in New York City. One of the Alliance social workers wrote a letter on the Waldsteins' behalf, emphasizing the competence of Ella's parents and reminding Bedford Hills of Ella's readiness to return home. Mr. and Mrs. Waldstein were united "in the one wish to have the girl back home again under the parental roof, certain that they would know how to manage her, and certain also that their daughter would now appreciate the love and care they intend to give her."[43] Similarly, Paula Brownell's step-father wrote, "I promise you in the name of the almighty that her mother and I will do every thing we can to keep her straight."[44] Taking a more blunt approach, Nora Patterson's husband vouched for his wife's good behavior, writing, "If she does not do what is wright I will have [her] put back in there again."[45] And Louise Peffley's mother vowed that "if she was not a good girl we would very quick bring her back.[46]

In rare instances family intervention worked, and the reformatories released young women ahead of schedule. Sometimes the family had found favor with the courts and the reformatories were forced to respect a judicial order declaring that there had been an irregularity in the commitment proceedings. In other cases reformatory officials found reason to honor the request of a family claiming to be in desperate need of a young woman's aid.[47] Myra Roundman, a twenty-five-year-old adulterer, thus was able to leave Albion early to care for her six small children, all living temporarily in the Oswego County Home while she was confined. Myra's husband had pleaded for his wife's release, certain that "to have her home would make us all feel happy, but the children would be the happiest." Myra's mother also urged the reformatory to parole her daughter, composing a heart-rending appeal to Albion's assistant superintendent. "Mrs. Coon her children need her so bad and want her so much it is pitaful to hear them Daddy when is mother is mother comming home I want my mother." With assurances from the Oswego County probation office that Myra would return to a decent home, and promises from the inmate that she was ready to resume the responsibilities of marriage and motherhood, Albion's board of managers authorized her early release.[48]

Most families, however, were not so lucky. Though their pleas were heartfelt and insistent, the great majority of interventionist families discovered that reformatory authorities were unwilling to consider early parole or other special requests, preferring to release inmates on a schedule determined by the institutions' parole boards. To maintain public trust, the reformatories' superintendents could not ignore these appeals entirely, especially when they were made on behalf of family members by respected community organizations and leaders. Nonetheless, Albion and Bedford Hills usually had no legal obligation to honor families' requests and, indeed, believed that most requests for special favors were without merit. As Flora Daniels pointed out in one of her annual reports to the state legislature, parents and lawyers who wrote to Albion "asking that a certain girl be released because six months is long enough to punish any girl" simply misunderstood the reform process and failed to realize that the typical delinquent young woman required lengthy observation and training if she was ever to cope successfully with "the demands of outside life."[49]

Moreover, reformatory authorities had good reason to believe that many "contrite" young women claimed remorse only as part of a deliberate strategy to improve their chances for early parole. Rosa Covello was, in fact, a conscientious and cooperative inmate, but Sophie Polentz "exhaust[ed] all patience," Althea Davies was "sulky" and "noisy" though her work habits were fairly good, and Molly Garrison was "coarse and disruptive" and tried, during her second year at Albion, to escape from the reformatory.[50]

Whenever possible, superintendents replied to families' appeals for special treatment with polite but firm letters of refusal. Responding to Mrs. Peffley's respectful request for the early parole of her sickly daughter, Albion's superintendent Flora Daniels wrote a sympathetic note that was supposed to reassure the worried mother: "I think you do not need to worry about Louise's condition for she is having good care and I think will be all right after a while."[51] Similarly, when Althea Davies's sister asked about the possibility of an early parole, stressing the family's sincere interest in the girl and Althea's promise to be good, Bedford's Amos Baker replied, "I am very sorry I cannot comply with your request, but hope . . . Althea . . . will keep up her good record so that she may secure an early opportunity for being placed on parole."[52]

However, when family members became insistent or hostile, or when the inmate whose parole was in question was extraordinarily troublesome, the superintendents were inclined to reply in blunt and dismissive language. Thus, responding to the attorney who had written on behalf of Mr. and Mrs. Arlington to ask if their daughter Alice might be returned home to care for her sick and elderly mother, Albion's Flora P. Daniels wrote: "This girl is entirely unfit to live anywhere or with anybody, except under the strictest supervision. We have very few girls in the Institution who have given us as much trouble as Alice. I have tried in every way, to cure her of some of her bad habits . . . [and] to give her every advantage possible. If her parents did but know it, they can have greater peace of mind with Alice here, than they would have in all probability with her at home."[53] And when Mrs. Burrows insisted that Albion oblige the father of her daughter's baby to accept financial responsibility for his child, Albion's acting superintendent Nellie Coon replied with some irritation, "We have no authority or jurisdiction whereby we can prosecute 'suspected' fathers of babies, even if we desired to do so, which we do not . . . I request that you do not trouble me any further about the matter."[54]

The reformatories at Bedford and Albion assumed that family encouragement and support were instrumental to their inmates' reform. For this reason they invited families to take part in the reform process. Doubting, however, the character and competence of most parents and relatives, they monitored all correspondence between inmates and their families, weeding out negative comments and sometimes admonishing parents who wrote in an "inappropriate" tone or discussed "discouraging" subjects. Young women were to express repentance and gratitude for the second chance the reformatories and their families offered them; parents were to encourage and forgive their delinquent daughters, withholding anger, shame, and anxiety.

Frustrated with the small role they had been assigned, some families tried to take direct charge of the reform process. In highly prescriptive letters to the reformatory superintendents, they offered advice about how their daughters should be reformed or requested an early parole for young women who had "learned their lesson" well enough to return home. Their girls' prior conduct had caused them grief and convinced them that there was little to be found in urban youth cultures besides danger and immorality. But now, these families wanted the young women to return home and prove their renewed dedication to kin.

The reformatories were able to dismiss most interventionist letters and campaigns with ease; power was on the state's side. But though family campaigns failed to undermine the institutions' substantial authority, they are nonetheless significant for what they reveal about families' attitudes toward their offspring. The families wanted their daughters (or wives) to return home, and most made it clear that they did not consider it acceptable or reasonable to disown a young woman simply because she had been disobedient or sexually delinquent. All of these families were willing to forgive and admit affection for the girls; however, they rarely suggested the need to interrogate their own past conduct or expectations. Rather, families who asked to be reunited with their daughters assumed that it was up to the girls to prove that they had learned a lesson. And the assertions that families made in asking for inmates' release reveal that parents and other kin felt themselves better able to define the interests of the inmates than either the reformatory or the young women themselves. Mothers, fathers, sisters, brothers, and husbands assumed that they knew when it was time for inmates to return home and what they needed to do to reclaim their roles as daughters, sisters, or wives. They assumed that the young women's former unhappiness and disobedience were merely signs of insufficient self-control, readily overcome with proper training and discipline.

A few families admitted, directly or indirectly, that they had not provided their young women with sufficient protection or direction, perhaps believing that this was what the reformatories wanted to hear. For example, when Molly Garrison's mother wrote to Albion to ask for her daughter's early release, she confessed that because of the family's financial needs she had taken a job away from home, leaving Molly unsupervised and vulnerable to the "ruf girls" who lived in Malone, New York. Now, however, the Garrison family had moved to a rural setting where there were few immoral temptations and Mrs. Garrison was again a full-time homemaker, well prepared to oversee her girl.[55]

Yet the interventionist families did not know how to recognize or acknowledge more complicated family problems and dynamics. They found it impossible, at least within the constricted avenues of communication available to them, to admit or discuss the "misdeeds" or abuses of a father, mother, or sibling that may have shaped or provoked a young woman's rebellion. Similarly, the interventionist families did not know how to analyze the changing character of female adolescence and were unable to probe the misunderstandings and tensions between young women and their relatives as girls were pulled by cultural and economic forces into a world of wage work, mass consumption, and public recreation.

Ultimately, families' restricted participation in the reform process helps to demonstrate one of the paradoxes of state-mandated reform: family-inmate interaction was carefully scripted and carefully monitored, but it was never completely mastered. State censorship offered young women and their families no opportunity to discuss or mend their troubled relations and, by disallowing deliberate repair, the reformatories reduced their own control, for the old emotions, expectations, and dynamics continued to operate and find expression. Moreover, in dismissing the interventionist campaigns of working-class, immigrant, and African American families, the reformatories frustrated, but could not deny, familial expectations and claims. Once released from the reformatories, young women confronted these expectations head on, and while some parolees would find it possible (and agreeable) to concede the merit of their families' demands, others would refuse to accept the authority of kin who had changed little and undergone few "reforms" in their absence. The path to "final discharge" often traveled through dangerous terrain as parolees struggled to reestablish relationships with kin.

CHAPTER FIVE

"I've Chosen a New Road to Travell":
The Challenges of Parole

In the spring of 1926 Anna Tercillo, a paroled inmate, wrote to Bedford Hills to ask when she might expect the "free papers" that would deliver her from state supervision. After years of challenging the reformatory's authority because she did not like the jobs and housing it found for her, two lengthy "disappearances," a humiliating return to Bedford as a parole violator, and rejection by once-hopeful but now-exasperated parents, Anna felt sure she had turned a corner. Her conduct in recent months had been above reproach and she was finally able to declare, "I can assure you I'll never go wrong again. Because it does not pay. Bedford has taught me my lesson and I think twice up there is enough for any girl. When you go straight you dont have to be afraid of anyone following you around or be afraid to go anyplace." Anna looked forward to receiving her "free papers" not "to do wrong . . . [but] to get in good with my people again."[1]

Parole was the most decisive phase of the reformatory sentence in the early twentieth century, presenting female delinquents the task of re-establishing a sense of self in the world. Prior to and during their incarceration these young women had been viewed by parents, police, social reformers, judges, and reformatory personnel as agents of disorder whose rebellion and moral indifference endangered the stability of family and society. However much their experience also reflected the consequences of social disadvantage, individual misfortune, or cultural turmoil, in public discourse each young woman was a "girl problem" in need of containment.

Now, released from the physical confinement of the reformatories, these same young women had to try to decipher and resolve their relationship to dominant cultural representations of female sexuality and disorder. They needed to think about how they wanted to be seen or treated by families and communities, had to determine how to construct the social identities of the individuals they wanted to become.[2]

The newly released inmates were not free agents: they remained under state surveillance for months or years while Bedford Hills and Albion tested their ability to conform to the lessons in morality and industry that had been taught them in reformatory cottages and classrooms. More specifically, the reformatories used the political authority vested in them by the state to oblige parolees to choose between a stark set of opposing cultural narratives: "successful" parolees modeled deference, hard work, and moral virtue in their interaction with family members, parole officers, and employers; in contrast, "parole violators" returned to the self-indulgence, the cheap amusements, and the sexual irresponsibility that claimed the bodies and souls of so many other other working-class, immigrant, and African American women. The reformatories' "successful" parolees salvaged their reputations and achieved social "respectability"; by comparison, their dissolute counterparts earned harsh scorn while risking arrest and reinstitutionalization. Finally, parolees in "good standing" forswore claims to personal autonomy and moral authority, understanding (unlike their wayward sisters) that their prior "delinquencies" and humble social origins were proof of moral frailty. They accepted their status as dependents, looked to their superiors for direction and approval, and accommodated authoritative social ideologies and traditions. "Successful" parolees thus became "obedient" daughters, "tractable" workers, "docile" blacks, and "educable" immigrants, demonstrating "virtue" through humility, loyalty, and self-sacrifice.

Presented with such sharply drawn images of failure and success, it is not surprising that Anna and many other young women found parole a daunting experience. For instead of obvious choices, clear paths marked "compliance" and "transgression," the parolees encountered circumstances and personalities that confounded moral certainty and made the reformatories' renderings of life on the outside appear warped and contrived. The reformatories' model of success assumed, for example, that parolees would be answerable to superiors who deserved their loyalty and respect. But as even the reformatories came to know, many young women returned to homes in which the old conditions prevailed: relations with parents and husbands were marred by hostility, misunderstanding, even threats of violence.[3] Likewise, young women on parole sometimes encountered employers who seemed to take unfair advantage and were impossible to please. What were parolees to do in circumstances like these? Was it wrong for them to challenge their superiors, to withhold allegiance from those who seemed not to deserve it?

Most significant, the parolees returned to a culture in flux. Americans were a people embattled over a long-standing social hierarchy that deemed all women unequal to men and some women unequal to "true womanhood" because of their class, ethnicity, or public demeanor. The nation was divided over women's morality and sexuality, torn over conceptions of feminine virtue and vice. The parolees would encounter individuals who believed in women's obligation to remain "pure" and who refused to forget the parolees' past indiscretions or recognize their present rectitude. But they would also meet men and women who measured young women's "popularity" and social worth on the basis of unchaperoned participation in sexualized and commodified youth subcultures. To some parolees it would seem hard, even unfair, to be asked to contend with such contradictory values. Why should they abjure social autonomy, masculine attention, commercial recreation, and fashionable clothes if, despite their efforts, they were still likely to face hostility and suspicion? And how could it be so wrong and dangerous to want what other young women considered appropriate and necessary to social success?

Expected to uphold the reformatories' exacting definitions of feminine decency, yet unable to ignore social and cultural conditions that eclipsed singular definitions of virtue, New York's female parolees were at times confused and angry. Eighty-nine of the one hundred young women in my sample went out on parole (the rest having left the reformatories under circumstances that precluded or did not require continued surveillance), and at least thirty-eight of the paroled group were at some point designated "parole violators."[4] These young women changed jobs without prior approval, took lovers, married without the reformatory's permission, failed to report to parole officers, disregarded curfews, disobeyed parents, ran away from home, wore cosmetics and seductive clothes, and (re)turned to prostitution. Many other young women who were never named parole violators also challenged reformatory policy or became involved in disputes with kin, employers, or parole agents over their work and family obligations, attitudes, and interests.

Despite the parolees' numerous infractions and "mistakes," the reformatories managed, in the long run, to do as they had hoped, that is, to "fit the girls to meet the future and to make them useful citizens."[5] Seventy-three of the eighty-nine parolees eventually constructed "respectable" lives, situating themselves within households and workplaces as dutiful daughters, honest employees, and loyal servants. And a few of this group married, or planned to marry, while on parole. (In contrast, only a small minority of women who had married prior to incarceration returned to their husbands, having realized that their spouses were disagreeable, undependable, or abusive, and part of the past they wanted to leave behind.)[6] No doubt, the parolees were growing up and perhaps losing interest in adolescent rebellion. More to the point, they came to realize that urban and youth subcultures lacked cultural authority and provided neither the economic opportunity nor the social security that assured real autonomy; indeed, outright rebellion was likely to lead to a new police arrest, a second or third stay in a reformatory, familial rejection, and harsher community ostracism than they had yet endured.[7] Responding to state surveillance and the pressures of family and community, most of the parolees thus accepted the idea that "freedom" was best won by conformity and accommodation. Like Anna Tercillo, they acknowledged the close link between social acceptance and self-respect and learned to define their needs and identities in the context of normative familial, class, ethnic, and race relations.[8]

Still, the reformatories' triumph was incomplete. Although the parolees were hedged in by overt political controls and, in Judith Walkowitz's words, "bound imaginatively by a limited cultural repetoire," they nonetheless managed to "reshape cultural meanings within certain parameters."[9] As we shall see, many "successful" parolees refused to accept without comment or question the reformatories' definition of virtue. While embracing a life of respectability, these young women demanded to play a role in delineating its terms. They wanted to be the judge of their own moral reformation, to rid themselves of skeptical overseers. Neither unassertive nor fainthearted, the "successful" parolees expected parents, employers, and reformatory superintendents to treat them with consideration and respect. Reconciled to overwhelming demands for conformity, they yet demanded some right to autonomy and self-definition.

Just as important, Bedford Hills and Albion had insufficient power or inclination to ease the material, social, or cultural disadvantages that rendered respectability a fragile and easily upset accomplishment; some of the young women who desired to "keep straight" were ultimately unable to sustain the effort. And a substantial minority of young women simply rejected state definitions of respectability, preferring to live at the margins of society as sexual and social outlaws regardless of the attendant hazards.

In many respects the circumstances of parole changed considerably between 1900 and 1930. Until the 1910s the parole systems at Bedford Hills and Albion were quite rudimentary, with each institution relying on a single overworked parole agent to investigate employment and residential prospects for women leaving the reformatory. Unable to keep up with the heavy case loads, the parole agents passed much of their work on to the reformatory superintendents, who, in turn, wrote letters to the inmates' families to ask for suggestions and recommendations. Albion's Superintendent Curtin thus corresponded with Sarah Oliver, the unmarried aunt of inmate Elizabeth Oliver, hoping to learn something about the suitability of Elizabeth's father's home in Tonawanda, New York, as a parole residence.

> I think that if everything is satisfactory in Elizabeth's home that I can get a parole for her early in May. Mrs. Meldrum [the parole agent] went to Tonawanda with the intention of seeing Elizabeth's father but the house was closed and she did not have your address. Do you think Elizabeth will be able to keep house for her father? and will you and her other relatives vouch for her conduct and keep us informed of same. . . . If you think she can be well protected please let me hear from you.[10]

As Curtin's letter reveals, Albion was also unable to provide regular supervision to young women after they left the reformatory. Parolees from Albion were expected to write to the institution every month, but beyond that, the reformatory generally depended on unsolicited and infrequent communications from employers, relatives, or neighbors for news of the parolees' progress or, as sometimes happened, of their return to a degenerate life. Curtin was no doubt happy to learn, for example, that the sister of parolee Charlotte Cooke was "well pleased with her." But the superintendent must have been disheartened to hear of Elizabeth Oliver's disastrous parole to her father. Five months after Elizabeth's parole began, Sarah Oliver wrote that "in the past two months she has been anything but good. . . . she has had one of the girls named Frieda with her for about four weeks. . . . they would go out nights, get drunk, and act very bad." Now, Sarah reported, Elizabeth had run away, and the whole family was "entirely disgusted and will be only to glad to send her back with you."[11]

In these early years, Bedford's supervision of parolees was probably little better than Albion's, though its parole agent was supposed to visit parolees on a "frequent" basis.[12] The reformatories were not content with the status quo, however, and during the 1910s and 1920s they attempted to standardize and improve their parole systems. By this time the institutions' superintendents were well aware that paroled women often made a renewed acquaintance with immorality; indeed, Bedford's annual reports revealed a system in dire need of repair. For example, fifty-five of the 199 women placed on parole between October 1, 1914, and September 30, 1915, were returned to the institution for violation of parole; another forty-four violated parole but were never found.[13]

Hoping to reduce parole violations, both institutions began to investigate and evaluate the homes and neighborhoods of family members and potential employers with great care. This trend coincided with the emergence of modern social work, which offered the reformatories a model for systematic home visits. Parole agents or the representatives of social agencies affiliated with the reformatories visited prospective employers, called at the homes of family members, and interviewed neighbors and ministers before deciding where to place individual young women. Thus, when it came time to parole Althea Davies, the West Indian teenager brought up in Harlem by her married sister, the Church Mission of Help sent a social worker to the sister's home. Amy Prevost found Mrs. Crowe to be "an exceptionally pleasing intelligent young woman" but would not consider paroling Althea to her because she worked during the day and was in no position to prevent Althea, now a young mother, from resuming her old habit of entertaining men at home while the adults were away. Another sister, married and a full-time homemaker, was thought to offer a more suitable residence.[14]

Members of the reformatory staff also talked with prospective parolees to ascertain the girls' preferences and to evaluate the "mental and educational equipment" and "personal characteristics" that might make one placement option better than another.[15] If, like Althea, a young woman had a baby with her in the reformatory, the staff also talked with her about childcare arrangements and the option of adoption. Careful attention to the "individual needs" of parolees was especially important to Bedford Hills in the 1920s after it dramatically shortened the typical stay of inmates at the reformatory and lengthened the time spent on parole.[16]

In the name of "individualized" parole assignments, the reformatories also took advantage of structural changes in the economy which were expanding employment options for working-class women. Although Albion consistently paroled the great majority of its inmates to domestic positions in middle-class households or in their old homes to help their families with housework and childcare, by the 1920s the reformatory was paroling a few young women each year to positions in stores, offices, or factories. Bedford

Hills made an even greater effort to give its parolees nondomestic employment alternatives, recognizing the diminishing appeal of domestic service to young women living in a modern industrial society. Bedford's annual report for 1925 shows forty-five of the ninety-nine parolees working in other than domestic employment; their ranks included file clerks, factory workers, a piano instructor, dressmakers, dental workers, and store clerks. Eight other parolees were "at home," presumably caring for their families. Five women were employed as domestic workers on a "day's work" (live-out) basis. "General housework" (live-in domestic service) was still the most common occupation, listed for forty-one women, but it was no longer as important as it had been in years past.[17]

Yet for all they tried to improve parolees' residential and employment options, the reformatories did not seek to modify or "modernize" the rules of parole. Indeed, the rules governing parolees from Bedford Hills and Albion remained constant throughout the early twentieth century, preserving and idealizing Victorian moral values and social relationships. Inmates paroled to domestic positions were expected to be obedient servants, eager to learn from and please their white middle-class mistresses. They were not to take any recreation or go out at night without the explicit approval of their employers, and they were not to make friends or visit family members without the consent of the superintendent, parole agent, or mistress of the household. Women who took factory, clerical, or other employment were also expected to be good, dependable workers. And since most of the nondomestic wage earners lived at home, they were obliged to be dutiful daughters or sisters who conformed to the dictates of their older relatives or guardians in matters of social deportment, courtship, and recreation.[18] Parolees with babies or small children were further expected to be attentive and responsible mothers. Finally, parolees were required to be frugal consumers, opening savings accounts or returning a portion of their wages to the institutions for safekeeping. Young women who wanted to buy new clothes or make other "irregular" purchases were suppposed to justify their need for these goods; those without sufficient cash on hand had to ask the reformatory superintendents to grant them access to wages "held in trust" for them.[19]

In short, parolees were required to prove to their social superiors (employers, parole agents, parents, superintendents) that they were "better" and "less selfish" girls than they had once been, able to recognize and fulfill the moral and social obligations of virtuous womanhood. They were to demons-

trate that "morally indifferent" young women from working-class, immigrant, and African American homes could be transformed into willing ad-
herents of middle-class morality.

Of course, neither institution could be sure that parolees conformed to
the prescribed standards. Without close supervision from parole officers, the
reformatories were hard pressed to provide adequate oversight. Albion asked
all domestic employers to read and sign parolees' monthly letters to the
reformatory and to open all mail sent and received by them. The reformatory also encouraged domestic employers to write to the Superintendent
with concerns or criticisms. But the reformatory's lone parole agent was
unable to pay regular visits to parolees and give them advice, encouragement, or a necessary reprimand. It sometimes asked local social agencies to
provide parolees with "friendly oversight," yet the care provided in these
cases was sporadic at best.[20]

Bedford Hills was better off than Albion, but it still lacked the ability to
supervise its parolees as closely as it wished. Throughout the late 1910s and
1920s the reformatory struggled along with only one full-time "field officer"
to supervise the dozens of women who were usually out on parole at any
time. She was assisted on an irregular and part-time basis by the reformatory
marshall, whose primary duty was to convey young women from the courts
to Bedford Hills and from the institution to parole residences. Bedford Hills
considered itself fortunate to receive additional assistance in both home
investigations and parole supervision from social workers/parole agents employed by Catholic Charities, the Jewish Board of Guardians, the (Episcopal) Church Mission of Help, and the City Mission Society.[21] But even with
this outside aid, the case files of Bedford inmates suggest that most parolees
saw a parole supervisor very infrequently.[22] Superintendent Amos Baker
admitted that without adequate staff "it is very difficult, well nigh impossible, to follow each girl a sufficient length of time to determine with absolute
certainty what the institution has accomplished."[23]

Still, it was not easy for parolees to escape oversight or sanction. Dutiful
parolees were never above suspicion and insubordinate parolees were seldom
beyond punishment. Complaints from parents or employers often came later
than the superintendents would have liked, but they nonetheless provided a
critical link between parolees and the reformatories. The New York City
Police Department also took a hand in locating Bedford parolees who
"disappeared" from their homes or places of employment. It was not impossible to avoid punishment for violating parole; certainly some women man-

aged to do so. But the majority of those who abridged the rules of parole were at some point punished for their misconduct.

In truth, rebellion and misconduct were not on the minds of most new parolees. More than half of the parolees in my sample made resolute efforts to achieve respectability. From the start of their parole, these forty-eight young women endeavored to fulfill obligations to kin, to perform well as employees, and to adhere to the rules of the reformatories. Like so many other young women of their generation, they had challenged the identities prescribed for them by their families and communities and had tried to develop a new set of social and moral values. But having experienced unhappiness at home, vulnerability on the streets, and humiliation in the reformatories, they began parole having made up their minds to endorse orthodox representations of the "girl problem," to view their previous pursuits as misguided and dangerous. Conforming to conventional definitions of female respectability (as mediated by class, race, and family) became preferable to a flawed and perilous autonomy.

Some of these earnest and accommodating parolees were fortunate enough to return to homes in which relatives decided not to hold their delinquencies against them. They faced neither ostracism nor frequent reminders of previous misconduct and were allowed to move beyond their troubled histories quickly and gracefully. Thus Eva Pomering, the wayward minor who had shocked her family by running away and taking an Italian lover, was accepted without question when she returned home. Eva's sister had tried unsuccessfully to engineer her early release from Albion, and the Pomerings quickly made evident their enduring affection for the parolee. Writing to Albion's parole agent, Eva reported that "Mother and father are very good to me. . . . I am getting along very nicely. and I thank you for letting me go home." Eva's parole went very smoothly, though she had been one of Albion's most difficult inmates.[24] Cynthia Romer's parents were also "extremely anxious" to have their formerly wayward daughter at home, though they had not tried to secure her early release. Cynthia quickly settled into a comfortable and thoroughly conventional routine: she worked during the day as a switchboard operator, spent evenings with her parents and siblings, and attended Catholic services every Sunday.[25]

The conforming parolees' successful reintegration into their families required effort by all concerned: parents or guardians had to forgive and forget; the parolees had to be contrite and willing to conform to their families' expectations.[26] Parolees were also more likely to adjust to home life if their relatives overcame or resolved difficulties that the young women had previously found distressing. Sarah and Mary Walton, sisters who had been admitted to Albion together for prostitution, returned to parents who had finally reconciled their differences, mending a home that was previously torn by bitter quarrels and marital separation. Both girls completed their paroles without difficulty. And Myra Henning returned to a home that was no longer oppressed by her father's presence, a violent alcoholic and poor provider who apparently separated from her mother while Myra was away. Spared the anxiety that her father had provoked, Myra established stable relationships with her mother and siblings and trained to become a telegraph operator, writing to Bedford's Amos Baker that she was "on the road to success. I don't think Dr. Baker, that there is any need to worry about my ever becoming mixed up in any trouble any more as I have a real interest now & have learned my lesson quite thoroughly."[27]

In at least one case, a parolee engineered favorable changes in her family after she returned home. Mildred Pomrenke was deeply ashamed of her incarceration and wanted to be reunited with her family despite her father's abuse and her mother's admission that "the home life is far from pleasant." Determined to overcome the disgrace of being a reformatory girl, "Mildred . . . made an excellent record . . . [and] helped improve the home. She was very fond of her father and was the only one who could control him." Proud of what she had accomplished, Mildred told Bedford's superintendent Leo Palmer that her parole worker "was more than pleased the condition she found my home, She said there sure was some change since I came home."[28]

Having previously found much to deplore in their families, remorseful young women who returned to relatively stable and forgiving homes sometimes felt indebted not only to the kin who welcomed them but to the institutions that had "reformed" them. As the comment by Myra Henning suggests, they came to view their reformatory experiences as a valuable lesson that taught them to appreciate the merits of hard work and filial obedience. Thus Eleanor Hamlisch, a parolee who gladly took charge of caring for her ailing mother, made clear her gratitude to Bedford Hills when she told Superintendent Helen Cobb, "My opinion is, Every girl has a fair chance while in Bedford and if she dont take it she has her self to blame."[29] And Nora Patterson realized after returning home to her parents' "warm welcome" that Bedford Hills "taught me a great lesson, obedience for one which I think is the greatest of all, I helped Mother clean house and we are almost finished now and then I expect to go to work not that I have to but

Mrs. Talbot I owe my mother a great deal and mean to help her in every way I can. . . . I cannot thank you enough and the only way to do so is to be good and do what is right."[30]

Of course, penitent parolees were not always willing or able to return to their own families. Many young women went to white middle-class homes as domestic servants because they did not want to return to parents who had mistreated them or because the reformatories decided that their relatives lacked the resources, patience, or moral integrity to supervise them according to state-prescribed norms. Others went to the homes of strangers or relatives outside of their immediate family knowing that their closest kin wanted nothing more to do with them. For example, Sallie Wilcox was paroled as a domestic servant after her foster mother wrote to Albion's superintendent Alice Curtin to say that "it *would not be agreable*" for "her & her [illegitimate] child to come here. . . . I have a young Grand daughter with me & don't want her under Sallie's influence. . . . I wish her no harm but she has *no* friends around here, & her own Sister is disgusted with her."[31] And Paula Lester was left without a family to return to after her mother made it clear that she was "not in a position to shelter or do anything" for her daughter. Paula's husband, at first eager for his wife's release from Bedford, also put aside dreams of reconciliation when he heard that his wife escaped from the reformatory and, before being recaptured, took another man for a lover. By the time her parole was due, Mr. Lester had "come to a definite understanding that Paula is a menace to the social life of his children and himself and he will under no circumstances take up home with her again." Paula was placed temporarily in the Deaconness Young Shelter until an aunt "promised her cooperation."[32]

Whatever the reason for their placement in a position away from home, young women who became live-in domestics were denied the emotional satisfaction of seeing the old family conflicts replaced by harmony and mutual respect. Nonetheless, many found a sense of accomplishment and security while providing competent and loyal service to white middle-class households. Sallie Wilcox proudly told Albion's Alice Curtin that she had been entirely responsible for the upkeep of her employer's house while her mistress was out of town and claimed that she "got along nicely with the work."[33] And Ester Bromwell, an African American, became a reliable and self-respecting servant, though she had previously disliked and avoided this obviously racialized field of work. In a letter to Bedford's superintendent Helen Cobb, Ester announced, "I feel as tho I ame the proudest girl you ever paroled. Because I enjoy being with Mrs. Tuxhill and family and I certainly enjoy doing my best. . . . I've tried hard to satisfy my people in every way and I've succeeded. . . . since I've been in your charge in your Institution I've become a better woman in every way. In other words I've chosen a new road to travell. . . . I've named it The Straight Road. which is the best after all."[34] Ester may well have overstated her enthusiasm, conjuring the loyal black "mammy" to win Cobb's praise; still, her excellent record on parole bespoke a new appreciation for outward conformity.

A few parolees apparently managed to obtain both security and surrogate kinship through domestic service, a development the reformatories heartily applauded. The reformatories had long assumed that inmates were most likely to "improve" in the "intimate home life of [the] cottage group" where "a matron of the right type can do much to help each girl meet her reponsibilities in the family circle"; it followed that a young woman paroled to domestic service would do best when treated "as a member of the family" and accorded "sympathetic and understanding supervision" by her mistress.[35] Albion's staff was thus pleased to learn that Patsy Belham "was like a daughter in the Porter household," and Bedford's superintendent must have been gratified to hear Nellie Roberts say that her domestic employer was "very nice to me" and "it seems like home."[36]

Signs of "familial" attachment between servant and employer were especially evident in the letters of Susanna Nedersen, who wrote to Bedford's superintendent Helen Cobb and parole officer Bella Murphy, "[The] people I work for are just like parents to me and the children are as nice as they can be. . . . I will never forget what you have done for me and want to now thank you. I could not find anyone so good to me as Mr. and Mrs. Jackson. . . . Mrs. Jackson is my . . . guiding angle [sic] for she tells me all the things that I want to know & she is teaching me how to read the newspaper & to talk better than I did."[37] Susanna's filial loyalty to the Jacksons was determined largely by the severity of her former abuse: she had been sexually assaulted by her father and was convicted of perjury after bringing charges against him and then, under intense familial pressure, dropping them. Susanna had done very well at Bedford Hills, where staff members believed her story and offered their sympathy, and her position with the Jacksons offered a secure dependency and surrogates for the parents who had violated her trust.[38] Furthermore, Susanna could imagine no positive alternative to life with the Jacksons because her prior attempts to gain autonomy had proved disastrous: she had spent one terrifying week in New York City as a runaway—it was "too big a place and you get killed"—and was later raped, and became pregnant, by a man who hired her to clean his house and promised to give her large sums of money. The baby born of this pregnancy had been immediately taken from Susanna (who thought it was stillborn) by her mother; Mrs. Nedersen was later fined for concealing the death of the infant though the family's neighbors and an Albany probation officer claimed that the infant was alive at birth and that Susanna's mother strangled it.[39] Being a "good" servant/daughter to the Jacksons seemed to promise Susanna liberation from her past, and she saw no need to fret over her subordinate status in the household. Indeed, shortly before her final release from Bedford Hills, Susanna asked Superintendent Helen Cobb to do all she could to help her stay *with* the Jacksons and *away* from her own family.

> I heard that father was up to see you about my coming home. I don't want to go home for this reason if I go home I would not get the chance that I am getting down here with Mrs. Jackson and another thing is that when I was home I was always in trouble and I don't think I ought to go home for the people to point their finger at me and say there is *Susanna* who has been doing time in Bedford Hills and she is out and home with her father again. And just look at the *black Mark* that is on my name for me to cover again if I go home. I don't want to go home. I would very much like to see my mother again. I will some day soon but I don't know what day it will be. When I was home my father ill treated me and as for my poor mother she knowes and that [it] is his fault that I got in trouble. Hoping you will help me. I am very truly Susanna Nedersen.[40]

Yet for all their willingness to be obedient and good, as Susanna's poignant remarks demonstrate, the reformatories' "best" parolees were not necessarily able to step wholly away from their past troubles. A number of good parolees experienced or confronted the liklihood of conflict with members of their families, sometimes the very same relatives who had intervened for early parole claiming that they knew what was best for their daughters. These young women were required to acknowledge that their kin failed to live up to middle-class norms, were forced to revisit family dynamics that marked them as "deviant" females. Susanna, for example, could not escape the fear that a return home would lead to a repeat of the "mistreatment" she had previously suffered at her father's hands. Alice Arlington, whose parents hired an attorney to try to win her early release, realized shortly after her parole began that two years in Albion had not changed her relationship with her parents; she could not "get along at home" and went to Toronto to get work, risking chastisement or worse for moving without permission. Polly Overton, one of Albion's "feebleminded" girls, went home for a visit and was held "against her will" by a mother who was outraged that she had been sent to a domestic position; the young woman had to be "rescued" by reformatory authorities. And Emily Carrington's mother insisted that her daughter be paroled home but subsequently showed "no common sense in trying to gain the girl's affection"; Emily made a "great effort" to please her mother, but after three unhappy months she transferred to a domestic position, with Albion's assent.[41]

Moreover, because the parolees were objects of surveillance, dependent on others for direction and approbation, they could not rest secure in their new-found rectitude. However laudable their conduct, the parolees were vulnerable to hostility or distrust from members of their communities. They had been tainted by their incarceration and represented the forbidden "other," those women—adolescent, working-class, immigrant, African American, feebleminded—who were susceptible to moral corruption. Susanna Nedersen wanted to demonstrate loyalty to her "poor mother," but she could not do so without facing hostility from neighbors who were unlikely to have forgotten her "delinquencies." Doreen Cropper, another "good" parolee, discovered that everyone in Tarrytown, New York, knew her story and that local business owners were unwilling to give her a job. Doreen's mother became consumed by worry that she would "never get over the chagrin and humiliation of Doreen having a Bedford record" and, seeing no other option, moved with her daughter to another city to escape the neighbors' animosity.[42]

Hurt by the narrow-mindedness that made it hard for them to recover their names and self-esteem, even some of the "best" parolees nonetheless missed the excitement of city streets and the young friends they had known earlier. Ella Waldstein's parole letters to Superintendent Cobb had a wistful tone, suggesting that the former "incorrigible girl" was happy to be at home with her family but regretted that life was not as interesting as it had been when she spent every spare moment at Coney Island. In one letter she remarked, "I would write you more often but there is really nothing to write it is the same thing over and over again. I'm always home and go out very little so you can see Bedford has changed me quite a bit." Similarly, Evelyn Blackwell willingly returned to the semirural home of her widowed father to keep house and care for her two small children, but she could not overcome her feelings of boredom and isolation. Evelyn wanted to take a job in town to earn a little extra money and relieve the tedium and loneliness of housekeeping, but Bedford Hills "thought it was best" for her to stay home.[43] And Lena Meyerhoff expressed some disillusionment with respectability when she wrote to Superintendent Baker, "I stay home all the time I have know friends at all. Kindly let me know if I could have permission to stay out Saturday night till one o'clock. As the girls are all going to the Island."44

Lena Meyerhoff, Susanna Nederson, Doreen Cropper, Ella Waldstein, Evelyn Blackwell, and others managed to satisfy the terms of their parole despite its frustrations and to derive some satisfaction from conventionality. It would be inaccurate, however, to suggest that the "good" parolees played an essentially passive role in their relations with the reformatories. Precisely because they were so eager to be free of opprobrium, these young women demanded an active role in judging their own conduct and moral fortitude.

Occasionally, for example, "good" parolees defended actions that might be misinterpreted as a violation of parole. Thus Blanche Preston, an African American parolee and excellent domestic servant, insisted on the right to judge the propriety of her recent marriage, though she wed without Bedford's permission and could have been cited for violating the reformatory's rules: "I hope Dr. Baker that you will not scould me. . . . I did not have to get married But I loved the boy Because he loved me. . . . he is a nice young man he goes to Sunday School. . . . He has now bad habits he does not smoke or drink."45 Similarly, Lena Meyerhoff sought to avoid punishment for having some slight contact with a runaway parolee by explaining her "mistake" to Dr. Baker: "I never knew that you are not sipposed to have anything to do with and inmate until [my parole agent] told me. Cause if I know I knever would have had any bussines with . . . Maria. it was a shock to me which I have not got over. . . . It is a year the thirteen of this month since I am out and I sure do not care to go back."46

More often, "good" parolees insisted on the right to be free of the state's surveillance and interference after "proving" that they had fulfilled the terms of their parole. Writing to Bedford's superintendent to say that she had done everything she could to demonstrate the authenticity of her reform, Susanna Nedersen said she should be rewarded with an early final discharge so that she might follow her employers out of the state to their summer home in Connecticut. "Miss Murphy [the parole agent] . . . said I was a good girl and . . . I ought to be with Mrs. Jackson and I hope you will see that I get there." Merced Borja also wrote to Bedford Hills, telling Superintendent Leo Palmer that it was high time that the board of managers consider her for final discharge. "Now Dr. Palmer I've been keeping my Parole for almost a year and had never failed in my reports, so I will ask you to be kind enough and let me know if this is correct and that I will get my free papers as my behavior while in your institution was good and same while I been on Parole." And Gertrude Leavitt, a former inmate in Bedford's division for mentally defective delinquents whose parole was highly successful, wrote a series of impatient letters to Bedford Hills insisting that she be considered for final discharge. The second of these declared, "Well Dr. Baker did you take up my case I hope you will give me my New Years present my free Papers. I am waiting for them long enough and I think I deserve to hear good news from you."[47]

While most young parolees steadfastly followed the "straight road," others traversed a twisted path as they struggled to gain freedom from state surveillance. Young women who had been rebellious as reformatory inmates were often disinclined to be "good girls" on parole. Although they wanted to be rid of state controls they found it very difficult to make the compromises that family members, employers, and parole agents demanded. These young parolees did not want to put aside their own desires for the sake of a good record, did not want to forfeit autonomy and personal pleasure for obedience to authorities who might never be satisfied with their efforts.

For their part, reformatory superintendents, parole agents, and social workers *were* inclined to expect the worst of parolees who had been difficult inmates, often handling them with some severity. When Bedford Hills solicited advice from the Jewish Board of Guardians about Sophie Polentz, a most troublesome inmate who had just been paroled, Alice Menken replied, "Sophie should be carefully supervised; and . . . there should in no way be any temporizing on our part, and . . . refusal to go to work and contribute toward the support of the family should be sufficient ground to return the girl to the institution for violation of parole, since the financial condition of the home had been one of the factors influencing the Board to release her at this time."[48]

So, too, the families of some of the most disorderly parolees tended to be distrustful and judgmental. Sophie and some of her peers returned to kin who had sought their early release, but such intervention did not guarantee smooth relations on parole. Other young women faced outright ostracism or else encountered family members who were clearly reluctant to take them back, doubting that their conduct or attitudes had been improved. Unwilling to let her niece back into her home, Nanette Wilkins's cousin (and guardian) wrote to Bedford's superintendent Baker shortly before the young woman's parole to say that she would not cut the young woman off entirely but could not help her either. "She must be responsible for herself as far as support is concern. I am only willing to give her advice, that is if she obeys."[49] Anabel Rider's foster mother agreed to take the Albion parolee back into her home only after "many weeks" of careful thought and with assurances that the reformatory would help keep "close account of her." Simiarly, Anna Levinson went home to a father who had long felt that "the girl will never make good." And Cecilia Tomasi's father was apparently of the opinion that his daughter needed the "strictest discipline . . . as it was the only way that any success would be obtained as they have tried every other way to appeal to her without good results."[50]

Undoubtedly aware of the suspicion surrounding them and loath to seek approval from people who had been a source of unhappiness in the past, not surprisingly some young women disobeyed and disappointed their elders from the start of their parole. Anna Tercillo ran away less than a week after she was paroled to her parents; Cecilia Tomasi might as well have done so for all the distress and disruption she caused her mother and father. Reluctant to report Cecilia's misconduct (apparently because they feared that their immigrant daughter would be deported to Italy, and thus disgrace the entire family), her parents later admitted that Cecilia began misbehaving the second day after she was paroled "by staying out until 5 o'clock in the morning, going to dance halls frequented by an undesireable class of people, refusing to help about the house, defying her parents—at one time striking her mother, once getting out of an upstairs window to go to a dance, and another time smashing the front window when they didn't come in time to let her in the door."[51]

More frequently, however, young women who later had a difficult time on parole started out by making at least a half-hearted attempt to succeed at work and at home. Sent to a domestic position, Rae Rabinowitz won early praise from her employer and wrote a hopeful letter to Bedford Hills saying, "I am trying real hard now to do my best, and I know I shall succeed if I keep up." Ilene Sterling also made a good start as a domestic servant, writing to Bedford Hills, "I like my place very much, the people are very kind to me and I could not hope for any better." Janine Rosen was paroled to her father's home and quickly found a promising position with a local charity: the work was "very interesting," the environment was "pleasant," and the hours were "agreeable." Anabel Rider claimed that she liked being at her foster mother's "a lot better now than I did before . . . and I intend to be a much better girl too." Even Sophie Polentz showed promise at first. She found a job stringing pearls within a week of returning to her parents and seemed to get along with her father, though the two had clashed bitterly in the past. "I am glad to say that since I cam home my father feels much better. He also thanks you very much for paroling me home." Three months later, Sophie was still trying hard to succeed and "lost no time" finding a position with a biscuit manufacturer after she was laid off from her first job.[52]

Still, a good initial effort did not ensure success. Young women who had not yet internalized the moral values and conformist ethic of the reformatories, or who encountered faultfinding adults, often managed only a temporary accommodation with their families and employers. Persistent demands for self-sacrifice and obedience began to irritate the parolees, to seem "unfair" or "unreasonable." Thus, when Mr. Rosen began to complain that his paroled daughter had become "secretive" and "very snappy in her answers to inquiries as to her extravagances & how & where she spends her time," Janine did not hesitate to protest that her "parent's attitude makes life well nigh impossible at times."[53]

Similarly, Althea Davies complained to Superintendent Amos Baker that no matter how hard she tried to obey her kin and care responsibly for her baby girl, her sisters offered nothing but criticism. "Dr. Baker I tried very heard but I carn't make it, I have no one to help me, my family don't want me because I have brough a disgrace on them, I am an outcast." Marian Jacoby, also a Bedford parolee, complained after a single month as a pantry maid at the Bloomingdale Hospital in White Plains that she could not "stand this position any longer. I am like a regular slave. . . . I have the hardest floor in the building. . . . I don't want to break my parole but I certainly can't stand this job." Rae Rabinowitz did not have sufficient nerve to complain directly to Bedford Hills but confided to an older sister that she had been happier at the reformatory where "i was with the girls and wasn't lonesome. Here . . . I am their servant and am left to eat alone in the kitchen and I must always be alone and no one to say a word to while they all talk and play the piano and victrola and etc."[54]

With urban streets, commercial amusements, and youthful peers often close at hand, young women could fairly easily find forbidden outlets for their frustrations. The parolees' case files provide many examples of their attempts to explore avenues for self-expression, companionship, and sexual affection. Ilene Sterling did not want to antagonize or disappoint her domestic employers, but she was unwilling to give up a private life of her own and so began a surreptitious romance with a young trolley-car conductor who lived nearby. Marian Jacoby coped with her unpleasant job by becoming involved in "improper conduct" with her male coworkers, and Anabel Rider, tiring of a narrow domestic life, became involved in clandestine flirtations with neighborhood men. When she was finally confronted and chastised for her misconduct, Anabel told her foster mother that the older woman had no right "to tell her what to do." Ginger Trapp, another Albion parolee, developed the "habit" of frequenting one of Rochester's movie theaters and "[became] acquainted (through flirtation) with one of the ushers . . . a boy younger than herself." Even less discreet, Rae Rabinowitz "got herself talked about in town for going out with some undesireable men," and five months after her parole began she disappeared while shopping with her employer: "The earth swallowed her up." Janine Rosen and Sophie Polentz also disappeared from their homes without a trace, though the latter was suspected of going away "with a young man who was interested in her."[55]

All of these young women must have known that their actions were risky, and most of the disorderly parolees were eventually sent back to the reformatories for violation of parole. Anabel Rider managed to avoid a second stay at Albion largely because her foster mother was willing to assume principal responsibility for advancing the recalcitrant young woman's "reform," but Ilene Sterling, Ginger Trapp, Janine Rosen, Marian Jacoby, Rae Rabinowitz, and many others were not so fortunate. These women found that urban amusements and illicit romances, however pleasurable, jeopardized their security and eventually cost them the autonomy they wanted so much.

Disorderly parolees who lacked the courage or inclination to run away discovered that parents and employers had only to ask Albion or Bedford Hills to remove offending girls from their presence; thus, Ilene Sterling and Ginger Trapp were unceremoniously conveyed back to the reformatories after their misconduct became known to their mistresses.[56] And young women who "disappeared" from their homes or places of employment soon learned that it was no easy task to hide their whereabouts, disguise their identities, and resist capture or arrest, especially given their urgent need for income. One runaway parolee, Rachel Adelson, took the unusual route of trying to obtain financial assistance from the Girls' Service League; but she told a league worker so many "conflicting stories" that the agency got in touch with detectives and arranged for her return to Bedford Hills.[57] More often, runaway parolees in need of money turned to prostitution or jobs in speakeasies and nightclubs; too shrewd to trust social workers, they also knew better than to look for employment in factories, stores, or other legitimate businesses where they might be recognized by "unfriendly" coworkers or customers.

Still, the illicit sex and liquor trades afforded little security. Rae Rabinowitz, a complete amateur when it came to commercialized sex, found herself under arrest for solicitation just three months after she ran away.

Shunning the streets, Janine Rosen lasted nine months before the police found her working in a night club called the Rendezvous Inn. Anna Tercillo managed to stay out of the law's reach for almost a year after she disappeared from her parents' home, but she was an experienced prostitute. And Frances Brewer resisted arrest for thirteen months, undoubtedly because she was kept by a corrupt policeman who benefited from her return to prostitution and made it his business to stay informed of efforts to find her. Finally, Melanie Burkis, a former wayward minor who became involved with a black pimp in Harlem and posed as a "colored" streetwalker, eluded the police for nearly a year and a half.[58] With luck, experience, and assistance, some women evaded recapture for a time, but few did so indefinitely.

Bedford's Amos Baker tried to tell himself (and the New York State legislature) that parole violators who came back to the reformatory "did not feel any resentment" and instead "proved themselves to be orderly and helpful to the other girls of the Institution."[59] But certainly there were young women who felt and behaved otherwise. Twenty-six young women in this study returned to Bedford Hills or Albion for parole violations or for "unsatisfactory" work, and the fragmentary evidence suggests that they were less than fully cooperative.[60] Rae Rabinowitz was placed briefly in Bedford's psychopathic cottage for "unbecoming" conduct, and Marian Jacoby, also returned for prostitution, was sent temporarily to the state hospital for the criminally insane at Mattaewan after trying to escape and otherwise refusing to obey reformatory rules. Sophie Polentz was placed in Bedford's "segregation cottage" at least three times during her second nine-month stint at Bedford, and Melanie Burkis was so disruptive in her cottage that her cottage mates—themselves mostly parole violators—petitioned the superintendent to have her removed, "being that she cannot make a record of her own, she's trying to prevent others from doing likewise." Althea Davies, who returned to Bedford Hills voluntarily, thinking that the institution would be preferable to the homes of her disparaging aunt and sister, was "noisy, unwilling . . . resentful. . . . There are times when she seems very happy, and again when things don't go her way she will scream 'Oh God. . . . Why did I come back to this joint!'" And Frances Brewer was better during her second stay than her first when she had been "insolent, profane, and vulgar," but her conduct was still imperfect and she was punished at least once for "disregard of laundry rules and being painted up like a clown."[61]

Nonetheless, many of the second-termers eventually decided that "delinquent" conduct was not getting them anywhere. There is little evidence to suggest that their behavior or attitudes changed markedly while they were still inside the reformatories, although Marian Jacoby wrote to Amos Baker while she was at Mattaewan, "If I had to do it over again I would act different . . . because I was bad in Bedford that doesn't mean that I am insane."[62] And sometimes a second parole went as badly as the first, and a parolee returned to the reformatory yet again. Over time, however, the majority of these disorderly young women "went straight," realizing that the penalties for violating parole were so severe as to make nonconformity a burdensome liability.

Althea Davies, for example, returned to Bedford a third and then a fourth time after her sister complained that she was "pert and saucy," kept late hours, and continued to neglect her baby. But after her fourth stay at the reformatory, Althea was placed in a domestic position and under the pressure of overwork began to reevaluate her relationship with her family. Ready to make some concessions yet still assertive, she wrote to Superintendent Baker and asked for permission to return to her relatives: "I want to make good and I never want to come back to Bedford, but I surely won't stay hear and work myself to death, I can't do the work it is to hard for me with my baby." With Baker's consent, Althea went home again and finally proved herself capable of withstanding the varied demands of family, employer, and child; now nearly twenty, she realized that her daughter was a lasting and important responsibility and that her sister's support was crucial: "I have no one else to help me sopport my baby."[63]

Marian Jacoby also had a terrible second parole, disappearing from her new job within weeks and marrying a man who had been institutionalized previously for theft, drug addiction, and feeblemindedness. But after eight months "at large," she voluntarily contacted her parole agent saying that "she intended to do well if given another chance." She left her husband because he was "no good," went to live with her sister, found another job, and successfully finished her parole.[64]

And Anna Levinson decided after her second stay at the reformatory that opposing her father and mother was no longer worthwhile. She chose, however grudgingly, to put aside her claims to independence, adopting a social identity that permitted her to draw support and approval from her kin and parole supervisor. During her first parole, Anna had frustrated her parents and parole worker by refusing to help with the housework or to find a job and by spending many idle hours at a Brooklyn beach. But Anna's parole worker noted that the young woman's second parole was completely different from her first. "It is gratifying to note that Anna's attitude towards her family has changed completely; whereas formerly she always spoke of them scornfully, [recently] she spoke most kindly of her father and with pride mentioned his importance in the community."[65]

Still, even as they conceded the normalizing authority of family, state, and community, the parolees did not become compliant or submissive. Rather, having reevaluated their options and interests, they struggled to defend their right to be treated with all the consideration of individuals who had never fallen under a moral cloud. These once-refractory but now-"rehabilitated" parolees rejected complete moral dependency and refused to allow others to treat them as flawed or tainted because of past transgressions.

Having decided to pursue respectability, Anna Tercillo opted to postpone, perhaps indefinitely, a marriage that had already been approved by Bedford Hills. She did not trust her fiancé to treat her with the courtesy she deserved and was determined to protect herself from unfair criticism by a marriage partner. Writing to Amos Baker she explained, "I have refused him. I told him that I will not get married until I am free of Bedford and if he is willing to wait until then I will gladly get married. You see I don't want him to think that he has to marry me and I don't want him to have anything . . . he could throw up to me after we're married."[66] Anna Levinson was less concerned about skeptical men than about unfair state surveillance; she refused to accept without comment a letter that arrived from Bedford's superintendent Palmer, reprimanding her for the brevity of her monthly reports and implying that she was hiding some kind of immorality. Speaking very plainly, Anna endeavored to set the record straight: "Your letter received and I was surprised to find I did not give enough information about myself. You see Dr. I am working constantly and therefore haven't much news to give about myself outside of the fact that I am all the institution would want me to be, and am living strictly to the rules. Miss Chaskin [parole worker] will vouch for the truth of this statement. I am sure."[67]

Nanette Wilkins, too, sought to defend herself against sanctimonious relatives who wanted to deny her a position of dignity in her own home. After being cut off by her cousin Winifred, Nanette was placed in domestic service, returning to Bedford three separate times for doing her work unsatisfactorily and for staying out late at night. Eventually the young woman settled into a position with a domestic employer who was disinclined to look for signs of insubordination in her African American servant, preferring to treat Nanette as the object of a Victorian rescue mission: the teenager was "young and alone in the world" and in need of sympathetic advice and direction. Nanette may well have had to compromise her sense of self in order to get along with her employer, but it was better than going back to Bedford Hills or returning to Winifred, who had suddenly changed her mind and asked Nanette to come home. Appropriating a metaphor of bondage to describe Winifred's intent, Nanette tried to explain to Bedford's superintendent why she could not return to her family: "We could never get along at home together. . . . Why should I humble myself to be a slave for her husbin and child Im able to take care of myself now. and also made a women of myself. . . . Dr. Baker dont you think I can travle in this world alone ther are lots has did et beside me and have gone ahead."[68]

Respectability, however, could not be sustained by everyone who desired it. Sometimes poverty, abuse, and public distrust exhausted and mocked "reformed" young women's resolve; sometimes the reformatories had to admit that their "victory" was incomplete. Twelve of the young women in this sample worked hard to prove that they had chosen the "straight road" only to see social approbation and security slip from their grasp.

Possibly these young women deliberately constructed a facade of social conformity to get out from under the reformatories and get on with the "fast" lives they preferred. One could, for example, read the fragmentary data on Ginger Trapp as "proof" of dissemblance and fabrication: Ginger did "very well" on her second parole after being returned to Albion for an illicit romance, but soon after her final discharge she was "ordered out" of Rochester for solicitation and seen picking up a strange man in Syracuse. The authorities at Albion concluded that "Ginger was not *thoroughly* reformed."[69]

The more ample documentation on some of the other backsliders, however, points to a different interpretation: the actual circumstances of their lives just didn't fit the identities they pursued; they confronted dilemmas borne of social disadvantage that diminished and wore away at their "virtue." Families, employers, communities, and reformatories were able to persuade the parolees to accept dominant representations of female virtue and vice, but they could not obviate the obstacles that tended to impair the respectability of working-class, immigrant, and African American women.

The richest evidence on "backsliding" concerns Rae Rabinowitz and Nellie Roberts and reveals the ways in which familial, economic, and cultural pressures combined to undermine young women's hold on respectability. Rae's second stay in Bedford Hills was worse than her first, and she stayed in the institution until the end of her term, never going out again on parole. Nonetheless, after her final discharge, Rae conceded the importance of conformity and, according to her sister, tried to "be straight and do the right thing" by adopting the role of a "respectable conventional married woman." But the marriage was troubled: Rae's husband became disabled and seemed to lose all interest in supporting her. Before long he began to "mistreat" her and then deserted her and their small child. Rae quickly remarried and had another child, but her second husband also became ill and failed to support her. Six years after receiving her "free papers" from Bedford Hills, Rae was destitute, dependent on public charity, and unable to prevent the social workers to whom she applied for help from investigating her former delinquencies. Her respectability survived by a mere thread.[70]

The small measure of respectability that Rae managed to retain, Nellie Roberts failed to hold, though she should have done better than her peer. Nellie was never as difficult an inmate as Rae and she was a consistently well-behaved parolee, thankful for her "homelike" domestic position. Her employers, however, were not "real" parents and they had no obligation to protect her or retain her services. When Nellie's sister badgered her to return home after her final discharge, the girl reluctantly did so, though it meant confronting her alcoholic and "brutal" father. Just two weeks later, Nellie wrote to Bedford Hills, announcing that she had married "a fellow I used to keep company with before I went to Bedford." The hastily arranged marriage meant escape from her family, but Nellie was not at all sure that she had acted wisely and begged Superintendent Florence Jones not to abandon her: "It seems strange not to sign my own name . . . but I think i will be happy don't forget please Mis Jones to write and tell me if I can come down [to visit with husband] I am your good little girl. . . . it seems so strange to wear my too rings and Mrs. Lark I cant get use to it. *please please answer.*"[71] There is no evidence to show that Jones answered Nellie's plea for advice and comfort, and, not surprisingly, the marriage did not last. A letter from Port Jervis's justice of the peace shows that Nellie and her husband separated after less than two years together; they had a baby boy by then, and Nellie was thought to be supporting him through prostitution. Two years later she was arrested and committed to Bedford Hills on a new charge of solicitation and, for the second time, had to decide how to respond to the state's demand that she pursue a "moral" and "useful" life.[72]

If Bedford Hills and Albion found that some of their former inmates were thrust from the ranks of the respectable despite strenuous effort and good intentions, the reformatories' triumph over the "girl problem" was further diminished by parolees who stubbornly refused to heed the rules of parole or to concede the merits of conventional respectability. A small minority of young women—thirteen in this study—were simply unwilling to compromise their individuality or autonomy to satisfy their mentors.

Among them was Rachel Adelson, a former wayward minor who could not resolve her antagonistic relationship with her stepmother and was sent back to Bedford Hills after she ran away from home. Released from Bedford Hills a second time, Rachel went to a live-in position as a mother's helper, but the job displeased her; she disappeared after two weeks and was never found. Nola Pearce, an African American prostitute, also refused to conform to the rules of parole though, unlike Rachel, she enjoyed a close relationship with her mother. Hired as a cleaning woman by the same property owner on Manhattan's Upper West Side who employed her mother, Nola made a good start on parole, dutifully reporting to her white parole worker at the Church Mission of Help, sometimes accompanied by her mother. But mother and daughter resented the surveillance of the state. After a few months of cooperation the two disappeared from their home and work, and though the reformatory wrote various letters to the Pearces' Harlem address declaring Nola a "fugitive from justice," the young woman was never recovered.[73]

As a last example, Julia Kramer, another wayward minor, found it impossible to accept the work and living conditions of her housekeeping position at New York's Lying-in-Hospital. According to her parole worker from the Jewish Board of Guardians, Julia "talked about her 'rights' continually, and tried to incite others to rebel, until they had to discharge her." After being fired, Julia went to live with her married sister and took a job at a pleating and hemstitching company and, when that job did not work out, with an electric and radio company. But less than a month after leaving the hospital, Julia was out of work and blaming her situation on her employers' "peculiarities." By this time Julia's sister was so disgusted with the parolee's refusal to pay board or help with the housework that she asked her to move. Julia subsequently found another live-in job as a hospital ward maid, but was fired within weeks for spending two successive nights at Coney Island and failing to report to work. She had had enough by this time and, collecting her belongings, she disappeared from Bedford's sight.[74]

To varying degrees, each of these young women rebelled against conditions of work, family life, or state surveillance. They refused to submit to the state's efforts to transform them into useful and virtuous women. Still, it is important not to overstate the parole violators' investment in rebellion or their triumph as cultural nonconformists. Because most of these young women disappeared on parole and were never found, we are left knowing little about the definition they gave to their lives after their flight. Rachel, Nola, Julia, and some of the others may have tried eventually to fashion fairly quiet and "respectable" lives; once free of odious parole agents, parents, or employers they may have forged an accommodation with conventional morality that was of their own making.

If they did take this route, however, the successful runaways would still have had to use subterfuge to avoid discovery and disrepute. And artifice was risky, as Sophie Polentz found out after a second stay in Bedford Hills. Released to a domestic position because neither she nor the reformatory seemed to have any hope that she could repair her dreadful relationship with her father, Sophie still found the constraints of parole unbearable. She disappeared after three weeks and was never returned to Bedford Hills although the reformatory heard occasional reports of her. Working at first as a streetwalker, Sophie later married and tried "to live a decent respectable life." But having taken refuge from family and state in New York City's street life, she found it impossible to disengage herself from her underworld associates and was forced to pay "hush money" to the couple she had worked for while prostituting, lest her husband be told of her past habits. When she missed a few payments her spouse was confronted with information about her former career; he tried to "forgive her for her lie" but the marriage gradually fell apart and Sophie began to see how her "immorality" could haunt her.[75]

Sophie's experience may not have represented the experience of other "disappeared" parolees, but it is nonetheless instructive. Resistant to reformatory discipline, Sophie simultaneously found it burdensome to construct a safe alternative to conventional respectability. She had not been reclaimed and transformed, but neither had she gained sufficient security to dismiss or disregard prevailing notions of female delinquency.

Conclusion:
The Social Inequities of Female Adolescence

The history of New York's female delinquents highlights the inequities that shadowed young women's efforts to reinvent the meaning of female adolescence during the early twentieth century. Throughout the early twentieth century, working- and middle-class young women tried, with varying degrees of success, to use new sites of work (factories, department stores, offices, high schools, colleges), new places of residence (rooming houses and apartments), and new forms of commodified leisure (dance halls, amusement parks, movies, dating) to challenge the identities prescribed for them by their families and communities and to develop an alternative set of moral and cultural values. The young women who became inmates in New York's reformatories were engaged in an especially difficult and hazardous version of this quest for a modern social identity. At home and on the streets they discovered firsthand the perils of reinventing the self; so too, they came face-to-face with cultural authorities and state agencies that insisted on containing their resistance to convention.

Most of the young women who were committed to New York's reformatories at Bedford Hills and Albion came from families burdened by economic hardship, cultural dislocation, and social prejudice; their families knew as well the acute distress produced by marital discord, physical violence, severe illness, and untimely death. Wanting relief from domestic adversity, New York's female delinquents tried to disassociate themselves from home and kin, seeking amusement with other young people and sexual adventure on city streets. Their behavior often provoked conflict with families who could not tolerate (and feared they could not survive) the rebellion of their adolescent daughters. In turn, this estrangement from family prompted the young women to invest in the life of the street with little thought to its dangers, accentuating their vulnerability both to exploitation and state intervention.

New York's delinquents arrived at the state's reformatories for women by two distinct routes. The majority were committed to Bedford Hills or Albion after arrest by the police and conviction in court, usually on charges of prostitution, vagrancy, or disorderly conduct. Others were handed a reformatory sentence after angry and frustrated parents dragged their rebellious offspring into court and requested that they be "sent away." Whichever route they traveled, and whatever their legal offense, these young women discovered that New York's criminal-justice system viewed them through a single lens, condemning their indifference to Victorian standards of feminine virtue. Convinced that unruly adolescent females posed a grave moral danger to themselves, their families, and society, the state sought to foil their efforts at self-definition.

New York's response to disorderly adolescent females was not fueled by unmitigated hostility. The Progressive reformers who fashioned New York's campaign against the "girl problem" wanted not only to protect society from immorality but also to shield young women from the "living death" of prostitution. Their commitment to protection and prevention was manifested in a range of girls' clubs, protective leagues, sex-education campaigns, and delinquency-prevention programs. In assuming that female adolescent rebellion and sexual adventure led necessarily to prostitution, however, these male and female reformers proclaimed the inviolability of Victorian definitions of female sexual morality and denied young women's right to modify the moral status quo. Reflecting these values, New York's criminal-justice system deliberately cast a wide net around rebellious young women, also treating filial disobedience and casual sex as variants of or steps toward a career in prostitution. Indeed, the state discounted unruly young women's vulnerability and confusion, instead interpreting their perilous quest for self-actualization as a willing endorsement of moral degeneracy.

Significantly, state efforts to contain the "girl problem" were class and race specific. By the 1920s, as middle-class Americans realized that their own daughters were swept up in the currents of social change, their overt hostility to young women's remodeling of adolescence turned to a concerted search for a more permissive ideology of female adolescence. Within the middle class the ideal of purity waned as did the intense fear that prostitution must be the fate of all young women who deviated from a life of strict sexual control. The narrative of female adolescence written by mental hygienists freed some middle-class parents from fears of uncontrolled adolescent sexuality; the new "experts" stressed young women's need for sexual and social autonomy but also emphasized adolescent girls' willingness to bend budding sexual desires to societal norms. In this new script the role of parents was to help girls achieve a "healthy" adjustment to the values of the society around them. Female adolescent sexuality lost the power to shame or terrify middle-class Americans as mental-health professionals urged parents and educators to foster rather than repress adolescent girls' sexual "development." At the same time, mental-hygiene clinics replaced reformatories as the recommended site of treatment for sexually "maladjusted" girls.

And yet as the histories of young women committed to Bedford Hills and Albion so clearly illustrate, the reworking of societal norms and treatment modalities by mental-hygiene professionals did not displace preexisting correctional systems designed to cope with the "girl problem" as it was observed among working-class, immigrant, and African American young women. While the middle-class learned to cope with the rebellion of its own daughters, a significant minority of disadvantaged young women continued to be arrested for breaking older norms. State authorities and professionals in deliquency prevention continued to look for evidence of sexual delinquency in the neighborhoods of the poor, knowing that prostitution had not disappeared, not trusting disadvantaged girls to explore heterosexuality without drifting into lives of vice. The young women arrested were not necessarily the most promiscuous on city streets, or those most experienced in prostitution, but those least able to evade police surveillance and apprehension.

Inside the walls of the reformatories and on parole, delinquent young women encountered intense pressures that compelled many of them to attach new value to caution and social acceptability. The reformatories resisted the values of the new sexual order, wanting their inmates to adopt Victorian standards of middle-class womanhood, in part because Victorian values were so firmly institutionalized in the state setting, in part because reformatory personnel assumed that working-class or nonwhite young women would abuse a permissive standard of behavior. Reformatory personnel wanted to protect their charges and keep them from lives of immorality, censure, and abuse. Just as important, they were compelled to protect society from female delinquency.

Although the reformatories resisted liberal sexual values, they adopted modern psychological testing procedures and made selective use of mental-hygiene principles, for example, the principle that "antisocial" behavior was related to poor parenting and antagonistic relations at home. These procedures and principles were used to assess and maximize inmates' ability to respond to reformatory programs and expectations; at the same time, the results of tests and psychiatric interviews confirmed reformatory personnel's assumptions about the inferior inheritance and character training that young women received from lower-class, immigrant, and black parents.

The inmates' response to the reformatories was complex. These young women were coming of age in an era of widespread confusion and disorientation about gender, sexuality, and the meaning of female adolescence as a life stage; their response to the reformatories reflected acute sensitivity to the power of these institutions as well as indecision about their own social identity. Although nearly all of the inmates learned that they must show at least minimal respect for the authority of the state in order to win a timely parole, they reacted to the reformatories' social agenda in a variety of ways. Many young women resented the invasion of privacy and the social stigma that came with being reformatory inmates but did not entirely reject their keepers' social and gender values. Others actively resisted the reformatories' gender expectations. Still other young women deliberately sought the protection and social guidance of women reformatory officials.

Young women's response to the reformatories was also influenced by their relationships with their families. New York's inmates could not correspond or visit with friends or lovers, but they were allowed carefully scripted contact with family members. The evidence suggests that many inmates were uncomfortable about their status as "delinquents." They did not want to think of themselves as "bad" women or girls, resenting state officials and family members who defined them in this way; yet they depended on reformatory personnel and kin to change their designated status, to redefine them as "good" girls. At the same time, both inmates and kin had to contend with policies of censorship and control that left them little opportunity to repair misunderstandings or overcome conflicts. Daughters and parents might speak of repentance and forgiveness, but more than a few young women left the reformatories without having altered parents' expectations or won their trust.

On parole, young women found that their social choices and identities were shaped by continued reformatory surveillance, persisting family obligations, and the limited opportunity urban environments provided for economic independence or the evasion of state and family authority. Some paroled young women actively sought the approval of parents and some depended on the continued guidance of the reformatories, looking to female parole officers and superintendents as models and caretakers. But other young women continued to resist the authority and values of family members, reformatories, and employers in various ways—changing jobs without prior approval, making friends and taking lovers, running away from home, wearing cosmetics, (re)turning to prostitution. Other young people and criminal subcultures helped some young women evade reformatory surveillance, at least for a while. In a few instances, family members encouraged young women to break parole and protected them from the police and reformatory authorities.

Urban subcultures, however, provided young women with little social or economic security. Many parolees suffered recapture and a second stay in the reformatories. And few were able to gain complete autonomy or freedom from family obligations. Delinquent girls were not powerless; they struggled to assert themselves as individuals and managed to win some concessions from the reformatories and from their families. But their agency was limited: as inmates, parolees, and daughters, most learned to make conservative choices about their conduct, defining their needs and interests within the context of traditional family, class, and ethnic relations. These young women had experienced so much grief, abuse, and disappointment as rebellious adolescents that many of them eventually decided that conformity was easier and more satisfying than resistance, accepting the idea that freedom was to be gained through obedience to conservative cultural norms and conventions.

Bibliographic Essay

This essay is intended as a guide to the secondary literature on female adolescence, the family, womanhood, and reformers' efforts to control sexuality in early-twentieth-century America. I have not tried to be exhaustive; rather, I have selected those works that were foundational to my research. A few are mentioned more than once because of their wide-ranging utility. Within the categories described below, titles are listed in order of date of publication.

On the changing character of family life and adolescence in modern America see, Paula Fass, *The Damned and the Beautiful: American Youth in the 1920's* (New York: Oxford University Press, 1977); Joseph Kett, *Rites of Passsage: Adolescence in America, 1790 to the Present* (New York: Basic Books, Inc., 1977); Peter G. Filene, *Him/Her/Self: Sex Roles in Modern America* (Baltimore: Johns Hopkins University Press, 1986); Reed Ueda, *Avenues to Adulthood: The Origins of the High School and Social Mobility in an American Suburb* (Cambridge: Cambridge University Press, 1987); Beth Bailey, *From Front Porch to Back Seat: Courtship in Twentieth-Century America* (Baltimore: Johns Hopkins University Press, 1988); Steven Mintz and Susan Kellogg, *Domestic Revolutions: A Social History of American Family Life* (New York: Free Press, 1988); John D'Emilio and Estelle B. Freedman, *Intimate Matters: A History of Sexuality in America* (New York: Harper & Row, 1988); John Modell, *Into One's Own: From Youth to Adulthood in the United States, 1920–1975* (Berkeley: University of California Press, 1989); Ileen A. DeVault, *Sons and Daughters of Labor: Class and Clerical Work in Turn-of-the-Century Pittsburgh* (Ithaca: Cornell University Press, 1990); David Tyack and Elisabeth Hansot, *Learning Together: A History of Coeducation in American Schools* (New Haven: Yale University Press, 1990).

Young women's reinvention of female adolescence took place amid wide-ranging challenges—social, sexual, political, and economic—to conventional models of womanhood. The varied manifestations of "new womanhood" (and of a new female adolescence) in the working class have been described and analyzed in, Leslie

Woodcock Tentler, *Wage-Earning Women: Industrial Work and Family Life in the United States, 1900–1930* (New York: Oxford University Press, 1979); Joanne Reitano, "Working Girls Unite," *American Quarterly* 36 (Spring 1984): 112–34; Elizabeth Ewen, *Immigrant Women in the Land of Dollars: Life and Culture on the Lower East Side, 1890–1925* (New York: Monthly Review Press, 1985); Alice Kessler-Harris, "Independence and Virtue in the Lives of Wage-Earning Women: The United States, 1870–1930," in *Women and Culture in Politics: A Century of Change*, ed. Judith Friedlander, Blanche Wiesen Cook, Alice Kessler-Harris, and Carroll Smith-Rosenberg (Bloomington: Indiana University Press, 1986): 3–17; Kathy Peiss, *Cheap Amusements: Working Women and Leisure in Turn-of-the-Century New York* (Philadelphia: Temple University Press, 1986); Susan Porter Benson, *Counter Cultures: Saleswomen, Managers, and Customers in American Department Stores, 1890–1940* (Urbana: University of Illinois Press, 1988); Freedman and D'Emilio, *Intimate Matters*; Joanne Meyerowitz, *Women Adrift: Independent Wage Earners in Chicago, 1880–1930* (Chicago: University of Chicago Press, 1988); Susan A. Glenn, *Daughters of the Shtetl: Life and Labor in the Immigrant Generation* (Ithaca: Cornell University Press, 1990); and Stephen H. Norwood, *Labor's Flaming Youth: Telephone Operators and Worker Militancy, 1878–1923* (Urbana: University of Illinois Press, 1990).

New womanhood in the African American community also took diverse forms. On new sexual values see Daphne Duval Harrison, *Black Pearls: Blues Queens of the 1920s* (New Brunswick, N.J.: Rutgers University Press, 1990). On black women's reform efforts readers should consult Beverly W. Jones, "Mary Church Terrell and the National Association of Colored Women," *Journal of Negro History* 67 (Spring 1982): 20–33; Jacqueline Jones, *Labor of Love, Labor of Sorrow: Black Women, Work, and the Family from Slavery to the Present* (New York: Vintage Books, 1985); Cynthia Neverdon-Morton, *Afro-American Women of the South and the Advancement of the Race, 1895–1925* (Knoxville: University of Tennessee Press, 1989); Dorothy C. Salem, *To Better Our World: Black Women in Organized Reform, 1890–1920* (Brooklyn, 1990); Anne Firor Scott, "Most Invisible of All: Black Women's Voluntary Associations," *Journal of Southern History* 66 (1990): 3–22; Linda Gordon, "Black and White Visions of Welfare: Women's Welfare Activism, 1890–1945," *Journal of American History* 78 (1991): 559–90; and Evelyn Brooks Higginbotham, *Righteous Discontent: The Women's Movement in the Black Baptist Church, 1880–1920* (Cambridge: Harvard University Press, 1993).

Black women's reform activities were devoted in large measure to undermining racism. Significant studies of racism and the black experience in the late nineteenth and early twentieth centuries include Mark H. Haller, *Eugenics: Hereditarian Attitudes in American Thought* (New Brunswick, N.J.: Rutgers University Press, 1963), 144–59; Gilbert Osofsky, *Harlem, The Making of a Ghetto: Negro New York, 1890–1930* (New York: Harper and Row, 1971); C. Van Woodward, *The Strange Career of Jim Crow* (New York: Oxford University Press, 1974); Herbert G. Gutman, *The Black Family in Slavery and Freedom* (New York: Pantheon, 1976), 433–60; Jones, *Labor of Love, Labor of Sorrow*; and Neil R. McMillen, *Dark Journey: Black Mississippians in the Age of Jim Crow* (Urbana: University of Illinois Press, 1990).

New patterns of conduct, belief, and activism among middle-class women have generated a great deal of scholarly interest. Important works include James McGovern, "The American Woman's Pre-World War I Freedom in Manners and Morals," *Journal of American History* 55 (1968): 315–33; Linda Gordon, *Woman's Body, Woman's Right: Birth Control in America* (New York: Penguin, 1977); Sheila M. Rothman, *Woman's Proper Place: A History of Changing Ideals and Practices, 1870 to the Present* (New York: Basic Books, 1978); Rosalind Rosenberg, *Beyond Separate Spheres: Intellectual Roots of Modern Feminism* (New Haven: Yale University Press, 1982); Paula Baker, "The Domestication of Politics: Women and American Political Society, 1780–1920," *American Historical Review* 89 (1984): 620–47; Carroll Smith-Rosenberg, *Disorderly Conduct: Visions of Gender in Victorian America* (New York: Alfred A. Knopf, 1985); Nancy Cott, *The Grounding of Modern Feminism* (New Haven: Yale University Press, 1987); Seth Koven and Sonya Michel, "Womanly Duties: Maternalist Politics and the Origins of Welfare States in France, Germany, Great Britain, and the United States, 1880–1920," *American Historical Review* 95 (1990): 1076–1108; Robyn Muncy, *Creating a Female Dominion in American Reform, 1890–1935* (New York: Oxford University Press, 1991).

The early twentieth century's emerging culture of consumption was critical to the changing experience of women and girls. Useful and provocative works on this subject include Larry May, *Screening out the Past: The Birth of Mass Culture and the Motion Picture Industry* (New York: Oxford University Press, 1980); 105–9; T. J. Jackson Lears, *No Place of Grace: Antimodernism and the Transformation of American Culture, 1880–1920* (New York: Pantheon, 1981); *The Culture of Consumption: Critical Essays in American History, 1880–1980,* ed. Richard Wrightman Fox and T.J. Jackson Lears (New York: Pantheon, 1983); Peiss, *Cheap Amusements;* and Susan Strasser, *Satisfaction Guaranteed: The Making of the American Mass Market* (New York: Pantheon, 1989).

The antiprostitution movement of the Progressive Era gave voice to the anxieties of middle-class men and women who opposed, among other things, the sexualization of female adolescence. See John Connelly, *The Response to Prostitution in the Progressive Era* (Chapel Hill: University of North Carolina Press, 1980); David Pivar, "Cleansing the Nation: The War on Prostitution, 1917–21," *Prologue* 12 (1980): 29–40; Ruth Rosen, *The Lost Sisterhood: Prostitution in America, 1900–1918* (Baltimore: Johns Hopkins University Press, 1982); Allan Brandt, *No Magic Bullet: A Social History of Venereal Disease in the United States since 1880* (New York: Oxford University Press, 1985); Barbara Meil Hobson, *Uneasy Virtue: The Politics of Prostitution and the American Reform Tradition* (New York: Basic Books, 1987); and Freedman and D'Emilio, *Intimate Matters.*

A related literature examines the legal and cultural definitions of juvenile and adolescent delinquency that Americans devised in the late nineteenth and early twentieth centuries. See Anthony M. Platt, *The Child Savers: The Invention of Delinquency* (Chicago: University of Chicago Press, 1969); Robert M. Mennel, *Thorns and Thistles: Juvenile Delinquents in the United States, 1825–1940* (Hanover, N.H.: University Press of New England, 1973); Steven Schlossman and Stephanie Wallach, "The Crime of Precocious Sexuality: Female Juvenile Delinquency in the Progressive Era," *Harvard Educational Review* 48 (1978): 65–94; Peter Tyor, "Denied the Power to Choose the Good: Sexuality and Mental Defect in American Medical

Practice, 1850–1920," *Journal of Social History* 10 (1979): 472–89; and Mary E. Odem and Steven Schlossman, "Guardians of Virtue: The Juvenile Court and Female Delinquency in Early 20th-Century Los Angeles," *Crime and Delinquency* 37 (1991): 186–203.

Acting independently of men, female reformers in the late nineteenth and early twentieth centuries created and institutionalized a variety of programs explicitly intended to keep young women from lives of sexual immorality and degradation. To some extent they drew upon earlier models. On "rescue" work in the antebellum era see Ruth M. Alexander, "'We Are Engaged as a Band of Sisters': Class and Domesticity in the Washingtonian Temperance Movement, 1840–1850" *Journal of American History* 75 (1988): 763–85; and Carroll Smith-Rosenberg, "Beauty, the Beast, and the Militant Woman: A Case Study in Sex Roles and Social Stress in Jacksonian America," *American Quarterly* 23 (1971): 562–84. On "preventive" and "rescue" work in the late nineteenth century see David J. Pivar, *Purity Crusade, Sexual Morality, and Social Control, 1868–1900* (Westport, Conn.: Greenwood Press, 1973), 99–103, 105–9; Estelle B. Freedman, *Their Sisters' Keepers: Women's Prison Reform in America, 1830–1930* (Ann Arbor: University of Michigan Press, 1981), chap. 3; Barbara M. Brenzel, *Daughters of the State: A Social Portrait of the First Reform School for Girls in North America, 1856–1905* (Cambridge, Mass.: MIT Press, 1983); Nicole Hahn Rafter, *Partial Justice: Women in State Prisons, 1800–1935* (Boston: Northeastern University Press, 1985); Peiss, *Cheap Amusements*; 164–71; Meyerowitz, *Women Adrift*, 46–53; Peggy Pascoe, *Relations of Rescue: The Search for Female Moral Authority in the American West, 1874–1939* (New York: Oxford University Press, 1990); and Salem, *To Better Our World*. Joan Brumberg examines "rescue" work with middle-class young women in "'Ruined' Girls: Changing Community Responses to Illegitimacy in Upstate New York, 1890–1920," *Journal of Social History* 18 (1984): 247–72. The professionalization of "rescue" work is examined by Pascoe in *Relations of Rescue* and by Regina G. Kunzel in *Fallen Women, Problem Girls: Unmarried Mothers and the Professionalization of Social Work, 1890–1945* (New Haven: Yale University Press, 1993).

On the dynamic between clients and caregivers at welfare agencies see Linda Gordon, *Heroes of Their Own Lives: The Politics and History of Family Violence, Boston, 1880–1960* (New York: Viking, 1988); and Beverly Stadum, *Poor Women and Their Families: Hard Working Charity Cases, 1900–1930* (Albany: State University of New York Press).

Over time, early-twentieth-century Americans attempted in various ways to accommodate the changing social and sexual habits of America's adolescent girls, though ideological and practical obstacles to young women's autonomy did not disappear. D'Emilio and Freedman examine the sources of the "liberal" response to young women's reinvention of female adolescence as well as to some of the constraints they encountered in *Intimate Matters*. The controversy over sex education in the early twentieth century is discussed in Nathan G. Hale, Jr., *Freud and the Americans: The Beginning of Psychoanalysis in the United States, 1876–1917* (New York: Oxford University Press, 1971), 250–58; Christina Clare Simmons, "'Marriage in the Modern Manner': Sexual Radicalism and Reform in America, 1914–1941" (Ph.D. diss., Brown University, 1982), 17–44; and Allan Brandt, *No Magic Bullet: A*

Social History of Venereal Disease in the United States since 1880 (New York: Oxford University Press, 1985), 23–31. Efforts to devise new moral standards and new methods of parenting are examined in Fass, *The Damned and the Beautiful*; Kett, *Rites of Passage*; Margo Horn, "The Moral Message of Child Guidance, 1925–45," *Journal of Social History* 18 (1984): 25–36; Ewen, *Immigrant Women in the Land of Dollars*; Peiss, *Cheap Amusements*; William Graebner, "Outlawing Teenage Populism: The Campaign against Secret Societies in the American High School, 1900–1960," *Journal of American History* 74 (1987): 411–37; Ueda, *Avenues to Adulthood*; Bailey, *From Front Porch to Back Seat*; Kathleen W. Jones, "As the Twig Is Bent: American Psychiatry and the Troublesome Child, 1890–1940" (Ph.D. diss., Rutgers University, 1988); Meyerowitz, *Women Adrift*; Modell, *Into One's Own*; Robert L. Griswold, "'Ties That Bind and Bonds That Break': Children's Attitudes toward Fathers, 1900–1930," in *Small Worlds: Children and Adolescents in America, 1850–1950*, ed. Eliott West and Paula Petrik (Lawrence: University Press of Kansas, 1992), 255–74; and Vicki Ruiz, "'Star Struck': Acculturation, Adolescence, and Mexican-American Women, 1920–1950," in *Small Worlds*, 61–80.

Works focusing on the constraints imposed by modern sexual ideologies include Elizabeth Lunbeck, "'A New Generation of Women': Progressive Psychiatrists and the Hypersexual Female," *Feminist Studies* 13 (1987): 513–43; George Chauncey, Jr., "From Sexual Inversion to Homosexuality: Medicine and the Changing Conceptualization of Female 'Deviance,'" in *Passion and Power: Sexuality in History*, ed. Kathy Peiss and Christina Simmons (Philadelphia: Temple University Press, 1989), 87–117; Christina Simmons, "Modern Sexuality and the Myth of Victorian Repression," in *Passion and Power*, 157–77; and Pamela Haag, "In Search of 'The Real Thing': Ideologies of Love, Modern Romance, and Women's Sexual Subjectivity in the United States, 1920–40" *Journal of the History of Sexuality* 2 (1992): 547–77.

Notes

Works appearing in the Bibliographic Essay are cited in short form here.

Introduction

1. By law the two institutions admitted women between the ages of sixteen and thirty; however, the great majority were at the lower end of that range. Series 14610-78 Albion Correctional Facility Inmate Case Files, 1894–1968; Series 14610-77B Bedford Hills Correctional Facility Inmate Case Files, 1915–30, 1955–65; Records of the Department of Correctional Services, New York State Archives and Records Administration, State Education Department, Albany, N.Y. In compliance with New York State Department of Correctional Service regulations (7 NYCRR §5.24 (b)(10)–.25) governing researchers' access to restricted records, the inmate case file numbers have been dropped from this work and I have created fictitious names for the inmates and their associates. In the notes, the date after each inmate's name is the date of admission to the reformatory.

2. In the case of Bedford Hills, systematic sampling was altogether impossible as no files survived from 1901 to 1916 and the inmate files from 1917 to 1930 were either in very rough chronological order or in no order at all. Moreover, some of the surviving files contained copious documentation, others very little. The Albion records are in better chronological order, but here too the quantity and quality of documentation varies so widely that a strict sampling procedure seemed both unwise and impractical.

3. Because I selected well-documented files, my book may be biased toward trouble-makers or toward inmates whose families tried to intervene in the reform process (regardless of their girls' conduct). The latter is the more likely because conduct records never accounted for more than a small portion of the material in inmate files. Familial intervention is discussed at length in Chapter 4.

4. Having discarded representative sampling as a possibility, I have not, however, ignored the benefits of quantification. For each of the cases in my sample I coded and

tabulated data on the inmates' socioeconomic status, family and work histories, criminal records, and institutional and parole records.

5. The Laboratory of Social Hygiene is also discussed in Freedman, *Their Sisters' Keepers,* 111–21. The laboratory staff conducted extensive interviews with each new inmate and sought additional information from immediate family members, other relatives, neighbors, teachers, employers, and community agencies.

1. "Going Around with a Bad Crowd of Girls": Young Women and the Lure of City Streets

1. Nellie Roberts, New York State Reformatory for Women, Bedford Hills, 1917, Laboratory of Social Hygiene, staff meeting (quote), information concerning patient; record of conviction.

2. In 1917 and 1918, hoping to prevent venereal infection from undermining the fighting strength of America's armed forces, the federal government became actively involved in fighting prostitution and female promiscuity around military bases. See Connelly, *The Response to Prostitution in the Progressive Era,* 137–50; Hobson, *Uneasy Virtue,* 165–66, 172–75, 180; Pivar, "Cleansing the Nation," 29–40; Brandt, *No Magic Bullet,* chap. 2.

3. On middle-class and affluent female adolescents' rebellion against Victorian social and sexual mores during the first two decades of the twentieth century see McGovern, "The American Woman's Pre-World War I Freedom in Manners and Morals," 315–33; Rosenberg, *Beyond Separate Spheres,* 190–92; Lewis Erenberg, *Steppin' Out: New York Nightlife and the Transformation of American Culture, 1890–1930* (Chicago: University of Chicago Press, 1981), 77–83.

4. Nellie Roberts, Bedford Hills, 1917, information of patient (Nellie's comment on the soldiers was paraphrased by a Bedford social worker); mental examination.

5. Nellie Roberts, Bedford Hills, 1917, girl's statement; verified history; mental exam; information of patient.

6. Ibid., mental exam.

7. The precise income levels of the inmates' families are impossible to determine. The inmate case files usually listed fathers' and mothers' occupations; sometimes staff members also offered an imprecise assessment of a family's financial and physical circumstances: "destitute," "fair," "comfortable," "very comfortable," etc. These assessments must, of course, be used with great care, as a "comfortable" home in an immigrant neighborhood on Manhattan's Lower East Side was probably quite different from a "comfortable" home on Manhattan's Upper West Side, a residential area dominated by middle-class professionals. The largely working-class background of female offenders in the early twentieth century has been well established by numerous studies, both contemporary and historical. For contemporary studies of the socioeconomic standing of young women delinquents see Maude E. Miner, *Slavery of Prostitution: A Plea for Emancipation* (New York: Macmillan), 36–38; George J. Kneeland, *Commercialized Prostitution in New York City* (New York: Century Company, 1913, 1917; repr., Montclair, N.J.: Patterson Smith, 1969), 178, 215–18; Mabel Ruth Fernald, *A Study of Women Delinquents in New York State* (New York: Century Company, 1920), 5–6, 525–27; Herrick Committee, *Women and Girl Offenders in Massachusetts* (Boston: Massachusetts Child Council, Inc.,

1938), 13–15; Mabel Agnes Elliott, *Correctional Education and the Delinquent Girl: A Follow-up Study of One Hundred and Ten Sleighton Farm Girls* (Harrisburg, Pa.: 1928), 28–30. For historical studies see Rosen, *Lost Sisterhood*, 147–61; Freedman, *Their Sisters' Keepers*, 111–15, 121–25.

8. In 1900 only 5.6% of all married women were in the labor force. That figure rose to 10.7% in 1910, dropped to 9.0% by 1920 and rose again to 11.7% by 1930. See U.S. Department of Commerce, Bureau of the Census, *Historical Statistics of the United States: Colonial Times to 1970* (Washington, D.C., 1975), pt. 1: 133.

9. Deborah Herman, Bedford Hills, 1925, history blank, (Episcopal) Church Mission of Help summary report, October 31, 1925.

10. Thirty-two of the 100 young women in this study had completed six or fewer grades in school; another 35 had never gone beyond the eighth grade. For national statistics on high-school education in the twentieth century see *Digest of Educational Statistics* (Washington, D.C.: National Center for Educational Statistics, Autumn 1979), 47. Historians are somewhat divided over working-class girls' access to secondary education. Leslie Tentler argues that working-class girls made fewer gains educationally than working-class boys during the 1920s—the decade during which high schools registered their most dramatic gains in attendance—because working-class parents did not recognize the value of education for girls. Tentler draws on census reports for 1930 which show that girls in New York City, Chicago, and Philadelphia were somewhat less likely than boys to attend high school. Italian immigrant parents were especially likely to limit their daughters' access to education, but Polish and Jewish parents also worried that too much education would make their girls unfit for marriage. Still, over 50% of sixteen- and seventeen-year-old girls in these cities attended school. Tentler, *Wage Earning Women*, 95–104. In contrast, Ileen DeVault's work highlights working-class parents who were well aware of the values of secondary vocational education for daughters. In turn-of-the-century Pittsburgh, working-class girls and boys attended classes in the public high school's Commercial Department in nearly equal numbers, despite boys' brighter prospects in the white-collar work force. Forty-two percent of the students in the commercial program were the native-born children of foreign-born parents. DeVault, *Sons and Daughters of Labor*, 37, 42–44. And Miriam Cohen points out that, over time, even Italian parents came to value secondary education for daughters, especially when it involved vocational training. Miriam Cohen, "Changing Education Strategies among Immigrant Generations," *Journal of Social History* 15 (1982): 443–60.

11. Anna Levinson, Bedford Hills, 1924, investigation of Levinson home by Anna Stolper, social worker, Jewish Board of Guardians, March 18, 1925.

12. Caroline Browning, Bedford Hills, 1924, admission record, history blank; Sonya Arnett, Albion, 1922, intake interview and admission ledger.

13. Lizabeth Cohen, *Making a New Deal: Industrial Workers in Chicago, 1919–39* (Cambridge: Cambridge University Press, 1990), 53–97; John Bodnar, Roger Simon, and Michael P. Weber, *Lives of Their Own: Blacks, Italians, and Poles in Pittsburgh, 1900–1960* (Urbana: University of Illinois Press, 1982), 198–203; John Bodnar, *The Transplanted: A History of Immigrants in Urban America* (Bloomington: Indiana University Press, 1987), 85–115, 120–30, 184–89; John W. Briggs, *An Italian Passage: Immigrants to Three American Cities, 1890–1930* (New Haven: Yale University Press, 1978), 139–62; T. J. Woofter, *Negro Problems in Cities* (New York, Doubleday, Doran, 1928; repr., New York: Negro

Universities Press, 1969), 143–48, 158–70; Ewen, *Immigrant Women in the Land of Dollars*, 83–91; Judith E. Smith, *Family Connections: A History of Italian and Jewish Immigrant Lives in Providence, Rhode Island, 1900–1940* (Albany: State University of New York Press, 1985), 99–107, 124–65.

14. Sophie Polentz, Bedford Hills, 1924, history blank; Ester Bromwell, Bedford Hills, 1917, Laboratory of Social Hygiene, home conditions.

15. Other scholars are also aware that prostitutes and female sex offenders frequently came from broken or fragile families. See, for example, Rosen, *The Lost Sisterhood*, 145–47, Timothy J. Gilfoyle, *City of Eros: New York City, Prostitution, and the Commercialization of Sex, 1790–1920* (New York: Norton, 1992), 289–90; Gordon, *Heroes of Their Own Lives*, chap. 7.

16. Mildred Pomrenke, Bedford Hills, 1928, investigation by Catholic Protective Services, June 16, 1928.

17. Deborah Herman, Bedford Hills, 1925, Church Mission of Help summary report, October 31, 1925. The (Episcopal) Church Mission of Help was one of the few social-work agencies in New York which assisted African American delinquent girls.

18. Deborah Herman, Bedford Hills, 1926, Church Mission of Help summary report, October 31, 1925.

19. Sophie Polentz, Bedford Hills, 1924, Jewish Board of Guardians report, May 27, 1925.

20. Anabel Rider, Albion, 1923, admission ledger; intake interview; letter from guardian to Superintendent Flora P. Daniels, May 9, 1925.

21. The best study of working-class young women's pursuit of leisure is Peiss, *Cheap Amusements*. See also Tentler, *Wage-Earning Women*, 107–14; Meyerowitz, *Women Adrift*, 106–16; Ewen, *Immigrant Women in the Land of Dollars*, 208–24.

22. On the constraints of nineteenth-century girlhood and young womanhood see Mary Ryan, *Cradle of the Middle Class: The Family in Oneida County, New York, 1790–1865* (Cambridge: Cambridge University Press, 1981), chap. 4; Ann Boylan, "Growing Up Female in Young America, 1800–1860," in *American Childhood: A Research Guide and Historical Handbook*, ed. Joseph M. Hawes and N. Ray Hiner (Westport, Conn.: Greenwood Press, 1985): 153–84; Carroll Smith-Rosenberg, "Puberty to Menopause: The Cycle of Femininity in Nineteenth-century America," *Feminist Studies* 1 (1973): 58–72; Deborah Gray White, *Arn't I a Woman?: Female Slaves in the Plantation South* (New York: Norton, 1985), 93–99; Faye E. Dudden, *Serving Women: Household Service in Nineteenth-Century America* (Middletown, Conn.: Wesleyan University Press, 1985), 193–212; Thomas Dublin, *Women at Work: The Transformation of Work and Community in Lowell Massachusetts, 1826–1860* (New York: Columbia University Press, 1979), 74–85, 165–69, 188–97, 198–207.

23. John D'Emilio and Estelle Freedman, *Intimate Matters: A History of Sexuality in America* (New York: Harper and Row, 1988), 70–71, 93–104; Nancy Cott, "Passionlessness: An Interpretation of Victorian Sexual Ideology, 1790–1850," *Signs* 4 (1978): 218–36; Carroll Smith-Rosenberg, "Sex as Symbol in Victorian Purity: An Ethnohistorical Analysis of Jacksonian America," in *Turning Points: Historical and Sociological Essays on the Family*, ed. John Demos and Saran Spence Boocock (Chicago: University of Chicago Press, 1978), 242–44; Deborah Gray White, *Arn't I a Woman*, 27–46; Harriet A. Jacobs,

Incidents in the Life of a Slave Girl, Written by Herself, ed. Jean Fagan Yellin (Cambridge: Harvard University Press, 1987).

24. Lee Virginia Chambers-Schiller, *Liberty a Better Husband: Single Women in America, The Generations of 1780–1840* (New Haven: Yale University Press, 1984); Anne Firor Scott, "The Ever Widening Circle: The Diffusion of Feminist Values from the Troy Female Seminary, 1822–1872," *History of Education Quarterly* 19 (1979): 3–25; Nancy Cott, *The Bonds of Womanhood: Woman's Sphere in New England, 1780–1835* (New Haven: Yale University Press, 1977), 125; Thomas Dublin, *Women at Work,* chaps. 6 and 7; Christine Stansell, *City of Women: Sex and Class in New York, 1789–1860* (Urbana: University of Illinois Press, 1987), 83–101; Deborah Gray White, *Arn't I a Woman?* 97–98.

25. Peiss, *Cheap Amusements;* Ewen, *Immigrant Women in the Land of Dollars,* 208–24; Kessler-Harris, "Independence and Virtue in the Lives of Wage-Earning Women, 3–17; Glenn, *Daughters of the Shtetl,* 159–66.

26. Harrison, *Black Pearls,* 18–22; Hazel V. Carby, "'It Jus Be's Dat Way Sometime': The Sexual Politics of Women's Blues," in *Unequal Sisters: A Multicultural Reader in U.S. Women's History,* ed. Ellen Carol DuBois and Vicki L. Ruiz (New York: Routledge, 1990): 238–49; E. Franklin Frazier, *The Negro Family in the United States,* rev. and abr. ed. (Chicago: University of Chicago Press, 1966), 273–75.

27. Ueda, *Avenues to Adulthood,* 132–36; Modell, *Into One's Own,* 71–72; McGovern, "The American Woman's Pre-World War I Freedom in Manners and Morals," 315–33; Rosenberg, *Beyond Separate Spheres,* 190–92. George Kneeland, "Asks Women to Aid Girls in Vice Peril," *New York Times,* June 17, 1914: 3; Winthrop D. Lane, "Under Cover of Respectability: Some Disclosures of Immorality among Unsuspected Men and Women," *Survey,* March 25, 1919: 746–49; Edith Livingston Smith and Hugh Cabot, M.D., "A Study in Sexual Morality," *Journal of Social Hygiene* 4 (October 1919): 534–36; Erenberg, *Steppin' Out,* (quote) 77–78; Mabel Ulrich, Lectures to Social Morality Institute, "First Lecture," February 25, 1915, (quote) p. 12, "Constructive Preventive Work through Moral Education," February 25, 1915, (quote) p. 8, Record Files Collection, Reel 155.3, YWCA of the U.S.A., National Board of Archives, New York.

28. Jane Deeter Rippin, "Social Hygiene and the War: Work with Women and Girls," *Journal of Social Hygiene* 5 (January 1919): 136. Many of the camp followers were detained by the government for prostitution or infection with venereal disease, and these young women usually had little education and few occupational skills. But according to observers, many young women from middle-class homes also joined the ranks of the camp followers. Madeleine Hooton, a probation officer in Binghamton, New York, reported in 1919 that the "wayward girls she had worked with before the war came from the poorest classes," but since the war "the wayward girls with whom I have had to deal come from different classes, namely: from the middle and so-called upper classes." Hooton's observations were echoed by Henrietta Additon, the assistant director of the federal government's detention program, who remarked that some of the camp followers were the daughters of "well-to-do" families. These young women were not prostitutes who received money for sex; rather, they were "charity girls" who "[go] with the soldier in return for dinner, automobile rides, or any present" he might give them. And Jennie Harris, a physician involved in the government's campaign against venereal disease,

complained that "girls apparently of good families drive up in their cars and invite the soldiers who happen to be along the roadside near the camp to come to supper to a roadhouse or the nearest city." Hooton is quoted in Mrs. Mortimer Menken, Chair, "The Wayward Girl," *Proceedings of the New York State Conference of Probation Officers* (1919): 285; Henrietta S. Additon, "Work among Delinquent Women and Girls," *Annals of the American Academy of Political and Social Science* 79 (1918): 155; Jennie H. Harris, M.D., "The Prostitute in Relation to Military Camps," *Woman's Medical Journal* 27 (1918): 125.

29. Modell, *Into One's Own*, 85–96; Fass, *The Damned and the Beautiful*, 201–3, 262–68; Phyllis Blanchard and Carlyn Manasses, *New Girls for Old* (New York: MacCaulay, 1930), 1–3, 66–72. Robert S. Lynd and Helen Merrell Lynd, *Middletown: A Study in Modern American Culture* (New York: Harcourt Brace Jovanovich, 1929), 134–43.

30. William Graebner, "Outlawing Teenage Populism: The Campaign against Secret Societies in the American High School, 1900–1960," *Journal of American History* 74 (1987): 411–35; Lynd and Lynd, *Middletown*, 211–22; Fass, *The Damned and the Beautiful*, 84–86; Blanchard, *New Girls for Old*, 25, 36–40, 45.

31. Peiss, *Cheap Amusements*, 108–14; Meyerowitz, *Women Adrift*, 102–4; D'Emilio and Freedman, *Intimate Matters*, 197, 242–48; Mary Richmond, *The Adolescent Girl: A Book for Parents and Teachers* (New York: Macmillan, 1925), (quote) 113; Blanchard and Manasses, *New Girls for Old*, 77, 82, 89, 90–91; Modell, *Into One's Own*, 115–18; Fass, *The Damned and the Beautiful*, 262–68; Lorinne Pruette, "The Flapper," in *The New Generation: The Intimate Problems of Modern Parents and Children*, ed. V. F. Calverton and Samuel D. Schmalhausen (New York: Macaulay, 1930), 379.

32. Peiss, *Cheap Amusements*, 63; Mary Ryan, *Womanhood in America: From Colonial Times to the Present* (New York: Franklin Watts, New Viewpoints Press, 1979), chap. 5; Joan Jacobs Brumberg, *Fasting Girls: The Emergence of Anorexia Nervosa as a Modern Disease* (Cambridge, Mass.: Harvard University Press, 1988), 238–48; Bailey, *From Front Porch to Back Seat*, 25–31; Modell, *Into One's Own*, 85–88, 89, 92. Mary Louise Roberts offers a nuanced analysis of fashion in 1920s France in "Samson and Delilah Revisited: The Politics of Women's Fashion in 1920s France," *American Historical Review* 98 (1993): 657–84.

33. Peiss, *Cheap Amusements*, 68–72; Ewen, *Immigrant Women in the Land of Dollars*, 208–11; Smith, *Family Connections*, 94–107; Marjorie Roberts, "Italian Girls on American Soil," *Mental Hygiene* 13 (1929):757–68; Ruth S. True, *The Neglected Girl* (New York: Russell Sage, 1914), 104–13.

34. Julia Kramer, Bedford Hills, 1928, history blank; Sophie Polentz, Bedford Hills, 1924, history blank; Janine Rosen, Bedford Hills, 1926, history blank; Rosa Covello, Bedford Hills, 1926, history blank.

35. D'Emilio and Freedman, *Intimate Matters*, 259.

36. Althea Davies, Bedford Hills, 1924, history blank; Margaret Jackson, Bedford Hills, 1924, history blank.

37. According to Steven Mintz and Stephanie Kellogg, the new ideal offered children "greater freedom from parental control, greater latitude in expressing their feelings, and increased interaction of adolescents with peers." *Domestic Revolutions*, (quote) 114, 115–17; D'Emilio and Freedman, *Intimate Matters*, 229–35; Marilyn Dell Brady, "The New Model Middle-Class Family (1815–1930)," in *American Families: A Research Guide and*

Historical Handbook, ed. Joseph M. Hawes and Elizabeth I. Nybakken (Westport, Conn.: Greenwood Press, 1991), 103–8.

38. Mabel A. Wiley, *A Study of the Problem of Girl Delinquency in New Haven* (New Haven, Conn.: The Civic Federation of New Haven, 1915), 16–17; see also D'Emilio and Freedman, *Intimate Matters,* 263.

39. John Modell, "Dating Becomes the Way of American Youth," in *Essays on the Family and Historical Change,* ed. Leslie Page and Gary D. Stark (Arlington: Texas A & M University Press, 1983), 95–102, (quote) 109, 115; Bailey, *From Front Porch to Back Seat,* 87–96.

40. Peiss, *Cheap Amusements,* 69–72; Ewen, *Immigrant Women in the Land of Dollars,* 212–14; Meyerowitz, *Women Adrift,* 104.

41. Lena Meyerhoff, Bedford Hills, 1924, Jewish Board of Guardians report, September 8, 1924. Nora Patterson, Bedford Hills, 1919, girl's statement. Nora's statement to a Bedford staff member was transcribed as follows: "Wanted to marry each other but parents thought they were too young so they had sexual intercourse."

42. Ella Waldstein, Bedford Hills, 1917, Laboratory of Social Hygiene, information concerning the patient, staff meeting, October 13, 1917.

43. Louisa Parsons. See file of sister, Margaret Parsons, Albion, 1924, letter from father to Governor Smith, June 6, 1923, about daughter Louisa, who was sent to Albion two years before Margaret; the letter was forwarded to Albion and placed in the file of Margaret Parsons. I was not able to locate Louisa's file.

44. Rae Rabinowitz, Bedford Hills, 1917, intake interview; Laboratory of Social Hygiene, information concerning the patient, girl's statement, verified history.

45. Eleanor Hamlisch, Bedford Hills, 1917, Laboratory of Social Hygiene, information concerning the patient. Cecilia Tomasi, Bedford Hills, 1928, letter to George Palmer, superintendent of Bedford Hills, from Rochester Catholic Charities, February 16, 1928. Mr. Tomasi's sentiments were paraphrased by a home visitor from the Rochester Catholic Charities who investigated Cecilia's home at the request of the Reformatory for Women at Bedford Hills.

46. Louise Peffley, Albion, 1915, intake interview.

47. Ella Waldstein, Bedford Hills, 1917, Laboratory of Social Hygiene, information concerning the patient, mental examination.

48. Although most delinquent young women's claims of rape were never investigated or validated, the staff at Bedford Hills accepted Rae Rabinowitz's account, noting that "her naive description of what happened would seem to indicate that she is truthful in making that statement." Rae Rabinowitz, Bedford Hills, 1917, Laboratory of Social Hygiene, staff meeting, mental examination.

49. Emily Carrington, Albion, 1925, admission ledger, court record, intake interview; Almira Danvers, Albion, 1919, admission ledger, intake interview; Myra Henning, Bedford Hills, 1924, New York City Probation Department investigation; Doris Sugarman, Bedford Hills, 1919, Laboratory of Social Hygiene, verified history, warrant of commitment.

50. Louise Peffley, Albion, 1915, intake interview.

51. Eileen McCarthy, Bedford Hills, 1926, psychiatrist's interview, January 30, 1929, p. 1.

52. Patricia O'Brien, Bedford Hills, 1922, New York City Probation Department investigation, intake interview, history blank.

53. Meyerowitz, *Women Adrift,* 39–84; Rosen, *The Lost Sisterhood,* 156–61; Tentler, *Wage Earning Women,* 13–25. Timothy Gilfoyle has argued that the rate of working-class young women's involvement in prostitution declined during the early twentieth century as wages gradually improved. Gilfoyle, *City of Eros,* 311.

54. Rosen, *The Lost Sisterhood,* 167.

55. Meyerowitz, *Women Adrift,* 141.

56. Eleanor Hamlisch, Bedford Hills, 1917, Laboratory of Social Hygiene, mental exam.

57. Nanette Wilkins, Bedford Hills, 1923, intake interview, history blank.

58. Marian Jacoby, Bedford Hills, 1919, girl's statement, case history.

2. "The Confusion of Standard among Adolescent Girls": Reformers Confront the Girl Problem

1. Mabel Ulrich, Lectures to Social Morality Institute, "The Child and the Young Girl," February 27, 1915, p. 10, Record Files Collection, Reel 155.3, YWCA of the U.S.A., National Board Archives, New York. The reference to prostitution as a "living death" was made by the Moral Survey Committee of Syracuse, *The Social Evil in Syracuse* (Syracuse, N.Y.: n.p., 1913), 16.

2. See Meyerowitz, *Women Adrift,*

3. Quotations are from Helen M. Slocum, "The Causes of Prostitution," *Woman's Journal,* January 18, 1879: 22. See also Ellen Battelle Dietrick, "Rescuing Fallen Women," *Woman's Journal,* May 27, 1893: 162; B. O. Flower, "Wellsprings and Feeders of Immorality," *Arena* 12 (May 1895): 337–51; Meyerowitz, *Women Adrift,* chap. 3; Freedman, *Their Sisters' Keepers,* 40–45.

4. Quotation from the mission statement of the (New York City) Salvation Army Rescue Home in New York State Board of Charities, *Manual and Directory of Charities* (New York: Wynkood Hallenbach Crawford Co., state printers, 1899), 563. Committee on the Elevation of the Poor in Their Homes, *Moral Elevation of Girls: Suggestions Relating to Preventive Work* (New York: State Charities Aid Association, 1885); Eugenia C. Lekkerkerker, *Reformatories for Women in the United States* (The Hague, Batavia: J. B. Wolters, 1931), chap. 5; Louise Rockwood Wardner, "Girls in Reformatories," *Proceedings of the Annual Conference of Charities* (1879).

5. Committee on the Elevation of the Poor in Their Homes, "Moral Elevation of Girls," 37–50, 58–65; New York State Board of Charities, *Manual and Directory,* 160, 194, 257–58, 348, 370–71, 388, 556–65, 574, 615–16, 618, (quote) 619, 620, 662–63, 719; Freedman, *Their Sisters' Keepers,* 57.

6. Committee on the Elevation of the Poor in Their Homes, "Moral Elevation of Girls," 18–19, 21; Peiss, *Cheap Amusements,* 170–78; See also Rev. Frank M. Goodchild, "The Social Evil in Philadelphia," *Arena* 15 (March 1896): 574–86.

7. Clifford Roe, "Warfare against the White Slave Trade," in *War on the White Slave Trade: A Book Designed to Awaken the Sleeping and to Protect the Innocent,* ed. Ernest A. Bell (Chicago: Charles C. Thompson, 1909), 141. Edwin A. Sims, "Menace of the White

Slave Trade," in ibid., 69; Connelly, *The Response to Prostitution in the Progressive Era*, 122–127; Rosen, *The Lost Sisterhood*, 42–43, 47–48, and chap. 7.

8. Harriet McDoual Daniels, *The Girl and Her Chance: A Study of Conditions Surrounding the Young Girl between Fourteen and Eighteen Years of Age in New York City* (New York: Fleming H. Revell, 1914), 9; Robert A. Woods and Albert J. Kennedy, ed., *Young Working Girls: A Summary of Evidence from Two Thousand Social Workers* (Boston: Houghton Mifflin, 1913).

9. Woods and Kennedy, *Young Working Girls*, 1, 4–5.

10. Ibid., 1–7, 101–12, 108.

11. G. Stanley Hall, *Adolescence: Its Psychology* (New York: D. Appleton, 1904; 2d ed., 1928), 1: xii–xiv, 342; 2: 72–73, 108–9, 625.

12. G. Stanley Hall, "Some Practical Points in the Psychology of Sex," in Committee on Hygiene of Sex, *Hygiene of Sex* (Boston: Health-Education League, 1910); G. Stanley Hall, *Educational Psychology* (New York: D. Appleton, 1911), 16. Hall's description of female adolescence is quoted in Dorothy Ross, *G. Stanley Hall: The Psychologist as Prophet* (Chicago: University of Chicago Press, 1972), 339; Hall, *Adolescence*, 1: 370–71.

13. Woods and Kennedy, *Young Working Girls*, 6–8.

14. Ibid., 2–3. In a similar study, the social worker Ruth True denounced parental practices that failed to keep adolescent girls in ghetto neighborhoods from recklessly pursuing fulfillment of their developing passions. Immigrant parents forced their daughters into employment at an early age, denying them any opportunity for recreation or pleasure. Homes became filled with "wrangling and spite" as daughters fought to retain control over their wages, their use of free time after work, and their choice of companions. And as True pointed out, once the bond between parents and daughter was broken, little stood between the girl and her search to satisfy the new and "insistent needs and desires of her womanhood." Ruth True, *The Neglected Girl* (New York: Russell Sage, 1914), 47–56, 58.

15. Woods and Kennedy, *Young Working Girls*, 6–8, 85–87.

16. See Rosen, *The Lost Sisterhood*, 15, 41–44; Connelly, *The Response to Prostitution*, 15–18, 35–38.

17. Committee of Fifteen, *The Social Evil; with Special Reference to Conditions Existing in the City of New York*, 2d ed. (New York: G.P. Putnam's Sons, 1912), 10; Massachusetts Commission for the Investigation of the White Slave Traffic, So-Called, *Report of the Commission for the Investigation of the White Slave Traffic, So-Called*. House Document 2281 (Boston: Wright and Potter State Printers, 1914), 43–44.

18. Rosen, *The Lost Sisterhood*, 41; Nicholas Fischer Hahn, "The Defective Delinquency Movement: A History of the Born Criminal in New York State, 1850–1966" (Ph.D. diss., State University of New York at Albany, 1978), 280–83, 324–26.

19. Pittsburgh Morals Efficiency Commission, *Report and Recommendations of the Morals Efficiency Commission* (Pittsburgh, 1913), 32, 34.

20. Wisconsin Legislative Committee on White Slave Trade and Kindred Subjects, *Report and Recommendations* (1914), 103.

21. Quoted in Daniels, *The Girl and Her Chance*, 7, 11.

22. True, *The Neglected Girl*, 58. See also Julian W. Mack, "Social Progress," *Survey*, July 6, 1912: 511–16.

23. Louise de Koven Bowen, *The Road to Destruction Made Easy in Chicago* (Chicago:

Juvenile Protective Association, 1916); New York Committee of Fourteen, *The Social Evil in New York City: A Study of Law Enforcement* (New York: Andrew H. Kellogg, 1910), 2–4. On prostitution as a business in which numerous parties (including the police) profited by flattering, making false promises to, or financially exploiting young women, see George Kneeland, *Commercialized Prostitution in New York City* (New York: Macmillan, 1913), chaps. 4 and 7; Howard B. Woolston, *Prostitution in the United States* (New York: Century Company, 1921; repr., Montclair, N.J.: Patterson Smith, 1969), 204–6; Massachusetts Commission, *Report of the Commission for the Investigation of the White Slave Traffic*, 20–22; Tessa L. Kelso, *Clause 79: Report to Committee of Woman's Municipal League of the City of New York* (New York, 1911), 16. On the pervasiveness of prostitution in the working-class and immigrant neighborhoods of New York City see Timothy Gilfoyle, *City of Eros: New York City, Prostitution, and the Commercialization of Sex, 1790–1920* (New York: Norton, 1992), 35–36, 39, 50–53, 213–18, 219–21, 239–41.

24. By World War I, forty-four states had passed laws against white slavery. See George E. Worthington, "Developments in Social Hygiene Legislation from 1917 to September 1, 1920," *Journal of Social Hygiene* 6 (1920): 558. On regulatory developments in New York City and other cities in New York see Committee of Fourteen, *The Social Evil in New York City*, 59, 68–70, (quote) 153–54, 193; Syracuse Vice Commission, *The Social Evil in Syracuse*, 90–91; "Dance Hall Law in Operation," *Survey*, April 11, 1911: 12; Maude Miner, "Social Hygiene," *Proceedings of the National Conference of Charities and Correction* (1914), 199–203; John P. Peters, D.D., "The Story of the Committee of Fourteen of New York," *Journal of Social Hygiene* 7 (1918): 347–88; Maria Ward Lambin, *Report of the Advisory Dance Hall Committee* (New York, 1924), 13–14, 18–22; Willoughby Cyrus Waterman, *Prostitution and Its Repression in New York City, 1900–1931* (New York: Columbia University Press, 1932; repr. New York: AMS Press, 1968), 151–53; Gilfoyle, *City of Eros*, 304–5; Peiss, *Cheap Amusements*, 179–80; Elisabeth Israels Perry, *Belle Moskowitz: Feminine Politics and the Exercise of Power in the Age of Alfred E. Smith* (New York: Oxford University Press, 1987), 41–56, 67–73.

25. "Protective Leagues for the Girls of New York," *The Survey*, January 31, 1914: (quote) 519; Maude Miner, "The Girls' Protective League," *Proceedings of the National Conference of Charities and Correction* (1915): 261–67; Sabina Marshall, "Girls' Protective Work," in *Social Work Yearbook, 1929*, ed. Fred S. Hall (New York: Russell Sage, 1930), 1: 176–78.

26. Daniels, *The Girl and Her Chance*, 74–84, 88–95; Albert J. Kennedy and Kathryn Farra, *Social Settlements in New York City: Their Activities, Policies, and Administration* (New York: Columbia University Press, 1935), chap. 2 and App. C; Helen J. Ferris, *Girls' Clubs, Their Organization and Management: A Manual for Workers* (New York: E.P. Dutton, 1918).

27. T. J. Woofter, *Negro Problems in Cities* (New York: Doubleday, Doran, 1928; repr., New York: Negro Universities Press, 1969), 253–57; Dorothy Salem, *To Better Our World: Black Women in Organized Reform, 1890–1920* (Brooklyn, N.Y.: Carlson, 1990), 45–46.

28. Wisconsin, Legislative Committee on White Slave Traffic and Kindred Subjects, *Report and Recommendations* (1914), 109. Kennedy and Woods, *Young Working Girls*, 94–95; Maude Miner, "How to Reach the Girls," in Committee on Hygiene of Sex, Massa-

chusetts State Conference of Charities, *Hygiene of Sex* (Boston: Health Education League, 1910): 21–25; Charles Bitwell, "The Current Movement for Sex Education and Hygiene," *Proceedings of the National Conference of Charities and Corrections* (1912), 264–66; Special Committee on Sex Education, "How Shall We Teach?" *Journal of Social Hygiene* 2 (1916): 573–81; Bryan Strong, "Ideas of the Early Sex Education Movement in America," *History of Education Quarterly* 12 (1972): 129–61.

29. Young Women's Christian Association, *Report of the Commission on Social Morality from the Christian Standpoint* (1913), 3–8, Record Files Collection, YWCA of the U.S.A., National Board Archives, New York. During the war the YWCA merged its sex-education efforts with the the federal government's Section on Women's Work, a part of the Social Hygiene Division of the Commission on Training Camp Activities. All together, the YWCA lecturers organized in the War Work Council gave 6,197 lectures to 969,217 women and distributed over 280,000 pamphlets. See Social Morality Committee, War Work Council, *Report, June 1917 to July 1919* (1919), 3–4, 67–69, 75–76, Reel 154.5, YWCA Record Files Collection.

30. Rachelle Yarros, "Experiences of a Lecturer," *Journal of Social Hygiene* 5 (1919): 213; Katharine Bement Davis, "Women's Part in Social Hygiene," *Journal of Social Hygiene* 4 (1918): 532–42; see also Anna L. Brown, "Facing Facts" (February 1918), 2, Reel 154.5, YWCA Record Files Collection.

31. Church Mission of Help, Jewish Board of Guardians (JBG), and New York Protective and Probation Association (NYPPA) are described in *The Greenwood Encyclopedia of American Institutions: Social Service Organizations*, ed. Peter Romanofsky (Westport, Conn.: Greenwood Press, 1978), 379–81, 331–34, 290–92. See also the published annual reports of the JBG and the NYPPA. Additional information may be gathered from Anne T. Bingham, "The Psychiatric Work of the New York Probation and Protective Association," *Mental Hygiene* 6 (1922): 539–74; Girls' Service League of America, *For Girls: Jobs, Friends, Shelter, Understanding* (New York, 1928): 1–25 and App. On the techniques of modern social work and the social worker's obligation to take account of individual differences see Mary Richmond, *Social Diagnosis* (New York: Russell Sage Foundation, 1917), esp. 365–70; William Healy, M.D., *The Individual Delinquent* (Boston: Little, Brown, 1915).

32. The best general discussion of the work of police women may be found in Chloe Owings, *Women Police: A Study of the Development and Status of the Women Police Movement* (New York: Frederick H. Hitchcock, 1925), ix-xviii, chap. 6 and 7. See also Maude Miner, "The Policewoman and the Girl Problem," *Proceedings of the National Conference of Social Work* (1919), 134–39; Mina Van Winkle, "Standardization of the Aims and Methods of the Work of Policewomen," *Proceedings of the National Conference of Social Work* (1929), 151–54; Maude Miner, "A Community Program for Protective Work," *Proceedings of the National Conference of Social Work* (1920), 141–48; Jane Deeter Rippin, "Social Hygiene and the War: Work with Women and Girls," *Journal of Social Hygiene* 5 (1919): 125–36.

33. Belle Lindner Israels, "The Way of the Girl," *The Survey*, July 3, 1909: 493.

34. Peiss, *Cheap Amusements*, 171–84; Meyerowitz, *Women Adrift*, 79–91.

35. Julia Kramer, Bedford Hills, 1928, letter from Jewish Board of Guardians to Superintendent George Palmer, March 2, 1928; Jewish Board of Guardians, social history, June 28, 1928; copy of letter from Girls' Service League to Inwood House, March 25, 1926.

36. On the efforts of other states to gain control of adolescent girls and boys see Lawrence Veiller, *The Adolescent Offender: A Study of the Age Limit of the Children's Court* (New York: Charity Organization Society of the City of New York, 1923), 27–33. On efforts in other states to remodel prostitution laws so as to make them reach "all promiscuous sex delinquents" see American Social Hygiene Association, *Social Hygiene Legislation Manual, 1921* (New York: 1921 with 1925 supplement), 18, 15–17, 51–55.

37. Roger Biles, "Lawrence Turnure Veiller," in *Biographical Dictionary of Social Welfare in America*, ed. Walter I. Trattner, (Westport, Conn.: Greenwood Press, 1986), 731–33; Pamela Roby, "Politics and Prostitution: A Case Study of the Formulation, Enforcement, and Judicial Administration of the New York State Penal Laws on Prostitution, 1870–1970" (Ph.D. diss., New York University, 1971), 129–33.

38. The Committee of Fourteen was made up of prominent religious leaders, activists in the Anti-Saloon League, and leaders of various community associations. By the 1910s the committee included six women: Mary Kingsbury Simkovitch, a prominent setttlement worker and advocate of parks and playground reform; Belle Lindner Israels, leader of the Committee on Amusements; Maude Miner, founder of the New York Probation and Protective Association; Mrs. John M. Glenn, a Charity Organization Society leader; Mrs. Barclay Hazard, a municipal reformer; and Ruth Standish Baldwin, a clubwoman interested in promoting probation work with African Americans. Waterman, *Prostitution and Its Repression in New York City*, 96; Perry, *Belle Moskowitz*, 67.

39. Ilene Sterling, Bedford Hills, 1917, Laboratory of Social Hygiene, staff meeting, verified history, information of patient, information of committing judge, information of mother, mental examination.

40. Rae Rabinowitz, Bedford Hills, 1917, Laboratory of Social Hygiene, staff meeting; Rosa Covello, Bedford Hills, 1926, record of commitment, history blank, admission record.

41. Evelyn Blackwell, Bedford Hills, 1926, history blank, letter from Gladys Mendum, social worker for State Charities Aid Association, to Amy Prevost, parole officer for Bedford Hills and the (Episcopal) Church Mission of Help, October 13, 1926. Deborah Herman, Bedford Hills, 1925, Church Mission of Help summary report, October 31, 1925, history blank—girl's statement.

42. Ella Waldstein, Bedford Hills, 1917, Laboratory of Social Hygiene, staff meeting; Lena Meyerhoff, Bedford Hills, 1924, preliminary investigation, New York City Magistrate's Court. After her arrival at Bedford Hills, Lena reported that she did not know who the father of her child was but that the father was not J. Smith. See admission record.

43. *Laws of 1882*, chap. 410, section 1466; *Laws of 1886*, chap. 353; *Laws of 1903*, chap. 436; *Laws of 1914*, chap. 445. For a brief discussion of the laws see Paul W. Tappan, *Delinquent Girls in Court: A Study of the Wayward Minor Court of New York* (New York: Columbia University Press, 1947), 44–47.

44. Parents outside of New York City could also place their daughters in private reformatories, often without going to the courts. By the late nineteenth century, private reformatories or asylums for "erring" women and girls operated in Albany, Brooklyn, Buffalo, Elmira, Rochester, Syracuse, Troy, and Westchester, as well as in Manhattan. New York State Board of Charities, *Manual and Directory*.

45. Millicent Potter, Albion 1900, see unlabeled printed form filled out by the police

justice of Tonawanda, N.Y.; Penelope Jaros, Albion, 1916, letter from mother to Superintendent Flora P. Daniels, October 15, 1917, warrant of commitment; Eva Pomering, Albion, 1918, record of conviction, intake interview, letter from Mrs. William More Decker, former employer of Eva's older sister, to Superintendent Flora P. Daniels, December 2, 1919.

46. New York, *Laws of 1923*, chap. 868. In the year ending June 30, 1921, only 7.69% of Bedford Hills's new inmates were "incorrigible girls," having been convicted of violating the New York City statute. By 1925, however, 23.6% of Bedford's new inmates were Wayward Minors; in 1928 the percentage was 26.6%. Commitments to Albion under the new law were slow at first. In the year ending June 30, 1924, only 7.8% of the inmates admitted that year were Wayward Minors; yet in 1928 28.6% of the new inmates at Albion were Wayward Minors. Although these statistics do not tell us who testified against the girls in court, it is probably safe to assume that parents, not police, acted as complainants in the majority of cases. New York State Reformatory for Women at Bedford Hills, *Twenty-first Annual Report* (Albany, 1922), 16, and *Twenty-fifth Annual Report* (Albany, 1926), 14; Albion State Training School, *Thirty-first Annual Report* (Albany, 1925), 16; State Commission of Corrections, *Second Annual Report* (Albany, 1928), 519.

47. Veiller, *The Adolescent Offender*, 35; Lawrence Veiller, "Senator Schackno's Wayward Minor Bill, Statement for the Governor's Legal Adviser," May 9, 1923, *Bill Jacket Collection 1923*, chap. 868, Reel 1923 8, New York State Library Legislative Reference Section, Albany, N.Y., pp. 2, 6. The preventive associations and women's groups endorsing the Wayward Minor Act included the Big Sisters (Protestant, Catholic, and Jewish divisions), Women's City Club, Women's Prison Association, Young Women's Christian Association, New York Probation and Protective Association, Women's Municipal League, New York City Federation of Women's Clubs, and the Harlem Council of Women, among others. The names of these organizations were listed in the statement Veiller prepared for Senator Schackno; researchers may also read the organizations' actual letters of support, which form part of the bill jacket collection.

48. *People v. Sullivan*, 200 N.Y. Suppl. 214 (1923).

49. Two years later the Wayward Minors Act was extended to apply to males as well as females. New York, *Laws of 1925*, chap. 389.

50. Bruce W. Cobb, *Inferior Criminal Courts Act, Annotated* (New York: Macmillan, 1925), 157–58; Lawrence Veiller, "Proposed Wayward Minor Bill, Statement for the Governor's Legal Adviser," January 26, 1923, *Bill Jacket Collection*, 1923, chap. 868, Reel 1923 8, pp. 1–2.

51. Young women were occasionally adjudged wayward minors and committed to reformatories on the basis of police rather than parental testimony. See, for example, Janine Rosen, Bedford Hills, 1926, history blank; Cynthia Romer, Bedford Hills, 1926, admission record, history blank.

52. Maude E. Miner, "The Problem of Wayward Girls and Delinquent Women," *Proceedings of the American Academy of Political Science* 2 (1911–12), 130, 135; Honorable William McAdoo, "Women Offenders in New York," *Proceedings of the National Conference of Charities and Corrections* (1912), 228–30; Jean Norris, "Methods of Dealing with Women Offenders," *NYU Law Review* 3 (March 1926): 31–39.

53. Comment by Alice C. Smith, Probation Officer, Night Court for Women, New York City, "Round Table Discussion: Girls and Women on Probation," in New York State Probation Commission, *Eighth Annual Report and Proceedings* (1914), 174.

54. Edwin J. Cooley, *Probation and Delinquency: The Study and Treatment of the Individual Delinquent* (New York: Thomas Nelson, 1927), 30. See also Edwin J. Cooley, "The Administrative versus the Treatment Aspects of Probation," *Proceedings of the National Conference of Social Work* (1920), 155.

55. Comment by Alice C. Smith, "Roundtable Discussion: The Relation of the Probation Officer to the Families of Probationers (with Special Reference to Women and Girls)," in New York State Probation Commission, *Ninth Annual Report and Proceedings* (1915), 296.

56. "Roundtable Discussion: Probation in Cases of Women," in New York State Probation Commission, *Sixth Annual Report and Proceedings* (1912), 244.

57. Anna Levinson, Bedford, 1924, report prepared by the Jewish Board of Guardians, March 18, 1925, and sent to Bedford Hills.

58. Roby, "Politics and Prostitution," 39–44.

59. Roby, "Politics and Prostitution," 66; Committee of Fourteen, *Annual Report for 1915* (New York, 1916), 3.

60. Under New York City's prohibition against "disorderly conduct," police were to keep prostitutes from "loitering or being in any thoroughfare or public place for the purpose of prostitution or solicitation to the annoyance of the inhabitants or passers-by." New York, *Laws of 1882*, chap. 410, sect. 1458. Elsewhere in the state police made fairly effective use of the state's vagrancy law to protect the public from harrassment and vice. See also Roby, "Politics and Prostitution," 65–68; Waterman, *Prostitution and Its Repression*, 12–13, 19.

61. Waterman, *Prostitution and Its Repression*, 13.

62. Cornelius Cahalane, *Police Duty: A Course of Study for Policemen Everywhere* (New York: Chief Publishing, 1912), 107; Kneeland, *Commercialized Prostitution in New York City*, chap. 7.

63. The Tenement House Act passed in 1901 and amended in 1909 and 1913 permitted the arrest of women who solicited or committed prostitution inside tenement houses, but detectives and police officers were reluctant to act against these women because of the difficulties involved in testifying in court. Entrapment was not yet an accepted legal practice; nevertheless, magistrates generally required that a police officer testifying against a woman in court "swear not only that he was solicited to enter, but that he did enter the tenement house, paid a money consideration, and that the prostitute actually exposed her person for the purpose named. . . . [The officers] are frequently subjected to rigid cross-examination . . . and efforts are often made by magistrates to belittle their testimony and they are ridiculed and humiliated." The police officers' reluctance to participate in entrapment also undermined a second intent of the tenement-house law: without proof that prostitutes were operating in tenements, the police could not prosecute tenement owners for permitting prostitution on their premises. Committee of Fourteen, *The Social Evil in New York City*, 14–15, 16–18; Waterman, *Prostitution and Its Repression in New York City*, 94–95.

64. Committee of Fourteen, *The Social Evil in New York City*, 5, 12–13. See also

Committee of Fifteen, *The Social Evil with Special Reference to Conditions Existing in the City of New York*, 152, 157.

65. Syracuse Moral Survey Committee, *The Social Evil in Syracuse*, 53.

66. Committee of Fourteen, *Annual Report for 1915*, 3.

67. In 1916 the newly amended Section 887.4 accounted for only 9.6% of all arraignments in the Manhattan Women's Court, the tribunal specially designated for females charged with prostitution, intoxication or drug use, incorrigibility, and petit larceny. Arraignments under the older laws accounted for 53.8% of the total. By 1920 the vagrancy arraignments had increased to 23.2% of the total, while arraignments under the old laws had decreased to 40.31%. And by 1930 vagrancy arraignments in the Women's Court had jumped to 57.7%, while charges under the other laws dropped to a mere 2.2% of the total. Board of City Magistrates, City of New York, *Annual Report for 1916*, 185, *Annual Report for 1920*, 118, *Annual Report for 1930*, 111.

68. Vice officers usually arrested women under the amended vagrancy statute, but the sanctioning of entrapment also enhanced their ability to arrest women under the tenement-house law and disorderly-conduct statutes. Waterman, *Prostitution and Its Repression*, 53–55.

69. Frances Brewer, Bedford, 1926, history blank.

70. Marian Jacoby, Bedford, 1919, case history, girl's statement.

71. Caroline Browning, Bedford, 1924, history blank.

72. Yvonne was discharged from Bedford six weeks after her commitment after successfully appealing her case. The particulars of the court appeal are not in her file. Yvonne Waters, Bedford Hills, 1917, Laboratory of Social Hygiene, girl's statement, information concerning patient, staff meeting.

73. Frank Harris, "The American Inquisition," *Pearson's Magazine*, (4-part series) February, March, April, May, 1917; Malcolm Cowley, "The Vice Squad Carries On," *New Republic*, (2-part series) June 25, 1930, July 2, 1930; (N.Y.) Supreme Court Appellate Division, First Judicial Department, *In the Matter of the Investigation of the Magistrates' Courts in the First Judicial Department and the Magistrates Thereof, and of Attorneys-at-law Practicing in Said Courts, Final Report of Samuel Seabury, Referee, New York, March 28, 1932* (New York, 1932).

74. Waterman, *Prostitution and Its Repression in New York City*, 126–30.

75. In an attempt to prevent venereal infection from undermining the fighting strength of American forces, Congress passed Section 13 of the Selective Service Act in May 1917, ordering the Commission on Training Camp Activities (CTCA) to suppress commercial prostitution near the nation's training camps. Later that year, the CTCA established the Committee on Protective Work for Girls (CPW) to supervise young women who went to the camps, ostensibly for legitimate employment, and to prevent them from engaging in illicit relations with soldiers. When the committee was deemed inadequate, having failed to protect girls "from the excitement and thoughtlessness produced by the emotions of war playing upon the emotions of sex," the CTCA did not hesitate to abandon "protection," placing "suppression" in its stead. The CTCA reorganized the CPW under a new name—the Law Enforcement Division of the Section on Women and Girls (SWG)—assigning it the task of apprehending all young women who were suspected of promiscuity, prostitution, or venereal infection. To aid the federal

government's campaign, some cities close to military camps imposed nine-o'clock curfews on all women. Other communities prohibited young women from spending time in the company of soldiers or sailors except where the men and women were related or where women carried a letter of permission from their parents or guardians. Connelly, *The Response to Prostitution*, 137–50; Hobson, *Uneasy Virtue*, 165–83; War and Navy departments, U.S. Commission on Training Camp Activities, *Documents Regarding Alcoholic Liquors and Prostitution in the Neighborhood of Military Camps and Naval Stations* (Washington, D.C., 1917), 5–6, 9–10, 14–15; Maude Miner, "Protective Work for Girls in War Time," *Proceedings of the National Conference of Social Work* (1918), 657–58; Lane, "Girls and Khaki: Some Practical Measures of Protection for Girls in Wartime," *The Survey*, December 1, 1917: (quote) 236; Henrietta Additon, "Work among Delinquent Women and Girls," *Annals of the American Academy of Political and Social Science* 79 (1918): 153.

76. Cobb, *Inferior Criminal Courts Act*, (quote) 151.

77. Fass, *The Damned and the Beautiful*, 15–51; D'Emilio and Freedman, *Intimate Matters*, chaps. 10 and 11; Hale, *Freud and the Americans*, 257–71; Modell, *Into One's Own*, 67–76.

78. George Kneeland, "Asks Women to Aid Girls in Vice Peril," *New York Times*, June 17, 1914: 3; Winthrop D. Lane, "Under Cover of Respectability: Some Disclosures of Immorality among Unsuspected Men and Women," *The Survey*, March 25, 1916: 746–49.

79. The growing prominence of mental hygiene in the 1920s is discussed in a number of secondary works, including Murray Levine and Adeline Levine, *A Social History of Helping Services: Clinic, Court, School and Community* (New York: Appleton-Century-Crofts, 1970), chap. 10; David A. Rothman, *Conscience and Convenience: The Asylum and Its Alternatives in Progressive America* (Boston: Little Brown, 1980), 303–6; Fred Matthews, "In Defense of Common Sense: Mental Hygiene as Ideology and Mentality in Twentieth-Century America," *Prospects* 4 (1979): 467–80; Margo Horn, *Before It's Too Late: The Child Guidance Movement in the United States, 1922–45* (Philadelphia: Temple University Press, 1989), 15–22; Hamilton Cravens, "Child Saving in the Age of Professionalism, 1915–1930," in *American Childhood: A Research Guide and Historical Handbook*, ed. Joseph M. Hawes and N. Ray Miner (Westport, Conn.: Greenwood Press, 1985), 453–62; Kathleen Jones, "'As the Twig Is Bent': American Psychiatry and the Troublesome Child, 1890–1940" (Ph.D diss., Rutgers University, 1988).

80. Gerald Pearson summarized the sentiments of his colleagues on repressive parenting, especially as it related to adolescence, when he wrote, "Serious problems in adolescence result in part from the way in which the pre-adolescent child has been prepared for adult adjustment and in part from the attitude of the parents during the adolescent period." Pearson, "What the Adolescent Girl Needs in Her Home," *Mental Hygiene* 14 (January 1930): 51. Important contemporary critiques of parenting may also be found in William Healy, *Mental Conflicts and Misconduct* (Boston: Little, Brown, 1917); Miriam Van Waters, *Youth in Conflict* (New York: Republic Publishing, 1926), chap. 2; Phyllis Blanchard and Carlyn Manasses, *New Girls for Old* (New York: Macauley, 1930), chap. 9; Helen Williston Brown, "The Deforming Influences of the Home," *Journal of Abnormal Psychology* 12 (April 1917): 49–57; Frankwood E. Williams, *Adolescence: Studies in Mental Hygiene* (New York: Farrar and Rinehart, 1930), chap. 3. On the relationship between

mental conflict and mental illness, especially in youths, see William A. White, M.D., "Childhood: The Golden Period for Mental Hygiene," *Mental Hygiene* 4 (April 1920): 258; Virginia P. Robinson, "A Changing Psychology in Social Casework" (Ph.D. diss., University of Pennsylvania, 1930), 35–36; Bernard Glueck, "Psychoanalysis and Child Guidance," *Mental Hygiene* 14 (1930): 816–18.

81. Matthews, "In Defense of Common Sense," 462. See also Van Waters, *Youth in Conflict*, 227–29; Robinson, "A Changing Psychology," chaps. 8 and 10.

82. Anne T. Bingham, "The Personal Problems of a Group of Workers," *Proceedings of the National Conference of Social Work* (1920), 351; White, "Childhood," 264–67; Mary C. Jarret, "Psychiatric Social Work," *Mental Hygiene* 2 (April 1918): 288–89; Bernard Glueck, "The Psychoanalytic Approach," in *Sex in Civilization*, ed. V. F. Calverton and S. D. Schmalhausen (Garden City, N.Y.: Garden City Publishing, 1929), 474–75; Cravens, "Child Saving," 458.

83. Phyllis Blanchard, *The Adolescent Girl: A Study from the Psychoanalytic Viewpoint* (New York: Moffat, Yard, 1920), 211.

84. Jessie Taft, "Mental Hygiene Problems of Normal Adolescence," *Mental Hygiene* 5 (1921): 741–43. Taft directed the Department of Child Study of the Children's Aid Society in Philadelphia, an important provider of social services to children, especially adolescent girls. See also Samuel D. Schmalhausen, "Family Life: A Study in Pathology," in *The New Generation*, ed. V. F. Calverton and Samual D. Schmalhausen (New York: Macauley, 1930), 287; John Burnham, *Paths into American Culture: Psychology, Medicine, and Morals* (Philadelphia: Temple University Press, 1988), 84–85.

85. Pearson, "What the Adolescent Girl Needs in Her Home," 42.

86. Winifred Richmond, *The Adolescent Girl* (New York: Macmillan, 1926), 43, 58; Taft, "Mental Hygiene Problems of Normal Adolescence," 747–49.

87. E. Van Norman Emery, "Revising Our Attitude toward Sex," *Mental Hygiene* 11 (1927): 329; Ruth Kimball Gardiner, "Your Daughter's Mother," *Journal of Social Hygiene* 6 (1920): 542. See also Blanchard and Manasses, *New Girls for Old*, 33, 94–96; Richmond, *The Adolescent Girl*, 42.

88. Richmond, *The Adolescent Girl*, 58.

89. Blanchard and Manasses, *New Girls for Old*, 44; Taft, "Mental Hygiene Problems of Normal Adolescence," 743, 750.

90. For example, Ruth Kimball Gardiner, a sex educator and ally of mental hygiene, observed that "mothers are often puzzled to know what in the world boys and girls find so interesting in the interminable, pointless, give-and-take conversations." Yet, Gardiner continued, "if the careless boy friendships can be continued through adolescence, it is a thing for which a mother may give thanks." Gardiner, "Your Daughter's Mother," 553.

91. On adolescent girls' essentially conformist goals see Blanchard, *New Girls for Old*, 13–14, 44–45; Van Waters, *Youth in Conflict*, 127–37; Richmond, *The Adolescent Girl*, 145. On the basic need of every individual to gain social acceptance and find a place in society, see Taft, "Mental Hygiene Problems of Normal Adolescence," 742; Bernard Glueck, "The Psychoanalytic Approach," in *Sex in Civilization*, 476–78; Bernard Glueck, "Psychoanalysis and Child Guidance," *Mental Hygiene* 14 (1930): 818; Williams, *Adolescence*, 13–18.

92. Blanchard, *New Girls for Old*, 44–45.

93. For Blanchard's comments on the positive results of petting, see ibid., 61, and "Sex

in the Adolescent Girl," in *Sex in Civilization*, ed, V. F. Calverton and S. D. Schmalhausen (Garden City, N.Y.: Garden City Publishing, 1929), 549. On girls' avoidance of intercourse, see Blanchard, "Sex in the Adolescent Girl," 542. A survey of adolescent girls conducted by Blanchard in 1929 and 1930 showed that most young women and girls were far too concerned with "personal security"—that is, with the threat of an unwanted pregnancy and social or familial ostracism—to engage in intercourse. Blanchard queried 252 young women, most of them college students, teachers, and clerical workers, about their opinions and practices in social and sexual matters. Only 20% of the 252 girls who answered her questionnaire considered petting or necking a "routine part of a girl's relationship with boys." Moreover, only 7% of the entire group "were willing to permit themselves indulgence in extra-marital intercourse." *New Girls for Old*, 69–70, 73–76, 138–39, 251–52, 263. See also Van Waters, *Youth in Conflict*, 249–56; Taft, "The Mental Hygiene Problems of Normal Adolescence," 749–50; Grace Loucks Elliott, *Understanding the Adolescent Girl* (New York: Henry Holt, 1929), 45–47.

94. Blanchard, "Sex in the Adolescent Girl," 557; Pearson, "What the Adolescent Girl Needs in Her Home," 47–48; Taft, "Mental Hygiene Problems of Normal Adolescence," 745–46, 749. See also Henry C. Schumacher, "The Unmarried Mother: A Socio-Psychiatric Viewpoint," *Mental Hygiene* 11 (1927): 779. William I. Thomas claimed that in most cases of sexual delinquency "sexual passion does not play an important role. . . . sexual intercourse is something submitted to with some reluctance and embarassment and something she is glad to be over with." William I. Thomas, *The Unadjusted Girl: With Cases and Standpoint for Behavior Analysis* (Boston: Little, Brown, 1923), 109. Thomas, a Chicago sociologist, did not work in a clinic setting, but he was an influential figure in mental-health circles and was particularly important in the professional development of Jessie Taft. See Rosenberg, *Beyond Separate Spheres*, 120–31.

95. Van Waters, *Youth in Conflict*, 249–56; Perkins, "Mental and Moral Problems of the Woman Probationer," *Mental Hygiene* 8 (1924): 512–14; Elizabeth Greene, "Results of Five Years' Psychiatric Work in New York City High Schools," *Mental Hygiene* 11 (1927), 551–56; Anne T. Bingham, "The Personal Problems of a Group of Workers," *Proceedings of the National Conference of Social Work* (1920), 349–51.

96. George S. Stevenson, "Psychiatric Clinics for Children," in *Social Work Yearbook, 1929*, ed. Fred S. Hall (New York: Russell Sage), 1: 339; Anne T. Bingham, "The Application of Psychiatry to High School Problems," *Mental Hygiene* 9 (1925): 1–27; Greene, "Results of Five Years' Psychiatric Work in New York City High Schools," 542–47; Austen Fox Riggs and William B. Terhune, "The Mental Health of College Women," *Mental Hygiene* 12 (1928): 559–68.

97. Bingham, "The Personal Problems of a Group of Workers," 346–52; Anne T. Bingham, "What Can Be Done for the Maladjusted?" *Mental Hygiene* 4 (1920): 422–35; Anne T. Bingham, "The Psychiatric Work of the New York Probation and Protective Association," *Mental Hygiene* 6 (1922): 539–74; Augusta Scott, "Three Hundred Psychiatric Examinations Made at the Women's Day Court, New York City," *Mental Hygiene* 6 (1922): 343–69; Eleanor Harris Wembridge, "Work with Socially Maladjusted Girls," *Journal of Abnormal Psychology* 17 (April-June 1922): 79–87; Jean Norris, "Methods of Dealing with Women Offenders," *New York University Law Review* 3 (1926): 31–39; Sabina Marshall, "Girl's Protective Work," *Social Work Yearbook*, 1929, 176–78. Alice Menken, *On the Side of Mercy* (New York: Covici, Friede,1933), 97; Girls' Service League

of America, *For Girls: Jobs, Friends, Shelter, Understanding* (New York:, n.p., 1928), 7, App.

98. Martha P. Falconer, "Report of the Social Hygiene Committee," *Proceedings of the National Conference of Charities and Correction* (1915), 248; Mrs. Mortimer Menken, *Proceedings of the New York State Conference of Probation Officers* (1915), 196; Hastings H. Hart, *Proceedings of the New York State Conference of Charities and Correction* (1917), 162–63. Some social workers and reformers recommended that feebleminded women be placed in custodial institutions for the duration of their fertile years to prevent them from bearing illegitimate children and burdening private and public welfare agencies with demands for economic and social assistance. See Nicholas Fischer Hahn, "The Defective Delinquency Movement: A History of the Born Criminal in New York State, 1850–1966" (Ph.D. diss., State University of New York at Albany, 1978), chap. 8. On the tendency to blame feeblemindedness for delinquency see Bernard Glueck, "The Causes of Delinquency," *Proceedings of the National Conference of Social Work* (1918), 157; Edith N. Burleigh, "Some Principles for Parole for Girls," *Proceedings of the National Conference of Social Work* (1918), 153.

99. Julia Kramer, Bedford Hills, 1928, summary of psychiatric exam provided to reformatory by Inwood House, February 21, 1928; Naomi Gorstein, Bedford Hills, 1927, preliminary investigation of New York City Probation Department.

100. Scott, "Three Hundred Psychiatric Examinations," 352, 366.

3. "Every Minute Is to Me Like Eternity": Inmates at Albion and Bedford Hills

1. Western House of Refuge for Women at Albion, N.Y., *Twenty-fifth Annual Report* (Albany: J. B. Lyon, 1919), 4.

2. Although Freedman, Brenzel, and Rafter highlight the social-control agendas of reformatory and prison founders and administrators, they recognize the potential for inmate resistance. None of these historians, however, has closely studied inmates' responses to institutionalization. As Freedman admits, "The most difficult problem in prison history is reconstructing the inmate experience" (*Their Sister's Keepers*, 100). Brenzel, *Daughters of the State*; Rafter, *Partial Justice*.

3. Women were committed to Bedford Hills and Albion, regardless of their specific offense, for a so-called "indeterminate" sentence that was to last for a maximum of three years. State law left it to the reformatories' boards of managers to decide, in consultation with reformatory staff, what portion of the three years each inmate ought to spend in the reformatory and what portion might be spent on parole. New York, *The State Charities Law*, chap. 605.

4. Western House of Refuge for Women, *Twenty-fourth Annual Report* (1918), 9; Amos Baker, "Modern Institutional Treatment of Inmates in a Women's Reformatory," *Proceedings of the New York State Conference of Probation Officers* (1925), 176.

5. Western House of Refuge for Women, *Twenty-fourth Annual Report* (1918), 9–10; Baker, "Modern Institutional Treatment," 176.

6. Western House of Refuge for Women, *Twenty-first Annual Report* (1915), 10; Baker, "Modern Institutional Treatment," 176.

7. Deborah Herman, Bedford Hills, 1925, history blank, intake interview.

8. Sophie Polentz, Bedford Hills, 1924, monthly reports.

9. Baker, "Modern Institutional Treatment," 176.

10. Freedman, *Their Sister's Keepers*, 56–57, 68–71, 131–32; Rafter, *Partial Justice*, 33–35; Brenzel, *Daughters of the State*, 24–25, 69–70; Eugenia C. Lekkerkerker, L.D., *Reformatories for Women in the United States* (The Hague: J. B. Wolters, 1931), 289–306.

11. Western House of Refuge for Women, *Twenty-seventh Annual Report* (1921), 10.

12. New York State Reformatory for Women at Bedford Hills, *Seventh Annual Report* (Albany: J. B. Lyon, 1908), 26–29; Western House of Refuge for Women, *Sixteenth Annual Report* (1910), 15–17.

13. Western House of Refuge for Women, *Twenty-fourth Annual Report* (1918), 10. At Albion, the reformatory's "scholastic" teachers specialized in different subjects, each working with the different grades. For example, during the mid-1920s, one teacher taught arithmetic, spelling, and civics; a second taught English, penmanship, and music; and the third taught reading, geography, physiology, and hygiene. Classes in the morning were for the first through fifth grades; in the afternoons, for those in the sixth through eighth grades. Throughout its history, Albion also gave individualized instruction in reading and writing to inmates who were illiterate or unfamiliar with the English language. Albion State Training School, *Thirtieth Annual Report* (Albany, 1924), 13, *Thirty-second Annual Report* (Albany, 1926), 10. Academic instruction at Bedford was similarly organized although it did not offer individualized instruction: inmates were placed in the reformatory's primary school (grades 1–3), intermediate school (grades 4–5), or advanced school (grades 6–9) according to their capabilities and prior instruction. According to Bedford's annual report for 1916–17, the primary school generally "contains foreigners just learning English, southern colored girls who have little education, and white Americans who have not attained a higher grade, usually because of inability to learn." New York State Reformatory for Women, *Seventeenth Annual Report* (1918), 17.

14. Katharine B. Davis served as Bedford's superintendent from 1901 until 1913, when she became the commissioner of correction for New York City. For further discussion of Davis's background and administrative goals and innovations see Freedman, *Their Sisters' Keepers*, 130–34. Changes in the vocational offerings at the two institutions were generally noted in their annual reports to the New York legislature.

15. Albion State Training School, *Thirty-third Annual Report* (1926), 10.

16. Baker, "Modern Institutional Treatment," 178; Albion State Training School, *Thirty-first Annual Report* (1925), 10, and *Thirtieth Annual Report* (1924), 13; New York State Reformatory for Women, *Fifth Annual Report* (1906), 31, and *Thirteenth Annual Report* (1914), 22–23.

17. Western House of Refuge for Women, *Tenth Annual Report*, (1904), 6; New York State Reformatory for Women," *Twenty-third Annual Report* (1924), 9–10.

18. For example, Albion inmates were supplied with a printed sheet titled "Rules Governing Girls of the Western House of Refuge." See illustration 2. Rules sheet in inmate case file for Eva Pomering, Albion 1918.

19. Albion imposed a centralized marking system in 1916. Prior to that year, each cottage had separate standards for removing the demerits on inmates' names. New York State Commission of Prisons, *Twenty-second Annual Report* (Albany, 1916), 104–6, and *Twenty-third Annual Report* (Albany, 1917), 93–94. Bedford implemented a somewhat different marking system in 1920, allowing inmates to accumulate marks (and recogni-

tion) for "good" behavior but penalizing them for "bad" behavior. This marking system underwent revision in 1922. New York State Commission of Prisons, *Twenty-sixth Annual Report*, (1920), 147; New York State Reformatory for Women, *Twenty-second Annual Report* (1922), 4.

20. According to Flora Daniels, these sanctions were not meant to inflict suffering; rather, they were intended "to help a girl to discipline herself . . . [and see] wherein she has done wrong and . . . that she is being justly punished." Western House of Refuge for Women, *Twenty-second Annual Report* (1917), 9–10.

21. (New York) State Commission of Prisons, "Report to the Governor Relative to the Investigation and Inquiry into Allegations of Cruelty to Prisoners in the New York State Reformatory for Women, Bedford Hills," *Annual Report* (1920), 67–103. The issue of brutal treatment at Bedford Hills is discussed at length below.

22. My understanding of the censorship system at the two reformatories comes entirely from my reading of the case files. All inmates at both institutions were required on arrival to sign statements giving permission to the institutions' censors to read all mail and open all packages. Further discussion of censorship as it affected the experience of the inmates follows in Chapter 4.

23. Ester Bromwell, Bedford Hills, 1917, Laboratory of Social Hygiene, mental examination.

24. It is difficult to be precise in judging and categorizing the behavior of inmates because descriptions of their conduct were sometimes inconsistent. An inmate described as generally "good" might still have been punished for numerous minor infractions. An inmate described as "fair" might have been an "honors" cottage resident who "had no disciplinary record."

25. Susan Rivington, Albion, 1901, admission ledger; Nellie Weston, Albion, 1915, admission ledger; Nora Patterson, Bedford Hills, 1919, conduct record; Merced Borja, Bedford Hills, 1926, conduct record.

26. Nora Patterson, Bedford Hills, 1919, letter to mother written in Jefferson Market jail, n.d.

27. All of Merced's correspondence was written in Spanish. Bedford Hills had it translated into English by an officer at Sing Sing Prison. The Bedford censor then read it and decided which letters ought to be retained and which might be sent to their intended recipients. Merced Borja, Bedford Hills, 1926, letter to female friend, June 21, 1926.

28. Grace Demerest, Bedford Hills, 1917, "Daily Notes." Treatment for gonorrhea in this case included sulpho-napthol douches, pertassium permanganate douches, applications of silver nitrate, and the use of ichthammol tampons.

29. Merced Borja, Bedford Hills, 1926, letter from Merced to Superintendent Amos Baker, November 9, 1926.

30. Patricia O'Brien, Bedford Hills, 1922, letter from Patricia to Superintendent Amos Baker, n.d.

31. Brenzel, *Daughters of the State*, 148–49; Freedman, *Their Sisters' Keepers*, 47–49.

32. Western House of Refuge for Women, *Eleventh Annual Report* (1905), 16.

33. New York State Reformatory for Women, *First Annual Report* (1902), 18.

34. Edward T. James, ed., *Notable American Women, 1607–1950: A Biographical Dictionary* (Cambridge, Mass.: Belknap Press of Harvard University Press, 1971), 1: 439.

35. New York State Reformatory for Women, *Fourth Annual Report* (1905), 24. Curtin is quoted in Western House of Refuge for Women, *Eleventh Annual Report* (1905), 17. See also the *Sixth Annual Report* (1900), 18, and *Seventh Annual Report* (1901), 6–7, 18–19.

36. At Albion, teachers and matrons also complained that refractory inmates disturbed the other girls and imperiled their reform. Western House of Refuge for Women, *Seventeenth Annual Report* (1911), 7. Staff members at Bedford complained that with the decline in the quality of their inmates they were often forced to labor for a full year or more "to bring a young woman into a state of mind where she is receptive of good influences." New York State Reformatory for Women, *Sixth Annual Report* (1907), 16–18. Throughout the 1900s and 1910s Bedford's concern with unmanageable and "hardened" inmates was also manifested in the statistical sections of its annual reports which obsessively enumerated the prior arrests and incarcerations of each inmate sent to the reformatory. According to the New York State Charities Law, judges were supposed to commit to the reformatories at Albion and Bedford Hills only those women who were "not insane or mentally or physically incapable of being benefitted by the discipline of either of such institutions." New York, *Laws of 1896*, chap. 546; *Laws of 1903*, chaps. 169 and 453.

37. New York State Reformatory for Women, *Sixth Annual Report* (1907), 17.

38. Susan Rivington, Albion, 1901, admission ledger.

39. Freedman, *Their Sisters' Keepers*, 116–21; Rafter, *Partial Justice*, 67–74; Nicholas Fischer Hahn, "The Defective Delinquency Movement: A History of the Born Criminal in New York State, 1850–1966" (Ph.D. diss., State University of New York at Albany, 1978), chaps. 3–5.

40. Western House of Refuge for Women, *Eighteenth Annual Report* (1912), 15, and *Nineteenth Annual Report* (1913), 15; New York State Reformatory for Women, *Eleventh Annual Report* (1912), 10.

41. Flora P. Daniels, who replaced Curtin in 1916, arranged for psychiatric and intelligence tests, which showed extraordinarily high rates of mental defect among Albion's inmates. The initial examinations showed that 152 (82.1%) of 185 inmates at Albion suffered from "nervous or mental abnormalities"; 62 of the 152 were distinctly "feebleminded." State Commission of Prisons, "Special Reports: Mental Disease and Delinquency," *Twenty-fourth Annual Report* (1918), 69–71.

42. Polly Overton, Albion, 1915, psychological examination.

43. On feebleminded inmates at Bedford Hills see Katharine Bement Davis, "A Study of Prostitutes Committed from New York City to the State Reformatory for Women, Bedford Hills," in George Kneeland, *Commercialized Prostitution in New York City* (New York: Century, 1913), 196–98, 234; New York State Reformatory for Women, *Ninth Annual Report* (1910), 21, and *Tenth Annual Report* (1911), 19–21, 53–58, 62–65.

44. Freedman, *Their Sisters' Keepers*, 118–19.

45. New York State Reformatory for Women, *Seventeenth Annual Report* (1918), 16.

46. Lekkerkerker, *Reformatories for Women*, 180.

47. Ilene Sterling, Bedford Hills, 1917, Laboratory of Social Hygiene, staff meeting.

48. Ester Bromwell, Bedford Hills, 1917, Laboratory of Social Hygiene, mental examination, staff meeting.

49. "Report to the Governor Relative to the Investigation and Inquiry into Allegations of Cruelty to Prisoners in the New York State Reformatory for Women, Bedford

Hills," in State Commission of Prisons, *Twenty-sixth Annual Report* (1920), 78. On the purpose and methods of treatment in the psycopathic hospital at Bedford Hills see Edith R. Spaulding, *An Experimental Study of Psychopathic Delinquent Women* (New York: Rand McNally, 1923), 1, 17, 50–51, 63.

50. After examining the impact of Davis's departure from Bedford Hills, Eugenia Lekkerkerker, the Dutch legal scholar, concluded, "It was hard to find a successor possessing the same ability to cope with the trying problems of the institution and at the same time having the same scientific vision of the work which Dr. Davis had." Lekkerkerker, *Reformatories for Women*, 108.

51. (New York) State Board of Charities, *Report of the Special Committee . . . to Investigate Charges Made against the New York State Reformatory for Women at Bedford Hills* (Albany, 1915), 7.

52. Ibid., 7–8, 10, 12–13, 18–19, 21, 26–27.

53. Lekkerkerker noted in her 1931 study that in the years following Davis's departure from Bedford Hills there was "no real co-operation between the Laboratory and the reformatory staff." Lekkerkerker, *Reformatories for Women*, 108.

54. State Board of Charities, *Report of the Special Committee*, 18.

55. Ibid., 18–19, 26–27; New York State Reformatory for Women, *Seventeenth Annual Report* (1918), 8, 16. For additional discussion of homosexuality among female prison and reformatory inmates see Margaret Otis, "A Perversion Not Commonly Noted," *Journal of Abnormal Psychology* 8 (1913): 113–16; Charles A. Ford, "Homosexual Practices of Institutionalized Females," *Journal of Abnormal Psychology* 23 (1929): 442–48.

56. I cannot determine the precise point at which black inmates began to be excluded from the reformatory's business classes but am fairly certain that this exclusion was routine during the 1920s. I have found two cases in which black inmates of "normal" intelligence asked pointedly for business training; staff members concluded, however, that they had reached their "limit" in education and recommended training in housework and industrial sewing. Caroline Browning, Bedford Hills, 1924; Margaret Jackson, Bedford Hills, 1924.

57. "Dr. Davis Answers Bedford Charges," *New York Times*, March 12, 1915: 16.

58. Western House of Refuge for Women, *Nineteenth Annual Report* (1913), 15; State of New York, Joint Committee of the Legislature, *Report of Investigation of the Joint Committee of the Legislature Concerning the Management, Conduct, and Affairs of the Western House of Refuge for Women at Albion, N.Y.* (Albany: J. B. Lyon, 1920), 7–8. On Bedford Hills, see Lekkerkerker, *Reformatories for Women*, 109.

59. New York State Prison Commission, *Thirty-first Annual Report* (1925), 167.

60. New York State Commission of Prisons, "Report to the Governor Relative to the Investigation into Allegations of Cruelty to Prisoners in the New York State Reformatory for Women, Bedford Hills," *Twenty-sixth Annual Report* (1920), 79. During the 1920s occasional mental tests and psychiatric interviews were conducted by nonresident practitioners to develop a "psychological profile" of inmates and thus, as in the decade before, suggest how they might respond to the demands of the reformatory. But frequently the exam or interview was not conducted until the inmate was to be considered for parole. (New York) State Commission of Prisons, *Thirtieth Annual Report* (1924), 155, and *Thirty-second Annual Report* (1926),137; Baker, "Modern Institutional Treatment," 177.

61. The division's significance lies primarily in the fact that the women committed to

it were subject, at least theoretically, to lifelong commitment. In fact, most of the inmates were paroled and eventually discharged and thus still followed the basic reformatory program, but at a slower pace than the other inmates. Nicholas Hahn argues that the extreme restlessness of the women in the Division for Mentally Defective Delinquents at Bedford was the principal reason that the state closed the division in 1931 and made Albion into an institution solely for mentally defective delinquent women. No longer surrounded by women who were expected to return to the outside world, the inmates at the redesigned Albion were expected to resign themselves to their confinement. Hahn, "The Defective Delinquency Movement," 468–71.

62. "150 Women in Race Riot at Bedford," *New York Times*, July 25, 1920: 1, 16. David M. Kennedy, *Over Here: The First World War and American Society* (New York: Oxford University Press, 1980), 281–84, 289; William M. Tuttle, *Race Riot: Chicago in the Red Summer of 1919* (New York: Atheneum, 1970).

63. State Board of Charities, *Report of the Special Committee*, see esp. pp. 27–28.

64. (New York) State Commission of Prisons, *Annual Report* (1918), 122. Albion also made special arrangements for difficult inmates, reserving ten cells along a "punishment corridor" in its reception building for the segregation of these young women. State Commission of Prisons, *Thirty-second Annual Report* (1926), 134.

65. "Dragged by Hair Bedford Girl Says," *New York Times*, December 13, 1919: 3.

66. State Commission of Prisons, "Report to the Governor Relative to the Investigation and Inquiry into Allegations of Cruelty to Prisoners in the New York State Reformatory for Women," *Twenty-sixth Annual Report* (1920), 67–105, (quote) 68; Rafter, *Partial Justice*, 80–81; "150 Women in Race Riot at Bedford," *New York Times*, July 25, 1920: 1, 16.

67. Bedford's board of managers declared the riot "the result of the legislative investigation, the newspaper accounts and the prominence given to some of the girls, which caused a spirit of insubordination and violence." New York State Reformatory for Women, *Twenty-first Annual Report* (1922), 1. During and after the legislative investigation, conditions at Bedford were discussed at great length in the public media. New York's governor Alfred E. Smith complained in the public media that "the handcuffing of young women and the so-called 'water cure' cannot be tolerated in the light of advanced thought. . . . in this enlightened age punishment of inmates of state institutions by the harsh and cruel methods of the Dark Ages cannot be tolerated." See "Asks Reformatory Heads Be Ousted," *New York Times*, March 19, 1920: 6. Eugenia Lekkerkerker concluded that Bedford's inmates exploited the "sensational fashion" in which the 1916 investigation was covered by the public media, and became increasingly rebellious over the next several years until the events of 1919 and 1920 forced the institution to alter its disciplinary procedures. Lekkerkerker, *Women in Reformatories*, 108–9.

68. "Plans Humane Bedford," *New York Times*, April 24, 1921: II, 6.

69. My assessment of Amos Baker is based on the reformatory's annual reports from the 1920s and, more important, on his correspondence with parolees, family members, and social workers. In comparison to Flora P. Daniels at Albion and Leo Palmer, Baker's successor, Superintendent Baker usually made an effort to understand the perspective of delinquent girls and their kin, sometimes bending the reformatory's rules when he felt

that it would be beneficial to do so. Interaction with family members and parolees is discussed at length in Chapters 4 and 5.

70. Rae Rabinowitz, Bedford Hills, 1917, conduct record; Melanie Burkis, Bedford Hills, 1928, monthly summaries.

71. Melanie Burkis, Bedford Hills, 1928, monthly summaries.

72. Rae Rabinowitz, Bedford Hills, 1917, letter to Rae from "Mama Blondie," November 11, 1920. This letter was sent to Rae during her second stay at Bedford, after she had been returned to the reformatory for violating parole.

73. Ella Waldstein, Bedford Hills, 1917, conduct record.

74. Florence Pirelli, Bedford Hills, 1927, monthly reports, summary of application for parole.

75. Rae Rabinowitz, Bedford Hills, 1917, conduct record.

76. Melanie Burkis, Bedford Hills, 1928, monthly report summaries, conduct record.

77. Marian Jacoby, Bedford Hills, 1919, disciplinary record.

78. Eva Pomering, Albion, 1918, rules sheet with notes to sister on front and back.

79. Ibid.

80. Lekkerkerker, *Women in Reformatories*, 237.

81. Renate Friedman, Bedford Hills, 1917, daily notes, application for parole.

82. Gertrude Leavitt, Bedford Hills, 1922, monthly progress report summaries, recommendation for recommitment, petition certificate of mental defect and orders, conduct record.

83. Bedford's annual reports show that 9 women were discharged from the regular reformatory and recommitted to the division for mental defectives in the first half of 1923, the first year of the division's operation. From July 1, 1923, to June 30, 1924, 11 women were recommitted. And from July 1, 1924, to June 30, 1925, 7 women were recommitted. Statistics for subsequent years were not published. The division closed in 1931 when Albion became an institution entirely for mentally defective female delinquents. New York State Reformatory for Women, *Twenty-third Annual Report* (1924), 16, *Twenty-fourth Annual Report* (1925), 16, and *Twenty-fifth Annual Report* (1926), 7.

84. New York State Reformatory for Women, *Twenty-second Annual Report* (1923), 3, 7.

85. Sophie Polentz, Bedford Hills, 1924, letter from Superintendent Amos Baker to Mrs. Menken at the Jewish Board of Guardians, December 15, 1925.

4. "I Live in Hopes of Her Come from There a Better Daughter": Families and the Reformatories

1. Of the 100 inmates in this study, at least 74 received and sent correspondence that was approved by institutional censors. Neither Bedford Hills nor Albion kept regular records of correspondence, and it is likely that young women for whom there is no clear evidence of correspondence also received and sent letters. I found evidence or mention of inmates' correspondence with family members or others outside the reformatories in censored letters, letters received from or sent to reformatory officials by family members or spouses, and (in some Bedford files only) lists compiled by staff of letters sent and received by individual inmates. Inmates corresponded often with a mother (20 of

74) or another female relative (22 of 74); less commonly with both parents (4), a father (4), male relative (2), spouse (5), fiancé (1), social worker (1), or past employer (1). In seven cases, I could not determine the identity of inmates' primary correspondent. Fragmentary evidence suggests that 6 inmates received letters weekly, 16 received letters biweekly, 9 received letters monthly, 7 received letters less than once per month. Inmates at both reformatories were usually allowed to write one or two letters per month. At least 39 of the 100 young women received visits from family members; as with correspondence, the records on visitation are incomplete and young women for whom there is no evidence of visitation may actually have received visitors. In most cases inmates were visited by their mothers, stepmothers, or other female relatives (22 of 39); sometimes these women were accompanied by the inmates' fathers, brothers, or spouses. Inmates were less commonly visited by fathers, male relatives, spouses, and fiancés unaccompanied by female relations (13 of 39). Finally, at least 65 of the 100 inmates had relatives who corresponded (sometimes frequently, sometimes very occasionally) with reformatory officials.

2. See for example the file of Anna Levinson, Bedford Hills, 1924, correspondence record. One of the reformatory officers noted on Anna's correspondence record that Mrs. Levinson "will have nothing more to do with her." But Mrs. Levinson decided to end contact with Anna only after the young woman had been returned to Bedford Hills for violating parole.

3. Alva Burrows, Albion, 1929, letter from Mrs. Burrows to Superintendent Flora P. Daniels, February 25, 1929.

4. Alva Burrows, Albion, 1929, letter from Mrs. Burrows to Superintendent Flora P. Daniels, July 30, 1929.

5. Alva Burrows, Albion, 1929, letter from Mrs. Burrows to Superintendent Nellie Coon, February 5, 1930.

6. Alva Burrows, Albion, 1929, reply to Mrs. Burrows from Superintendent Nellie Coon, February 14, 1930.

7. Estelle Freedman, Nicole Hahn Rafter, and Barbara Brenzel do not address the issue of parental intervention in the reform process in their recent analyses of women's prisons and reformatories. However, Kathleen W. Jones in her study of the Judge Baker Clinic in Boston found a fascinating dynamic between parents and mental-hygiene professionals. Middle-class parents who took their children or adolescents to the mental-hygiene facility for help in overcoming behavioral problems used the clinic "to foster their own positions and accommodate adult needs." But Jones found little evidence of confrontation between parents and professionals, and, in contrast to the reformatories, the mental hygienists proved highly responsive to the needs of middle-class parents. "Through their concerns and their needs, parents bent and shaped the profession's intent on scientifically studying and treating youths." In mental-hygiene clinics, parents were authentic clients who asked and paid for a service to be performed by psychologists or psychiatrists. In the case of the reformatories, the true client was the state, which depended on the reformatories to discipline delinquent girls. Jones, "As the Twig Is Bent: American Psychiatry and the Troublesome Child, 1890–1940" (Ph.D. diss., Rutgers University, 1988), 256, 258.

8. Nanette Wilkins, Bedford Hills, 1923, letter from Amos T. Baker to aunt, June 25, 1923. In later correspondence Nanette would refer to her guardian as her "cousin."

9. Edith Parnell, Albion, 1911, letter from Superintendent Alice Curtin to married sister of Edith Parnell, December 5, 1911.

10. Robert S. Pickett, *House of Refuge: Origins of Juvenile Reform in New York State, 1815–1857* (Syracuse, N.Y.: Syracuse University Press, 1969); Gordon, *Heroes of Their Own Lives*, chap. 2; Christine Stansell, *City of Women: Sex and Class in New York, 1789–1860* (Urbana: University of Illinois Press, 1987), chap. 10; Homer Folks, *The Care of Destitute, Neglected, and Delinquent Children* (New York: Macmillan, 1902).

11. *Young Working Girls: A Summary of Evidence from Two Thousand Social Workers*, ed. Robert A. Woods and Albert J. Kennedy (Boston: Houghton Mifflin, 1913), 2–3; Ruth True, *The Neglected Girl* (New York: Russell Sage, 1914), 47–56, 58; Eugene Kinckle Jones, "Negro Migration in New York State," *Opportunity*, January 1926: 10; Ethel McGhee, "The Northern Negro Family," *Opportunity*, June 1927: 176–78; Wisconsin Legislative Committee on White Slave Trade and Kindred Subjects, *Report and Recommendations* (1914), 103.

12. Phyllis Blanchard, "Sex in the Adolescent Girl," in *Sex in Civilization*, ed. V. F. Calverton and S. D. Schmalhausen (Garden City, N.Y.: Garden City Publishing, 1929), 557; Gerald Pearson, "What the Adolescent Girl Needs in Her Home," *Mental Hygiene*, 14 (1930): 47–48.; Jessie Taft, "Mental Hygiene Problems of Normal Adolescence," *Mental Hygiene* 5 (1921): 745–46, 749. See also Henry C. Schumacher, "The Unmarried Mother: A Socio-Psychiatric Viewpoint," *Mental Hygiene* 11 (1927): 779.

13. In my sample of 100 cases, reformatory authorities found that only 28 fathers had questionable or poor "habits," i.e., a history of chronic unemployment, drunkenness, or adultery. Ten fathers had been convicted or imprisoned for criminal activity. Even fewer mothers (13) were found to have questionable or poor "habits," and only 2 mothers had criminal records.

14. Eleanor Hamlisch, Bedford Hills, 1917, "Verified History."

15. Albion State Training School, *Thirtieth Annual Report* (1924), 9.

16. Alice Arlington, Albion, 1917, letter from Alice's mother to the inmate, February 20, 1919.

17. Eva Pomering, Albion, 1918, letter to Eva from younger sister, October 16, 1919.

18. Rae Rabinowitz, Bedford Hills, 1917, letter from Superintendent Anna Talbot to Rae's sister, February 4, 1921. The offending letter from Rae was withheld from the mail but not retained in Rae's file.

19. Blanche Preston, Bedford Hills, 1923, letter from Blanche addressed to "Dear Aunt," June 15, 1923.

20. Polly Overton, Albion, 1915, letter from Superintendent Daniels to Mrs. Overton, May 11, 1917. The letter sent to Polly from her mother read: "Oh Dear I am heart Broek. I lost one and you gone and this poor thing hear. there are days she feels good and yesterday she feanted and was up and down all day. . . . yesterday she said to me oh Mamma if I am going to be sick like this all the time I wish I would dye now. i try and laugh at her and make fun but it is killing me." Letter from Mrs. Overton to Polly, May 10, 1917.

21. For example, Margaret Slattery, a highly respected author of advice books for young women and their mothers, declared in 1913, "It is the right of every girl to receive the protection of wise parental authority." While they remained young, Slattery argued, girls should not be left "to decide life's most important questions, while parents, weak,

indifferent, or careless sleep until it is too late." Slattery, *The Girl and Her Religion* (New York: Pilgrim Press, 1913), 7.

22. Jones, "As the Twig," 222.

23. Lena Meyerhoff, Bedford Hills, 1924, letter from Superintendent Baker to Mrs. Meyerhoff, October 17, 1924.

24. Penelope Jaros, Albion, 1916, letter from Mrs. Jaros to Superintendent Flora P. Daniels, October 15, 1917.

25. Sophie Polentz, Bedford Hills, 1924, letter from Mr. Polentz to Sophie, June 17, 1925.

26. Ibid., letter from Mr. Polentz to Sophie, October 31, 1925.

27. David Rothman, *The Discovery of the Asylum: Social Order and Disorder in the New Republic*, rev. ed., (Boston: Little, Brown, 1990), 288.

28. The high frequency of intervention within my sample is probably not representative. In choosing inmate case files I tended to favor those with a lot of correspondence; otherwise my reading of the files would have turned up little of value. Much of that correspondence dealt with families' attempts to intervene in the reform process. Readers are thus warned not to attach too much importance to the frequency of intervention here. On the other hand, I do believe that the tone and nature of familial intervention is extraordinarily revealing of familial expectations and attitudes toward delinquent women.

29. Elizabeth Oliver, Albion, 1902, letter from Elizabeth's father to Superintendent Alice Curtin, January 3, 1904.

30. Alice Arlington, Albion, 1917, letter from attorney (Syracuse, N.Y.) to Superintendent Flora P. Daniels, April 18, 1918.

31. Sophie Polentz, Bedford, 1924, letter from Mr. Polentz to Superintendent Amos Baker, May 7, 1925.

32. Eva Pomering, Albion, 1918, letter from older sister to "President of Parole Board," December 3, 1919; letter from younger sister to Eva, April 20, 1920.

33. Paula Brownell, Albion, 1926, letter from Paula's stepfather to Superintendent Flora Daniels, July 8, 1927.

34. Letter from Louise's mother to William Dye, president of Albion's board of visitors January 29, 1917.

35. Althea Davies, Bedford Hills, 1924, letter from married sister to Superintendent Amos Baker, October 29, 1924.

36. Ella Waldstein, Bedford Hills, 1917, letter from Ella's brother to Miss Cobb, December 2, 1918.

37. Nora Patterson, Bedford Hills, 1919, letter from Mr. Patterson to Miss Cobb, November 30, 1919.

38. Sophie Polentz, Bedford Hills, 1924, letter from Mr. Polentz to Superintendent Amos Baker, May 7, 1925.

39. Rosa Covello, Bedford Hills, 1926, letter from Rosa's father, Mr. Covello, to Superintendent Amos Baker, August 13, 1926.

40. Molly Garrison, Albion, 1906, letter from Mrs. Garrison to Superintendent Alice Curtin, July 8, 1908.

41. Althea Davies, Bedford Hills, 1924, letter from married sister to Superintendent Amos Baker, October 29, 1924.

42. Eva Pomering, Albion, 1918, letter from older sister to Albion's parole board, December 14, 1919; letter from older sister to Eva, July 20, 1920.

43. Ella Waldstein, Bedford Hills, 1917, letter from Jacob Tarlew to Superintendent Cobb, February 12, 1919.

44. Paula Brownell, Albion, 1926, letter from Paula's stepfather to Superintendent Flora Daniels, July 8, 1927.

45. Nora Patterson, Bedford Hills, 1919, letter from Mr. Patterson to Superintendent Cobb, November 30, 1919.

46. Letter from Louise's mother to William Dye, president of Albion's board of visitors January 29, 1917.

47. Two of the 100 young women in this study were discharged by court order after their interventionist families sought legal assitance. Two other young woman were released conditionally (i.e., paroled) by a decision of Albion's Board of Managers after persistent intervention by their husbands. In both cases, the women had small children in need of their care.

48. Myra Roundman, Albion, 1927, letter from husband to Assistant Superintendent Coon, October 1928; letter from mother to Assistant Superintendent Coon, October 1928.

49. Albion State Training School, *Twenty-ninth Annual Report* (Albany, 1923), 9–10.

50. Rosa Covello, Bedford Hills, 1926, parole application, summary and monthly reports; Sophie Polentz, Bedford Hills, 1924, monthly reports; Althea Davies, Bedford Hills, 1924, conduct record; Molly Garrison, Albion, 1906, promotion cottage card; Hart cottage character cards.

51. Louise Peffley, Albion, 1915, letter from Superintendent Daniels to Mrs. Peffley, February 6, 1917.

52. Althea Davies, Bedford Hills, 1924, letter from Superintendent Amos Baker to married sister of inmate, October 31, 1924.

53. Alice Arlington, Albion, 1917, letter from Superintendent Flora Daniels to attorney Harley Crane, Syracuse, April 20, 1918.

54. Alva Burrows, Albion, 1929, letter from Superintendent Coon to Mrs. Burrows, February 14, 1930.

55. Molly Garrison, Albion, 1906, letter from Mrs. Garrison to Superintendent Alice Curtin, July 8, 1908.

5. "I've Chosen a New Road to Travell": The Challenges of Parole

1. Anna Tercillo, Bedford Hills, 1922, letters from Anna to Superintendent Amos Baker, April 30, 1926, and May 14, 1926.

2. For another fascinating analysis of the parolee's project of self-representation, see Paula S. Fass, "Making and Remaking an Event: The Leopold and Loeb Case in American Culture," *Journal of American History* 80 (1993): 919–51.

3. Albion State Training School, *Thirtieth Annual Report* (Albany, 1924), 10; New York State Reformatory for Women, *Eighth Annual Report* (Albany, 1909), 39.

4. Of the 11 nonparoled inmates, 3 were released early on court order or appeal; 4 were discharged unconditionally; one inmate escaped and was never found; one inmate was transferred to an institution for the criminally insane; one inmate was deported. The

circumstances of the eleventh inmate's release are unknown. I have been able to trace the postreformatory experience of 3 of the 11 nonparoled inmates.

5. New York State Reformatory for Women, *Twenty-first Annual Report* (Albany, 1922), 5.

6. Of the 24 women in this study who were married prior to their commitment, only 6 returned to their husbands after they left the reformatories; of this figure only 3 re-established stable relationships.

7. Twenty-seven of the 38 parole violators were reinstitutionalized at Bedford Hills or Albion, usually for a period of several months, before being released again as parolees.

8. Albion's annual reports provide statistics on parole violators but do not usually provide figures on the number of young women who eventually finished parole suc-cessfully (with or without parole violations). The only exception was the *Thirtieth Annual Report* (Albany, 1924), which showed that "of the 62 girls paroled during the fiscal year ending June 30, 1922, 49 finished their parole successfully" (p. 17). Bedford Hills, however, conducted a study of its parole system in the early 1920s and determined that 73.3% of the 725 women paroled between July 1, 1921, and June 30, 1925, "either have been honorably discharged from parole or are now in good standing on parole and doing satisfactorily." This study was conducted at a time when Bedford Hills was working hard to improve its parole system. My own study shows a higher rate of success (82%), but this figure should be treated as merely suggestive because my sample group is small and not strictly representative. New York State Reformatory for Women, *Twenty-fifth Annual Report* (Albany, 1926), 3–4.

9. Judith R. Walkowitz, *City of Dreadful Delight: Narratives of Sexual Danger in Late-Victorian London* (Chicago: University of Chicago Press, 1992), 9.

10. Elizabeth Oliver, Albion, 1902, letter from Superintendent Alice Curtin to Eliz-abeth's sister, April 18, 1904.

11. Charlotte Cooke, Albion, 1904, admission ledger; Elizabeth Oliver, Albion, 1902, letter from aunt to Superintendent Alice Curtin, October 2, 1904.

12. Bedford's parole agent was usually responsible for dozens of young women during a given year, and the parolees might reside in cites and towns scattered up and down the Hudson River. New York State Reformatory for Women at Bedford Hills, *Third Annual Report* (Albany, 1904), 14, 53, and *Eighth Annual Report* (Albany, 1909), 49.

13. Idem., *Fifteenth Annual Report* (Albany, 1916), 42–43.

14. Althea Davies, Bedford, 1924, letters from Amy Prevost, social worker with the Church Mission of Help, to Superintendent Amos Baker, January 9, January 10, 1925.

15. Albion State Training School, *Thirty-first Annual Report* (Albany, 1925), 13.

16. For contemporary discussions of young women and parole see Edith N. Burleigh, "Some Principles of Parole for Girls," *Proceedings of the National Conference of Social Work* (1918), 147–55; "On Parole," *The Survey*, January 15, 1924: 397–99; Alice Menken, *Delinquent Girls on Parole: A Study of Girls Paroled from Cedar Knolls School, 1909–1925* (New York: Jewish Board of Guardians, 1927[?]), 1–6.

17. Western House of Refuge for Women, *Twenty-sixth Annual Report* (Albany, 1920), 19; Albion State Training School, *Twenty-ninth Annual Report* (Albany, 1923), 15–16; New York State Reformatory for Women, *Twenty-fifth Annual Report* (Albany, 1926), 22. By way of contrast, Bedford's 1905 annual report showed that 20 of the 33 parolees in "good standing" were domestics. Only one woman worked as a nurse, one as a milliner,

one as saleswoman, and one as a dentist's assistant. The remaining 9 apparently helped keep house for their families. New York State Reformatory for Women at Bedford Hills, *Fifth Annual Report* (Albany, 1905), 54.

18. Bedford did not offer statistics in its annual reports on the residence of parolees. My reading of the Bedford case files shows that most women who worked in something other than domestic positions lived with their families and may have contributed to the family income. Those who did not live at home, or in the homes of domestic employers, usually worked in a facility such as a hospital that provided dormitory rooms for some of its workers.

19. My understanding of the reformatories' expectations of young women on parole comes primarily from a close reading of the correspondence and parole reports in individual case files. In addition, I was able to find files that contained printed lists of parole rules, lists that women usually took with them when they left the reformatories to begin parole. See, for example, Caroline Browning, Bedford Hills 1924, "Conditional Discharge" (Form G-232) and "Synopsis of Rules and Regulations"; Sallie Poster, Albion, 1917, "Parole Conditions."

20. Western House of Refuge for Women, *Twenty-fourth Annual Report* (Albany, 1918), 15; Albion State Training School, *Thirty-first Annual Report* (Albany, 1925), 13. I have found no evidence in the Albion case files of regular and frequent visitation to parolees by community social workers.

21. New York State Reformatory for Women, *Twenty-fifth Annual Report* (Albany, 1926), 4,7.

22. The case files used in this study show that only 11 of the 89 parolees were definitely visited by a parole agent or social worker, and 5 of the women in this small group received visits at infrequent intervals (bimonthly or less). It is, of course, possible that other young women were visited by parole officers or social workers but that the records of such visits were lost or destroyed.

23. New York State Reformatory for Women at Bedford Hills, *Twenty-fourth Annual Report* (Albany, 1925), 9.

24. Eva Pomering, Albion, 1918, letters from Eva to "Miss Leonard," October 25 and November 26, 1920.

25. Cynthia Romer, Bedford Hills 1926, letter from Mrs. Elizabeth Kjaer, social worker for the [New York] City Mission Society, to Superintendent Amos Baker, November 3, 1926; letters from Cynthia to Superintendents Amos Baker and Leo Palmer, January 12, February 3, 1927.

26. A few parolees appear to have "succeeded" on parole although they returned to families reluctant to take them. For example, when it came time for Susan Rivington to be paroled from Albion in 1904, her married sister wrote to Superintendent Curtin to say that she herself could not afford to bring the young woman out to her home in Kansas, and as for Susan's older brothers, "poor Susan cant espect anything from them they dont seem to ever think of her ever since she went astray." Curtin eventually persuaded one of these brothers to take Susan and supervise her parole, but he made it clear that he had no enthusiasm for the job. "Susan can have A home with me If she will do what is rite and be a god god servin girl. . . . She wil have to work out for hr liven the Same as my one children do." Susan apparently did well, despite her brother's cool welcome, for there is no evidence of parole infractions in her file. Susan Rivington, Albion, 1901, letter from

sister in Olean, New York, to Superintendent Alice Curtin, May 16, 1904; letter from brother to Superintendent Alice Curtin, n.d.; admission ledger.

27. Sarah Walton, Albion, 1913, admission ledger; Myra Henning, Bedford Hills, 1924, report from Associated Charities of Omaha, February 14, 1925; letter from Myra to Superintendent Amos Baker, April 1, 1926.

28. Mildred Pomrenke, Bedford Hills, 1928, preliminary investigation for court; summary of application for parole; Catholic Protective Services investigation, June 16, 1928; parole report; letter from Mildred to Superintendent Leo Palmer, February 25, 1929.

29. Eleanor Hamlisch, Bedford Hills, 1917, letter from Eleanor to Superintendent Helen Cobb, February 1, 1920.

30. Nora Patterson, Bedford Hills, 1919, letter from Nora to Acting Superintendent Anna Talbot, October 30, 1920. Nora was unconditionally discharged from Bedford Hills twelve months after she entered it. She was released early because she did not take part in the race riot of July 24, 1920. That fact earned her the praise of the reformatory's officers; more to the point, during the riot she apparently warned some black inmates of an impending attack, angering their white antagonists so greatly that her continued presence at Bedford was deemed unwise and unsafe.

31. Sallie Wilcox, Albion, 1910, letter from foster mother in Guilford Centre, N.Y., to Superintendent Alice Curtin, n.d.

32. Paula Lester, Bedford Hills, 1923, report from Jewish Board of Guardians, August 6, 1924; monthly parole summaries.

33. Sallie Wilcox, Albion, 1910, letter from Sallie to Superintendent Alice Curtin, October 13, 1912.

34. Ester Bromwell, Bedford Hills, 1917, letter from Ester to Superintendent Alice Cobb, February 1, 1920.

35. Western House of Refuge for Women, *Twenty-eighth Annual Report* (Albany, 1922), 9; Albion State Training School, *Thirtieth Annual Report* (Albany, 1924), 17, and *Thirty-first Annual Report* (Albany, 1925), 13.

36. Patsy Belham, Albion, 1921, admission ledger; Nellie Roberts, Bedford Hills, 1917, letter from Nellie to Acting Superintendent Anna Talbot, June 19, 1920.

37. Susanna Nedersen, Bedford Hills, 1917, letter from Susanna to Superintendent Helen Cobb, November 1919; letter from Susanna to Parole Agent Bella Murphy, September 17, 1919.

38. As an inmate, instead of resenting the reformatory's authority, Susanna spent her time at Bedford Hills trying to "improve" herself. "Yes, it is a lesson, I don't like the three years, [but] I don't mind it as much as other girls do. I don't cry and holler." The predictable routine and physical security provided by the reformatory allowed the young woman to put her unfortunate past behind her. Susanna Nedersen, Bedford Hills, 1917, mental examination.

39. Ibid., Laboratory of Social Hygiene, Mental examination, staff meeting, information of Mrs. Watkins, probation officer in Police Court, Albany, New York.

40. Ibid., letter from Susanna to Superintendent Helen Cobb, May 18, 1920.

41. Alice Arlington, Albion, 1917, letter from Alice to Superintendent Flora Daniels, September 12, 1920; Polly Overton, Albion, 1915, admission ledger; Emily Carrington, Albion, 1925, letter from the Westchester Child Welfare Department to Superintendent Flora Daniels, July 7, 1927, admission ledger.

42. Doreen Cropper, Bedford Hills, 1919, Church Mission of Help report.

43. Ella Waldstein, Bedford Hills, 1917, letter to Superintendent Alice Cobb, July 17, 1919, letter to Superintendent Alice Cobb, November 19, 1919; Evelyn Blackwell, Bedford Hills, 1926, letter from Rockland County State Charities Aid Association to social worker Amy Prevost at the Church Mission of Help, April 12, 1927, letters from Evelyn to Superintendent Leo J. Palmer, February 28, 1927, and May 31, 1927.

44. Lena Meyerhoff, Bedford Hills, 1924, letter from Lena to Superintendent Amos Baker, July 6, 1925.

45. Blanche Preston, Bedford Hills, 1923, letter from Blanche to Superintendent Amos Baker, March 22, 1924.

46. Lena Meyerhoff, Bedford Hills, 1924, letter from Lena to Superintendent Amos Baker, March 1, 1926. Actually Lena had not done anything wrong because she had not tried to aid the runaway parolee in any way. Baker assured her that she was not at fault, writing in reply to her letter, "There is no rule to the effect that one girl on parole is not to associate with another but there are times when it is undesireable for girls to keep up an acquaintance after they have left the Institution. Maria was not doing right and might have involved you in trouble. I think if you wished to keep up an acquaintance with a former girl you should first let me know about it and I would advise you properly. I would like to know if you have any idea where Maria is." Letter from Superintendent Baker to Lena, March 1, 1926.

47. Susanna Nedersen, Bedford Hills, 1917, letter to Superintendent Helen Cobb, n.d.; Merced Borja, Bedford Hills, 1926, letter from Merced to Dr. Leo Palmer, September 27, 1928; Gertrude Leavitt, Bedford Hills, 1922, letter from Gertrude to Superintendent Amos Baker, December 31, 1925; see also letters by Gertrude to Bedford Hills dated October 31, 1925, and March 31, 1927, and an undated letter, probably written in late April 1926.

48. Sophie Polentz, Bedford Hills, 1924, letter from Mrs. Alice Menken, Jewish Board of Guardians, to Superintendent Amos Baker, December 17, 1925.

49. Nanette's parents were dead; her aunt had raised her. Nanette was well-acquainted with her aunt's disapproval and she wrote a note to Superintendent Baker asserting that she had no interest in being re-united with her. "Dr. do you think it any pleasure for a girl to go to ther pople when there will never be any peice in the Home. We could never get along at home together. and another thing I might just as well face the world whyle Im young." Nanette Wilkins, Bedford Hills, 1923, letter to Superintendent Amos Baker, January 20, 1925.

50. Anabel Rider, Albion, 1923, letter from foster mother to Superintendent Flora P. Daniels, October 7, 1924; Anna Levinson, Bedford Hills, 1924, report by Jewish Board of Guardians, n.d.; Cecilia Tomasi, Bedford Hills, 1928, letter from Rochester Catholic Charities to Superintendent [Leo] J. Palmer. Father's comments are paraphrased by social worker.

51. Anna Tercillo, Bedford Hills, 1922, parole application summary; Cecilia Tomasi, Bedford Hills, 1928, record of parole. See also the (second) summary report on application for parole, which notes that Cecilia "demoralized" her younger siblings and "abused" her father.

52. Rae Rabinowitz, Bedford Hills, 1917, letter from Rae to Superintendent Helen Cobb, n.d.; the reply from Cobb to Rae, January 22, 1920, notes that the superintendent

is "glad to hear good reports of you and your work"; Ilene Sterling, Bedford Hills, 1917, letter to Superintendent Helen Cobb, October 30, 1919; Janine Rosen, Bedford Hills, 1926, letters from Janine to Superintendent Leo Palmer, March and April 1927; Anabel Rider, Albion, 1923, letter from Anabel to Superintendent Flora Daniels, January 7, 1925; Sophie Polentz, Bedford Hills, 1924, letters to Superintendent Amos Baker, December 22, 1925, and March 1, 1926.

53. Janine Rosen, Bedford Hills, 1926, letter from Mr. Rosen to Superintendent Leo Palmer, July 23, 1927; letter from Superintendent Palmer to parolee Janine Rosen, July 28, 1927; letter from Janine Rosen to Superintendent Leo Palmer, August 4, 1927.

54. Althea Davies, Bedford Hills, 1924, letter to Superintendent Amos Baker, July 10, 1925; Marian Jacoby, Bedford Hills, 1919, letter from Marian to "Miss Obrian," probably a case worker with the Central Committee for Friendly Aid to Jewish Girls (later the Jewish Board of Guardians), n.d.; Rae Rabinowitz, Bedford Hills, 1917, letter from sister to Superintendent Helen Cobb, November 11, 1919.

55. Ilene Sterling, Bedford Hills, 1917, letter from Ilene to boyfriend, c/o Westchester Trolley Company, n.d., letter from employer to Superintendent, May 5, 1920; Marian Jacoby, Bedford Hills, 1919, summary parole reports; Anabel Rider, Albion, 1923, letter from foster mother to Superintendent Flora Daniels, May 9, 1925; Ginger Trapp, Albion, 1914, report on visit to parolee, February 10, 1916; Rae Rabinowitz, Bedford Hills, 1917, copy of report sent to Mrs. Alice Menken, Committee for Friendly Aid to Jewish Girls, April 22, 1920, monthly parole reports; Janine Rosen, Bedford Hills, 1926, report by Jewish Board of Guardians, April 17, 1927, warrant for arrest, April 27, 1928; Sophie Polentz, Bedford Hills, 1924, monthly parole reports.

56. Ilene Sterling, Bedford Hills, 1917, parole report; Ginger Trapp, Albion, 1914, admission ledger; Rae Rabinowitz, Bedford Hills, 1917, letter from court probation officer to Superintendent Florence Jones, July 27, 1920.

57. Rachel Adelson, Bedford Hills, 1926, monthly summary reports.

58. Rae Rabinowitz, Bedford Hills, 1917, letter from Brooklyn Women's Night Court to Superintendent Florence Jones, July 27, 1920; Janine Rosen, Bedford Hills, 1926, report by Jewish Board of Guardians, April 17, 1928, letter from Superintendent Leo Palmer to Janine's father, June 8, 1928; Anna Tercillo, Bedford Hills, 1922, Parole Application Summary; Anna had been paroled to her mother and father on August 2, 1923; on August 7 the mother wrote to Bedford to say that Anna had disappeared: "Anna told me that she was taking a walk around the block and that she would return in five minutes and I have not seen her yet." Frances Brewer, Bedford Hills, 1926, monthly summaries; Melanie Burkis, Bedford Hills, 1928, monthly summaries.

59. New York State Reformatory for Women, *Twenty-third Annual Report* (Albany, 1924), 9.

60. The reformatories did not keep records of the inmates' conduct during second or third stays as consistently as they did for the first stay. Of the 26 women who returned to the reformatories, evidence survives on the conduct of only 9: 8 were troublesome or at least occasionally misbehaved.

61. Rae Rabinowitz, Bedford Hills, 1917, letter from Superintendent Anna Talbot to Rae's sister, February 4, 1921; Marian Jacoby, Bedford Hills, 1919, letter to Superintendent Amos Baker from Marian after her transfer to Mattaewan, October 3, 1921; Sophie Polentz, Bedford Hills, 1924, conduct record; Melanie Burkis, Bedford Hills, 1928, letter

from 11 women in Lowell Cottage to Superintendent Amos Baker, April 24, 1926; Althea Davies, Bedford Hills, 1924, unsigned, undated note (probably written by cottage matron); Frances Brewer, Bedford Hills, 1926, conduct record; monthly reports.

62. Marian Jacoby, Bedford Hills, 1919, letter from Marian to Superintendent Amos Baker, October 3, 1921; On the advice of the medical superintendent at Mattaewan, Dr. R. F. C. Kieb, Marian was released directly from that institution (after an eight-month stay) to a second parole position. Dr. Kieb also sent to Bedford a "certificate of mental restoration" which remains in Marian's file.

63. Althea Davies, Bedford Hills, 1924, notes of home visit, December 19, 1925; letter from Althea to Superintendent Amos Baker, July 27, 1926, and August 1926; monthly reports.

64. Marian Jacoby, Bedford Hills, 1919; Marian's remarks are paraphrased in a letter from Alice Menken (Jewish Board of Guardians) to Superintendent Amos Baker, March 9, 1923; see also letter from Marian to Superintendent Amos Baker, March 12, 1923; summary of parole reports; letter from New York City Magistrates' Court deputy chief probation officer Patrick Shelly to Superintendent Amos Baker, January 3, 1923; letter from Patrick Shelly to Amos Baker, January 5, 1923.

65. Anna Levinson, Bedford Hills, 1924, statement by social worker from Jewish Board of Guardians, typed on back of parolee's questionnaire for September 1927.

66. Anna Tercillo, Bedford Hills, 1922, letter from Anna to Superintendent Amos Baker, October 1925.

67. Anna Levinson, Bedford Hills, 1924, letter from Anna to Superintendent Leo Palmer, October 17, 1927.

68. Nanette Wilkins, Bedford Hills, 1923, letters from Nanette to Superintendent Amos Baker, January 5 and January 20, 1925; letter from employer to Baker, January 9, 1926.

69. Ginger Trapp, Albion, 1914, admission ledger.

70. Rae Rabinowitz, Bedford Hills, 1917, letter from Rae's sister to Bedford Hills, April 5, 1923; letter from Anna Stolper, Jewish Board of Guardians, to Superintendent Amos Baker, April 25, 1923; letter from United Jewish Society of Brooklyn to Bedford Hills, June 3, 1927.

71. Nellie Roberts, Bedford Hills, 1917, letter from Nellie to Superintendent Florence Jones, July 15, 1920.

72. Ibid., letter from Port Jervis justice of the peace to Bedford Hills, September 11, 1922. There is no formal record of Nellie's second arrest and commitment in her original case file; however, a physician's record card in the file has the following notation on its back: "admitted Oct 8 1924 as Nellie Roberts Lark. Married to Ernest Lark 7/14/20. Pt. Jervis, NY, Separated Nov 1921. Charge vagrancy—one child, Robert 3 yrs old." Bedford Hills probably opened a new case file for Nellie during her second incarceration but I was unable to find it.

73. Rachel Adelson, Bedford Hills, 1926, summary of monthly reports; Nola Pearce, Bedford Hills, 1923, letter from Nola to Superintendent Amos Baker, December 2, 1923; letter to Baker, March 2, 1924, letter from social worker Amy Prevost at the Church Mission of Help to Superintendent Amos Baker, March 13, 1924, letter from Superintendent Amos Baker to Mrs. Pearce, September 23, 1925.

74. Julia Kramer, Bedford Hills, 1928, summary of monthly reports.

75. Sophie's husband went to the Jewish Board of Guardians for assistance when he learned that his wife was being blackmailed as a former prostitute. The JBG did not tell him that his wife had also been at Bedford Hills and was a parole violator; indeed, Superintendent Palmer decided not to try to return Sophie to Bedford Hills because she was trying to lead a "decent" life. Palmer refused, however, to have her name cleared from the records because she would not consent to an interview with parole workers at the JBG. Sophie's husband did not learn that his wife had been at Bedford Hills until 1933. At that time the marriage collapsed entirely and Sophie's husband wrote to the reformatory claiming that his wife had stolen all of his belongings and gone back to prostitution. There is no reply to this letter in Sophie's file. A year earlier the reformatory had discharged Sophie (along with other "disappeared" parolees) in a sweeping effort to clear the institutional records. Sophie Polentz, Bedford Hills, 1924, monthly reports; letter from Sophie to Superintendent Leo Palmer, December 21, 1928; letter from Mrs. Hodes, Jewish Board of Guardians to Alice Menken, secretary of Bedford Hills Board of Managers, February 11, 1929; letter from Sophie's husband to Bedford Hills, September 8, 1933.

Index